Intimate Relationships in China in the Light of Depth Psychology

A Study of Gender and Integrity

Huan Wang

Routledge
Taylor & Francis Group

LONDON AND NEW YORK

First published 2020
by Routledge
2 Park Square, Milton Park, Abingdon, Oxon OX14 4RN

and by Routledge
52 Vanderbilt Avenue, New York, NY 10017

Routledge is an imprint of the Taylor & Francis Group, an informa business

British Library Cataloguing-in-Publication Data
A catalogue record for this book is available from the British
Library

Library of Congress Cataloging-in-Publication Data
Names: Wang, Huan, 1981- author.
Title: Intimate relationships in China in the light of depth
psychology : a study of gender and integrity / Huan Wang.
Description: Milton Park, Abingdon, Oxon ; New York, NY :
Routledge, 2020. | Includes bibliographical references and index.
Identifiers: LCCN 2019059500 (print) | LCCN 2019059501
(ebook) | ISBN 9780367369279 (hardback) |
ISBN 9780367369286 (paperback) | ISBN 9780429351945 (ebook)
Subjects: LCSH: Sex roles—China. | Marriage—China. |
Couples—China—Psychology.
Classification: LCC HQ1075.5.C6 W35 2020 (print) | LCC HQ1075.5.C6
(ebook) | DDC 305.30951—dc23
LC record available at https://lccn.loc.gov/2019059500
LC ebook record available at https://lccn.loc.gov/2019059501

ISBN: 978-0-367-36927-9 (hbk)
ISBN: 978-0-367-36928-6 (pbk)
ISBN: 978-0-429-35194-5 (ebk)

Typeset in Times New Roman
by Swales & Willis, Exeter, Devon, UK

To my mother, Zhou Guizhi

Contents

Acknowledgments

I would like to express my gratitude to Andrew Samuels and Kevin Lu. Working with them at the University of Essex was a great adventure for me. Andrew, in particular, has been the most brilliant and inspiring supervisor and lecturer I have ever met. Every discussion between us allowed me to hear my own voice clearly and without his wholehearted guidance and assistance, I could never have imagined publishing my work in English.

Profound gratitude goes to my former analyst, John Beebe. His companionship helped me to get through the most difficult times in my life over the past years. With his encouragement and emotional support, I made up my mind to start a new life in the UK in my thirties.

I am also hugely appreciative to my partner, Xiao Wang. His companionship has made my life in London much easier, and he has brought much fun to my life.

I owe a great deal to my parents, who have loved and supported me unconditionally. They are not traditional Chinese parents and did not ask me to be a filial daughter as normal Chinese parents do. They always encouraged me to do what I wanted and to follow my own path. When my father was alive, he expected me to study abroad, to broaden my horizons, and to gain certain achievements. Today, via this book, I have now, I hope, fulfilled his expectations. My mother has always been proud of my progress, and today, she has even more reason to be so.

Chapter 1

Introduction

In this introductory chapter, I attempt to establish the basis of this book, which sets out ideas and concepts which are, let us hope, important for understanding masculinity and femininity in intimate relationships in China. This leads to the development of a set of further ideas concerning work with Chinese couples therapeutically. For such understanding and future therapeutic work based on it, this book covers four main themes:

1   Exploring and critiquing some relevant basic Jungian and post-Jungian ideas in the Chinese context;
2   Understanding Chinese culture through a Jungian lens;
3   Developing appropriate and useful Jungian ideas in the clinical realm; and
4   Applying these ideas in both clinical work with patients and other related psychosocial arenas.

The study of national characteristics present in China has a long and controversial history, beginning in 1935 when Lin Yutang published his book *My Country and My People* to introduce China to the West. Jungian and post-Jungian ideas might be among the most efficacious psychological theories with which to facilitate our understanding of the Chinese psyche. Specifically, I will refer to the collective unconscious and the application of the concept of 'archetype', both of which will be discussed later. Further, the Jungian terms 'anima', 'animus', 'mother complex'[1], 'father archetype', etc., which of course need to be examined and discussed, can facilitate our understanding of men and women and the most basic relationships in both the intrapsychic and interpersonal realms. Based on my observation, Chinese therapists today welcome these concepts and ideas and have started to apply them liberally in their therapeutic work. Hence, exploring the applicability of Jungian psychology in Chinese settings and then developing relative ideas and techniques to work with Chinese people are both necessary and timely. This can deepen the dialogues between China and the West, which is significant for both China and the West's understanding of China.

In this book, I will focus on the realm of marriage, because couple relationships have become the basis of Chinese families in recent years due to Westernisation and the prevalence of small family structures. Furthermore, in my clinical observations, intimacy always emerges as the main issue raised by patients in therapy.

According to the *People's Daily* and the *Blue Book of Youth: The Development Report on Chinese Youth in the New Century*, since the late 1970s, divorce rates and the number of divorces in China have continued to rise annually. Since 2008, the rate and number have increased markedly, with the divorce rate increasing to 7.65 percent per annum. Most divorcees are between the ages of 22 and 35 (People's Daily, 2nd July, 2011; Blue Book of Chinese Youth Development, 2012), and it is important to note that the majority were born after 1978. Thus, it seems that young Chinese couples are facing a crisis in their intimate relationships at the current time and this phenomenon requires further examination.

The year 1978 was very important in modern China, marked as it was by the implementation of two major policies: first, The Chinese Economic Reform; and second, the one-child policy. Since then, the economic situation and family structure in China have undergone monumental shifts. The Reform and Opening-up policy brought to Chinese daily life the influences of modernisation and Westernisation. Meanwhile, a consequence of the one-child policy has been the decline of large families made up of grandparents and several siblings; these days, more families are composed of just three individuals (two parents and one child). As a result, intimacy issues seem to differ between the younger and older generations. On the one hand, the Chinese are retaining their old internal expectations and fantasies of intimate relationships, as informed by China's history and, I suggest, the cultural inheritance of older patterns of relationship; on the other hand, changes in daily life have led to new projections, expectations and dynamics in terms of relationships.

As a Chinese woman from a one-child family who grew up during this period of immense change, I have personally witnessed the effects of these great shifts. My main interest is to understand marriage issues in China from my cultural exploration and clinical observations and to interpret these issues from both Jungian and post-Jungian perspectives. I argue that the notions of femininity and masculinity, which are accompanied by particular fantasies of the 'other' and are constellated in Chinese marriages, are ambivalent. By adopting Jungian and post-Jungian lenses, I study traditional ways of viewing feminine, masculine and contemporary images that have been affected by both Westernisation and interventions from the political establishment in modern China. To sum up, my aims are to address the concepts and characteristics of the feminine and masculine by referring to intimacy in Chinese cultural and clinical settings and to decipher how Chinese society may cope with the difficulties encountered in its marital relationships today.

No doubt, there are a number of controversies here. China today is in a very complex situation: There have been tremendous collisions and fusions between older Chinese values based on its long history and new values that have been immensely affected by Westernisation and modernisation since 1911.[2] Meanwhile, marriage and intimacy issues are never simple. As Guggenbuhl-Craig argues, 'marriage is not a private matter' (1977, p.103). According to him, parents and relatives influence marriage and divorce and this is particularly the case in China where marriage is always affected by family, society and politics (Croll, 1978, p.26; 1981, p.83). The one-child policy has changed China's family structure, however, and accordingly, family dynamics have been modified. Chinese intimate relationships have been influenced by cultural factors, not only referring to rational factors but also including those which integrate the unconscious. Clinical psychological perspectives, particularly from the depth psychological perspective, are typically Western and are based on the study of individual cases. That being the case, we may query whether it is appropriate to apply these perspectives to the study of the Chinese psyche and Chinese relationships. Further, is it possible to figure out and deal with the shifts that have occurred in Chinese relationships? I would say that it is possible, and in the three following chapters, by critically reviewing the notion of femininity and masculinity from depth psychological perspectives and assessing the application of analytical psychology in China, I will show a) the complicity between the notions of femininity and masculinity and how they can be categorised at three different levels; b) how psychoanalysis and analytical psychology were imported and have developed in China, a non-Western context; and c) why the utilisation of a Western psychological lens to understand the 'East' is both timely and necessary.

Analytical psychology and the Eastern psyche

In *The Secret of the Golden Flower*, the Chinese Taoist classic, Jung wrote, 'it must be mentioned that just as the human body shows a common anatomy above all racial differences, so too, does the psyche possess a common substratum. I have called the latter the collective unconscious' (1931, para 88). According to Jung, human beings from different cultures have highly consistent inner worlds. The archetypes, the structures of the collective unconscious, are defined as being linked with instincts and also refer to a pattern of behaviour (CW18, para. 1228). It seems that the collective unconscious affects all peoples, irrespective of race and cultural difference. Further, a post-Jungian, Colman (2016), notes that behavioural and relational patterns included in archetypes have been revised by culture (pp.49–51). Thus, studying archetypes is a valid, universal approach to understanding and working on the psyche in different cultural settings.

Nevertheless, differences do exist between the Western and Eastern psychological worlds. As Jung said, 'Western man seems predominantly extraverted, Eastern man predominantly introverted' (MDR, pp.348–349). To this, Clarke adds that, 'the East's emphasis on inwardness, self-awareness, self-analysis, was perhaps as one-sided as the West's predominantly extraverted attitude' (1994, p.72). Jung and Clarke assume that Eastern introversion and Western extraversion, typical human characteristics, are both crucial for the development of an individual's psyche. However, these assertions in relation to the differences between East and West are divided and polarised and are not unproblematic. The difference between the East and West, and the validity of using Jungian and post-Jungian perspectives to understand issues arising from different contexts, in this case China, will be discussed in Chapter 4.

The importance of Jungian ideas has been increasing since the 1990s in China. The prevalence of such ideas and their growing influence in China merit, in part, the utility and application of a Western psychological lens to explore Eastern phenomena. However, how to use these Western concepts in non-Western contexts raises an important question, and what modifications must be made requires more discussion and research. These concerns have led to my own research – exploring the archetypal feminine and masculine in intimate realms in China through Jungian and post-Jungian lenses.

Femininity and masculinity in intimate relationships

According to Jung, feminine and masculine aspects are opposite yet equally important elements of the human psyche. He referred to the archetypal feminine in males as the *anima*, and the archetypal masculine in females as the *animus* (CW7, para. 296–340). They each have different psychological functions. Usually, 'the archetypal feminine is the province of relating and care giving […] [it] concerns joining, attachment and involvement' (Young-Eisendrath, 1984, p.12). It carries 'nurturing, vulnerable and care taking qualities' (Zweig & Wolf, 1997, p.26). The basic feature of the archetypal feminine is always considered to be involved with, and connected to, others. However, this description has over-emphasised the positive functions of feminine archetypes in contributing to human relationships and has assigned the possibility of relations between humans solely to the feminine province; consequently, it does not provide a whole picture of either femininity or of human relationships. If we explore archetypal images in a different setting, female images carry different characteristics and consequently have different functions. Even so, I admit that such images are not only an inner aspect of ourselves, but also contribute to the base of our relationships. Studying feminine images helps us to understand the intrapsychic structure, and further, to understand interpersonal relationships. In sum, these images play a crucial role in structuring the 'inter-subjective space'[3] in intimate relationships.

From a classical Jungian perspective, the archetypal feminine plays an important role in a man's development. (Jung depicted the integration of anima/animus as the bridge to the Self.) As von Franz argues, 'if a single man or if a whole civilization loses contact with the feminine element, that usually implies a too rational, too ordered, too organized attitude' (1970b, p.70). On the other hand, 'if a man neglects relatedness, she (his anima) at once regresses' (1970b, p.89). It is said that the feminine element works on a man's emotional and irrational life and is expressed in intimate relationships while his relatedness in turn affects his archetypal feminine. When he fails to connect internally with his femininity, it will harm his external relationships. However, there is no mention of women's femininity in the work of classical Jungians, implying that, for them, women's femininity is obvious and a woman must be born with knowledge thereof; hence, there is no need to explore it further. However, this is not the case.

As the post-Jungian scholar, Samuels, argues, '[w]omen and men also express an unconscious femininity and masculinity respectively' (1985b, p.215). The feminine archetype (the anima) is carried by both men and women. When I identify the importance of femininity in the clinical field, the couple therapist Young-Eisendrath emphasises the importance of 'understanding the repressed feminine'[4] in both men and women (1984, pp.91–100). A woman is not born familiar with feminine qualities; she also needs to learn how to relate to her archetypal feminine. Conflicts between women and their archetypal feminine also cause intimacy problems and produce psychological symptoms. Becoming more conscious of the feminine aspects of oneself is important and helpful for both men and women in clinical work.

Alternatively, when we refer to the archetypal masculine, Young-Eisendrath noted that Jung has a rather negative attitude to the woman's animus, emphasising the effects of 'a badly flawed masculinity' and highlighting that 'the strength of the animus ... was often overshadowed by its weakness'. Young-Eisendrath critiques this statement as essentialist and says that, among the first generation of Jungians, 'theorizing of anima and animus had all the problems of sexual stereotyping' (1998, pp.202–203). For example, according to von Franz, 'man in his primitive capacity as hunter and warrior is accustomed to kill', and the animus 'shares this propensity' (von Franz, 1970b/1996, p.169). From the perspective of classical Jungians, the archetypal masculine includes shadow, flaws, aggression, etc. and all these negative aspects are damaging to relationships. Positive animus perspectives are mentioned far less often than the negative animus experience, which was entangled with the unconscious tendency toward male chauvinism and stereotyping. Post-Jungians thus criticised the essentialist assignment of femininity and masculinity but share almost an identical attitude in relation to the archetypal masculine, which is held by both men and women, as 'the domain of distancing and separating', and characterised as 'binding off, separating from, and aggression toward nature and human beings' (Young-Eisendrath, 1984, p.12). Giegerich noted that the animus 'changes the direction' of marriage 'in a logically different status'. Both the man and woman in the marriage become inaccessible to each other; they are disconnected (2008, p.120). Based on these descriptions and assertions, the masculine has little to do with intimate relationships and when it is involved, there are negative effects. Completely contrary to the archetypal feminine, the archetypal masculine harms and destroys intimacy and marriage. However, these assertions are based on the divided and binary positions of masculinity and femininity that are rooted in Western culture and need to be expanded.

For example, one can question the extent to which it is possible to distinguish between psychological femininity and masculinity. Are their effects on intimate relationships different and contrary? Samuels states that 'anima and animus have certain characteristics in common' (1986, p.23) and they might also share common functions in relationships. According to Samuels, both men and women possess an anima and animus and, as Waddell points out, they 'offer the possibility for personal and culture gender expansion' (2006, p.161). Therefore, anima and animus might be better understood as comprising gender possibility and potential, not necessarily as carrying certain characteristics and facilitating certain functions. It seems unwise to define femininity and masculinity in a split and opposite way: The lines that separate the two are more fluid and permeable than Jung originally hypothesised. This topic will be discussed further in Chapter 2.

Moreover, Young-Eisendrath points out that 'gender varies from context, both between groups and within individuals over time' (1998, p.203). If this is the case, in different cultures and times, the contents and functions of the feminine and masculine would change; the images of anima and animus depend on one's environment, culture and historical context and their effects on intimate relationships might be interchangeable. In China in particular, due to the political and historical factors, the contents of femininity and masculinity are very complicated and ambivalent, as I will illustrate in the following chapters.

Feminine and masculine images in the imperial[5] Chinese context

In ancient China, feminine and masculine images can be divided into innocent and virtuous figures and sensual yet vile figures. This polarised and split phenomenon is quite common in Chinese legends, literature and history.

There are at least two typical Chinese feminine images of romantic relationships in traditional Chinese narratives. The first is the 'fairy ladies', who play a leading role in Chinese love stories. They are often from heaven or the water, or appear as flower spirits. These fairy ladies are attracted to decent, ordinary men who are usually vulnerable intellectuals. The fairy ladies actively court these men, helping them to overcome their troubles and assisting them to pass the examinations to become government officials. The second typical Chinese feminine image governing romantic relationships is the 'female ghost'. Sometimes, such ghosts could be another form of the 'fairy lady', who falls in love with a young graduate and offers him assistance. However, most of these characters are 'real' ghosts with grievances, and some are even devils or monsters, such as a snake or fox spirit. Crossing the path of a female ghost is usually dangerous, and they actively court, seduce, sleep with and suck the spirit of men. This may then result in the exhaustion or even death of the man.

In old Chinese love stories, most of the principal masculine characters are vulnerable intellectuals facing financial crisis. In such tales, being poor and weak is equated to being nice and considerate. On the other hand, in these love stories, warriors are rarely depicted and rich men who have sexual desires are depicted as villains. The former only value their friendships with other men and have no interest in intimate relationships with women. They believe that indulging in women and sex will harm their heroism. The latter are usually portrayed as negative characters – those who come into conflict with the dominant values of society and set obstacles for the young lovers due to their desire for the pretty woman. Such a man is 'the lecher', and all his endeavours fail by the end of the story.

These split archetypal images, which divide female images into the negative and the positive and male images into the poor but nice man and the rich yet vile man, not only exist in China, but are also common in other cultures. Such a simple division is the product of reductionism. When we survey men and women in intimate relationships, such images are far too anaemic to give us the full picture of the common complexity and ambivalence that occur in marriages. Chapter 5 will demonstrate that the typical Western male image – a man who simultaneously has the traits of aggression and tenderness – is now affecting Chinese people's vision of the ideal man. Chapter 6 will portray the idealised Chinese female image in opera, a mature form of literature that prevailed in the late period of imperial China. Such an image goes beyond dividing women into innocent and evil characters and depicts instead the development of the psyche.

The mother complex in China

Mother images are a very important part of femininity in the Chinese psyche. In old Chinese narratives, there are two typical mother images. The first is 'the great mother'. In Chinese stories, when compared with personal mothers, these mothers are usually widows who raise their sons for the glory of their husbands' families or for the benefit of the country. They are highly praised in history textbooks, such as *Lie Nv Zhuan*, edited by Liu Xiang, in the Han dynasty. The Chinese 'great mother' most often does not attend to her child's emotional life, or to the development of his individual interests. Instead, she emphasises the morals and values that will ultimately contribute to a collective life.

The second image is that of the 'personal mother'. In contrast to the 'great mother', the personal mother treats her sons as possessions and has a very close emotional bond with them. Separating these mothers from their sons is often difficult. From a psychological perspective, these sons are often unconsciously bonded to an unresolved mother complex and their mothers become obstacles to their intimacy with other women. There are many stories about the fights and struggles that ensue between mothers-in-law and daughters-in-law.

It is necessary to explore the specifically Chinese mother complex and its effects on the relationships of young Chinese couples. In old Chinese narratives, children were asked to obey and take care of their mothers. That is to say, Chinese people have traditionally been encouraged to be possessed by their mother complex. Consequently, individuals with a strong mother complex find it difficult to internally integrate their anima and externally to establish a healthy relationship with their spouse. The one-child family structure might have aggravated this issue by making the mother complex more prominent because there is no other child to share the mother's love and domination. The mother image has been traditionally over-bearing in China, and this has been further exacerbated by the one-child policy. Similar to archetypal images, cultural stereotypes and political intervention also play a role in shaping marital intimacy.

In contemporary China, the image of the personal mother is psychologically active in personal relationships and reflects popular culture. Contemporary Chinese literature describes such relationships, reflecting the historical and psychological shifts that have occurred in the Chinese psyche. For instance, in old Chinese narratives, there are few mothers who intervene in their daughters' marriages. Since the one-child policy, however, fights and struggles between sons-in-law and mothers-in-law have become noticeable. The image of a mother who has strong bonds with her only daughter is also appearing more frequently in clinical materials and popular culture. The mother complex in China revolves more around issues of possession of the single child, making the separation between mother and child an almost impossible task. The growing dominance of the mother complex is thus producing an impediment to intimate relationships in contemporary China. Chapter 5 will explore this particular manifestation of the relationship between mother and child in couples from one-child families compared with couples from families with multiple children. Further, Chapter 7 will use clinical materials to discuss how mothers affect their children's sense of self and others, and as a consequence, influence their children's marriages.

Father images and the father complex in personal development and relationships

Jung wrote, 'the normal person is fettered by more than one chain – the relationship to father and mother' (1985, p.230). Thus, the relationship with the father is equally as important as the relationship to the mother. Samuels points out that fathers are 'powerful inner agents' in a person's emotional life (1985a, p.2) and they naturally have an impact on the erotic life and behaviour of their children (1985a, p.27). Thus, we cannot avoid discussing fathers when exploring interpersonal dynamics and the social and cultural basis of these intrapsychic dynamics.

In more traditional narratives of the Chinese family, the father is often absent or much less important than the mother. The emphasis on filial piety in Chinese culture often transforms the absent father into an image of the idealised father. It might cause less guilt for the son to take the place of his father as master of the family. When fathers appear, it is usually in relation to the father's authority, and although they sometimes make mistakes, they are still good fathers. These images of the idealised, authoritative, all-good father are problematic, however. As Samuels suggested, 'an individual operating under the aegis of an all-good father image would not be able to handle authority or would feel hopelessly inferior to the paragon father or incestuously bonded to him' (Samuels, 1985b, p.31). In the traditional Chinese family, the child should love, respect and obey his father without question. The one-sided approach to fathers has produced problems, the effects of which are still prevalent amongst contemporary Chinese people.

Negative father images are also quite important from a Jungian perspective. According to Hillman, the father's negative traits are significant for the realisation of shadow and the development of the personality (1989, pp.220–221). Being trapped by an absent or dominating father hinders these processes and, in turn, prevents a more holistic and complete realisation of the personality. In China, the dominating image of the father is that of a 'false father' or 'senex',[6] which is accompanied by many negative connotations.

Failing to connect with our real, physical fathers would, arguably, harm our future relationships. Without the father's presence, children cannot separate from their mothers, which, in turn, deleteriously affects their ability to build meaningful relationships with the opposite sex (Samuels, 1985a, p.28, p.35; Seligman, 1986, pp.69–93). We could infer that, with the father's assistance, children have a greater possibility of overcoming their mother complex, affording them a greater opportunity to relate to others (particularly the opposite sex) more integrally. According to Freud, identifying with the father after the resolution of the Oedipus complex is the beginning of relating with others, once the ties from the mother have been severed.

We could even say that, for a daughter, her father is the first lover. He affects her sexual development, shapes her erotic tone and colours her intimacy (Samuels, 1985b, p.31, p.163; Hillman, 1989, p.219; Young-Eisendrath, 1993, pp.192–193). That is to say, a girl projects an image of her father onto her lover and husband. (The mother-son relationship was emphasised in old Chinese narratives, but the father-daughter relationship was rarely mentioned. From my clinical observation, it is difficult for a woman not to mention her father when we discuss her attitudes to men and her intimacy issues.) Chapter 6 will discuss how identifying with her father can facilitate a girl's individuation. This will be done by amplifying a Chinese opera, which is one of the few stories to depict the father-daughter relationship in China.

For a son, his father is 'a model persona' (Samuels, 1985b, p.163) – someone he should mimic in order to relate to the outer world. Further, Beebe suggests 'it is the unsuspected side of the father's anima that provides the greatest opportunities for the son's own anima development' (1985, p.101). This means that his projections onto all his intimate partners and his attitudes towards them are affected. Thus, identifying with the father – either too much or too little – will severely interrupt his intimate relationships. Chapter 7 will illustrate how a father affects his son's sense of self and his attitudes to women.

Romantic love and expectations in modern China

Throughout China's past, people emphasised loyalty to the extended family and country, valued the relationships between generations and tended to ignore the importance of individual endeavours. The importance of intimate relationships has also been neglected. In traditional Chinese narratives, erotic relationships beyond the aim of reproduction were not decent and usually led to disaster. Positive male and female figures never engaged in sexual activities solely for entertainment. Indeed, many romantic stories in traditional Chinese literature end with the separation of the lovers. In official history, romantic love is usually ignored, and is not valued by mainstream society. After 1911, however, with the onset of Westernisation and modernisation, the Chinese gradually came to realise the value of individual fulfilment, the importance of intimate relationships and the positive aspect of Eros.[7]

According to Hillman, romantic love is 'a meeting of images, an exchange of imagination' (1996, p.147) which can be projected through 'obsessive' and 'compelling' images, such as anima and animus (1996, p.141). When Jung talks about the four stages of anima, he names the second one 'Helen', the beauty of Troy who is on a romantic level. The first stage, named 'Eve', is a representation of sexual temptation (CW16, para. 361). From this development, we can see that the anima provides an image that enables us to acculturate our Eros, sexual desire and longing for attachment. Through this acculturation, anima shapes our relationships, transforming our sexuality from fertilising, primitive modes to culturally acceptable, and even civilising, modes. Thus, the literature on romantic love is often about the civilisation of Eros, not infrequently through frustration, disappointment and suffering (Hillman, 1996; Neumann, 1956; von Franz, 1970a). This pattern, indicative of more recent love stories, is becoming more common in modern literature.

Here, however, lies the great paradox of romantic love – 'it never produces human relationship as long as it stays romantic' (Johnson, 1983, p.133). Johnson continues: 'Romance is not a love that is directed at another human being; the passion of romance is always directed at our own projections, our own expectations, our own fantasy [...] it is a love not of another person, but ourselves' (ibid., p.193). Young-Eisendrath also points out that '[romantic] love was more than attachment bond, something more like a projection of an aspect of the self' (1993, p.70). It is for this reason that romantic love cannot last for long and often fails – a source of great disappointment. Instead of relating with the real other, we relate with a projected image of our own wishes and desires of romantic love and we can never be satisfied with such a relationship.

This paradox between long-lasting relationships and enthusiastic, but short-lived romances, highlights the issues pertaining to intimacy in the Chinese psyche. In the past, people married because it was a family requirement. Young couples needed to obey their parents (in most instances, the husband's parents), respect each other and take responsibility for the husband's family. Usually, they spent little time with each other and, consequently, there was little tension between them. Today, young people have different expectations of their partners, based on what they have learned from modern Chinese narratives which, I suggest, are influenced by Western narratives. They want to become deeply involved with the other, and project romantic love as 'the call', 'fate' and 'destiny' onto the relationship (Hillman, 1996/1997, p.145). They also anticipate that someone will identify with their ideal feminine or masculine images. This transition ushers in a conflict with traditional views of what constitutes a relationship.

In Chapter 5, I will explore the romantic expectations of young couples, in particular their images of femininity and masculinity as expressed through interviews. In Chapter 6, a romantic story from the Ming Dynasty will demonstrate how a girl's awakening sexuality and pursuit of love motivated her to find her path to individuation. Then, in Chapter 8, I argue that Westernisation in China is more likely cosmetic or has occurred more at the conscious level;

hence, although people are eager to procure romantic love, the deep root of Chinese relationships due to the collective will and the valuing of family intervention, continues to dominate, and this model is not at all romantic.

Political effects on Chinese families and relationships

Political interventions also work on young Chinese couples. Here, the main political intervention to which I refer is the one-child policy. Since the establishment of the People's Republic of China, politics have played a vital role in the development of Chinese families and marriages. Since the Communist Party took power in 1949, it has made arranged marriages illegal and has encouraged free-choice marriages (Croll, 1983, pp.80–82), which seem to offer the possibility of marriage based on romantic love. Meanwhile, the Communist Party has emphasised the political importance of marriage: A marital bond is not 'a personal affair or trifling matter of daily life', but 'provides for the birth, training and education of a new generation [,] [making] it a matter of vital significance to society' (Croll, 1981, pp.5–6). People tend to value 'revolutionary friendship' and 'love of comrades' in their intimate relationships, which means a 'good couple' is based on sharing the same political interests and devoting themselves to communism. In this 'friendship' and 'love', the difference between femininity and masculinity becomes blurred, if not non-existent.

Further, the most important political event shaping contemporary Chinese families and relationships is the one-child policy. This comprises direct 'state intervention' in the 'fertility decision[s]' and 'family plan[ning]' of an entire country (Croll, 1983, pp.90–91; 1985, pp.31–34). This policy has completely changed the family structure, family dynamics and children's perceptions of femininity and masculinity. This, in turn, has affected attitudes to sex and relationships in contemporary China. However, this does not mean that everyone has accepted the policy unconditionally.

Chinese people have developed their own strategies to resist the one-child policy, such as sending children to relatives and engineering false divorces (White, 2006, p.179). Further, because of the preference for sons, some Chinese families resort to female infanticide, infant abandonment and adoption and sex-selective abortion (ibid., p.199; Zhang, 2006, pp.63–82; Zhu, Lu, Hesketh, 2009, pp.920–923; Johnson, 1993, pp.61–87). All of these strategies and behaviours have tremendously influenced and even changed relationships and dynamics in the Chinese family, and the long-term effects are likely to last for several generations.

In a one-child family, without brothers and sisters, the child is totally affected by the mother and father. The mother brings a strong femininity and the father a strong masculinity. This polarised experience of masculinity and femininity will, I suggest, incite rebellion against traditional definitions of femininity and masculinity in China. The girl may become more masculine in the roles she plays in her own home as she grows up. In some cases, because of the son preference in Chinese tradition, the projection onto a girl that she is a boy may aggregate her masculinity. Furthermore, the boy, when he grows up, may be more feminine in the roles he adopts. Based on my observations of clients who have experienced a strong son preference in some shape or form, a boy's family is more likely to spoil the boy, worry about his security and forbid any risky behaviour. This stems from a fear of losing the only boy and hence, their only link to the future and the longevity of the family name. Meanwhile, a girl's family encourages her to be independent and competitive to prove she is not inferior to boys.

This transformation is challenging the traditional requirements of daughters and sons. A child from a one-child family will most likely be the centre of the family, regardless of gender (Zhai & Gao, 2010). Further, only daughters have unprecedented parental support to gain more power in society and in their endeavours (Fong, 2002). Hence, when these daughters grow up, it is very difficult for them to identify with traditional perceptions of what it means to be a wife. Furthermore, they have more resources to afford a divorce or to remain single. These empowered daughters have different attitudes to marriage and intimacy, or, they may be spoiled and remain dependent and 'entitled', barely separated from their parents.As a result of the emergence of these one-daughter families, in urban China, it is becoming increasingly common for a couple to live with the wife's parents (Pimentel & Liu, 2004). This phenomenon also challenges the old Chinese patriarchy, which only considered living with a husband's family 'normal'. Urban couples raised in such circumstances may be affected by the clash between ancient Chinese values and new family structures, which are the result of political interventions. This ongoing effect of the one-child family may cause more complicated dilemmas in their relationships. (On the one hand, the only child might receive all the love and attention from the parents; on the other hand, he/she might lack the ability to integrate into a group. This means his/her relationships with the other are governed by projections and unrealistic (and unmet) expectations of others.)

Intimate relationships in China today

'Femininity' and 'masculinity' in intimate relationships are never simple issues. From my discussion above, these issues can be addressed in China today. I argue that intimate relationships and sexualised images involved in relationships are affected by the inheritance of old traditions, the expectations based on Westernised romantic love and the interventions of political decisions that have changed the structure of family life.In modern China, one-child families are becoming more predominant. Some characteristics of these families are:

1   In small families, particularly in three-person families, the husband and wife can become closer to each other, without being distracted by older generations or multiple children.
2   In this small family structure, children have a closer relationship with their parents, particularly with their mothers, than in larger families (Chen & Ling, 2006). Furthermore, due to less financial stress, the father's absence can be reduced (presuming, of course, that the father is the main breadwinner). There are more opportunities for a father to get close to his child. Therefore, the psychosocial development of children will be affected by the father's increased physical presence, and the archetypal materials that are subsequently activated.
3   In one-child families, boys carry more femininity while girls carry more masculinity. This may redefine the concepts of femininity and masculinity and challenge the classical Jungian understanding of both. Post-Jungian perspectives offer more flexibility with respect to gender identification and sexual development. This development in China, accompanied by a suitable psychological lens to note the changes, could be the catalyst for a more fluid/integrative understanding of anima and animus in the Chinese context.

The final point is quite important for love. In our own time, the entire project of cultivating Eros via the patriarchal anima has been challenged by feminists, who see patriarchy as stifling the possibilities for women, forcing them to shape their bodies and personalities according to anima ideals. Hence, love in feminist times attempts to free women's lives, and even their desires, from the structures of the man's anima (Douglas, 1990). Many men are 'feminist-enough' to let their wives be who they are. In China today, many men agree that a wife should pursue her career development and live out her values. In return, this kind of attitude affects the roles of men in families and makes room for the animus as well as the anima. Thus, femininity and masculinity are no longer rigid and stereotyped concepts.

Nevertheless, problematic intimacy issues are still emerging. First, in one-child families, children might lack experience of relating to peers, so they lack enough knowledge required to share and negotiate central intimacy. (Even if they have peer companions in school, the partnership of schoolmates is different from that of siblings, which is quite important for the development of integral relationships in society.) Second, parents in one-child families may be more likely to interfere in their children's marriages, and children may remain dependent on their parents even after marrying and having their own family. This can lead to huge conflicts between couples from one-child families. Third, people carrying a strong mother/father complex are rarely satisfied with their spouses, because no one can compare with the inner image of the mother/father. When they feel disappointed, they are likely to give up their marriages easily, project the ideal spouse onto another person or do both simultaneously. According to the *Chinese Youth Development Report in the New Century*, most divorcees were born after 1978 (the year in which the one-child policy was implemented) and the main reason for divorce is infidelity (2012).

Furthermore, the ambiguity of the notions of femininity and masculinity makes young people expend more effort in developing their own sexual identification and relating to the opposite sex. This is a very new phenomenon for Chinese youth. It is not possible to return to the old Chinese way, or simply to copy Westernised ideals, and one cannot simply follow the pattern offered by the government. Therefore, this is also a good opportunity for young Chinese individuals to seek their own paths. For many years, Chinese people and their relationships within the family have served the community, state and system, that is, for a certain group, but not for themselves. Now, despite having more struggles and demonstrating more explicit pain during the process, this is not necessarily a bad thing. As mentioned at the outset, young Chinese people are facing a crisis in their relationships, but in Chinese, 'crisis' means that danger and opportunity coexist and, sometimes, opportunity is fostered by danger and follows it closely. Hence, there is a great possibility for young people to break free from the rigid frame and pattern of their marriages which used to establish and maintain collective benefits and instead find their own way to have an intimate relationship as independent individuals. Such exploration and discussion will be conducted in Chapter 8.

Outline of chapters

In the following three chapters, I discuss the basic relevant ideas and background of my study on femininity and masculinity among young Chinese couples today from a depth-psychological perspective. In Chapter 2, I discuss the notions of femininity and masculinity and explore the current debates on these notions from depth psychological perspectives. I address our ability to understand femininity and masculinity on three levels: first, as two abstract, interdependent potentials which assist our understanding of the world in a basic, dualist way. When it comes to our relationships, the contrasexual other represents the potential that we do not have now but we could have in the future. The second level refers to the culturally/socially assigned notions of femininity and masculinity. I argue that the characteristics and functions Jung assigned to the anima and animus are stereotypes of men and women rooted in Western culture. In different cultural and social contexts, however, such characteristics and functions can be different. The third level refers to real men and women, as explored in the clinical discussions of Freud and his followers. Based on this categorisation, I discuss the relevant issues in the clinical realm and demonstrate the situation of men and women in traditional Chinese society and how the picture of boys and girls has been affected by the one-child policy. All of the above comprise the basic knowledge with which to understand my further exploration and discussion regarding the Chinese categorisation of the feminine and masculine and attitudes towards men and women.

In Chapter 3, I illustrate how depth psychology – including both psycho-analysis and analytical psychology – has developed in China. I show the achievements that Chinese teams have attained in their training approach, academic area and clinical practice while discussing some external difficul-ties and possible problems of developing these two depth psychologies in a Chinese setting. This historical background allows readers to understand developments in China.

In Chapter 4, I discuss the applicability of depth psychology in China, which has never before been done by a Chinese therapist or researcher. Usually Chinese therapists' default depth psychology is applicable and apply it in their own way. I note that the debate regarding the differences between applying psychoanalysis in Chinese and Western settings has always existed, and Chinese teams have already made modifications and contributions, in particular the team of Shen Heyong. As an insider who grew up in China and completed my basic training there as an analytical psychology-oriented therapist, as well as a witness who spent the last five years obtaining Western academic training, I look back at events in China and attempt to establish a more neutral viewpoint from which to discuss the possible problems behind the fever of depth psychology in China and the rush to 'integrate' or 'localise' the two depth psychologies there. I also point out the challenges encountered by Chinese teams. Despite these problems, I conclude with a very positive attitude regarding the future and the hope that I have to continue my study of sexualised images and intim-ate relationships in China from the lens of depth psychology.

In Chapter 5, I interview eight urban couples who demonstrated curiosity in couple therapy and tried to work through their marriage problems or improve their marriages with the assistance of professionals. I identify their expectations and experiences of marriage, and the relevant female and male images they hold. The findings suggest that young Chinese people have rela-tively traditional female images when it comes to marriage but their idealised male images have obvious Western characteristics. Women from one-child families have different expectations of themselves compared with women from families with multiple children, while men from one-child families have closer relationships with their mothers. This study focuses on the exploration of issues relevant to intimate relationships among young Chinese urban couples from the level of their collective consciousness.

In the next chapter, to obtain a deeper understanding from the cultural level, I amplify the opera *The Peony Pavilion* to illustrate the function of sexuality and aggression in the process of individuation and the effects of attachment between parents and children in Chinese settings. Although this story was created 400 years ago, the heroine's sense of self and her relationship with her parents are more like those of a modern girl from a one-child family, and the obstacles in her way remain in China today, even though the external environment is quite different. She and her pattern of relating to a man chosen by herself has been an ideal for young Chinese people for many generations, and her experience of individuation can be borrowed by young Chinese people today who share similar family issues but are under less severe external pressure.

In Chapter 7, I study two clinical cases – one male patient and one female patient who came to me because of their marriage issues. To develop a deep understanding of both internal and external conflicts and specific difficulties among young people who have suffered in their relationships, I examine their stories, family dynamics and their relationship with me. In so doing, I come to the conclusion that a very typical cause of pain in Chinese marriage is that, due to the close bond with the extended family, young people with marriage issues have little sense of agency and cannot recognise their own or their spouse's subjectivity. Consequently, they retain an omnipotent fantasy as Giant Babies who are possessed by their mother complexes, and cannot resolve their Oedipal conflicts in order to enter a more mature level of relations as independent individuals.

In the reflection section, Chapter 8, I distinguish between the two ethical notions of 'integration' and 'integrity', which, at first glance at their linguistic forms, seem similar. I address marriage as a matter beyond the difference and cooperation between the masculine and feminine, men and women, and instead as that established between two distinct individuals. The core issue for Chinese marriage is the conflict between individual wills and collective requirements that are deeply rooted in traditional Chinese values and government interventions. I argue that a new approach to marriage is to find integrity for both partners, which means that both spouses can retain their self-consistency and boundaries, have amicable attitudes to each other, face their differences and conflicts and acknowledge the importance of them for a relationship. In return, such marriages could foster integrity in extreme circumstances and encourage individuation.

I would not venture to say that this book provides a complete picture of intimate relationships in China; rather, it offers a new perspective with which to examine the Chinese psyche and new angles for understanding young Chinese people, particularly those generations since the implementation of the one-child policy. However, China is a large country with many different regions and complex dynamics. I have not discussed many marriage issues in rural regions and among peasants, and the issues of this demographic could be quite different. A huge gap currently exists between rural and urban China and this gap is becoming ever bigger. Urban and rural China may be totally different worlds, both psychologically and physically. As a therapist who was born and grew up in large cities, my background and subjectivity make it difficult for me to gain in-depth access to people living in rural regions and to obtain authentic first-hand material, despite the fact that I spent several months living in the deep mountain region of Sichuan province after the major earthquake of 2008.

The interviews I conducted and the clinical materials I collected are from people living in cities and the opera I chose to amplify is well-known in affluent regions and among educated people. In a word, most of the research materials in this book are from regions of China which are more civilised and do not face survival issues. Hence, this book focuses more on marriage issues within a certain cohort of young Chinese people – educated couples living in cities. It examines their inner struggles, pain and difficulties and attempts to address the advantages and potential of the children from one-child families who have been raised under the shadow of a prevalent and pessimistic prejudice against their characters and capacities. I must concede that what first prompted me to study marriage issues among young Chinese people were the problems and difficulties I observed in my clinical work and heard in my surroundings. However, under deeper examination and further study, I gradually developed a more optimistic attitude towards this group and their problems and believe that subsequent generations will improve. This attitude will be demonstrated throughout the following chapters.

Notes

1   Compared with the *Oedipus complex*, the mother complex can be constellated in both daughters and sons. It affects the personality development of children, as well as their future relationships (CW9i, para. 162–163).
2   The Chinese Revolution of 1911 marked the end of imperialism in mainland China.
3   In the intersubjective space, the typical experiences are not only from individuals' own lives but also from their subliminal communication with others (Roesler, 2012, p.88).
4   In Jungian psychotherapy with couples, as Young-Eisendrath pointed out, there are three frames, 'reflect[ting] the gradual retreat of dominance-submission themes of power and the gradual appearance of attachment-separation themes of love' (1984, p.88). These two retreatments are important turning points in couple therapy. The three frames are characterised by 'the desire for possession and dominance', 'understanding the repressed feminine' and 'the power of free choice of love' (ibid.).
5   In this book, the 'imperial' period of China refers to the period from the first Qin dynasty to the last Qing dynasty. During this period, although one dynasty was replaced by another, the official governors of China were always emperors.
6   In most Chinese narratives, the father image is presented as an old man. He usually represents authority, playing a crucial role at big moments. However, he rarely shows up in daily life and has little emotional connection with individuals. Sometimes, he is quite rigid and relentless. The 'senex' is an archetypal image of an old man: 'When internally active as a withering self-critic, [it] has the same silencing and deadening effect on the feminine figure inside the man, the anima' (Beebe, 2011, pp.302–303).
7   Besides representing sexual relationships, Jung also defined Eros as 'interweaving' and 'relatedness' (CW13, para. 60).

Chapter 2

The notions of femininity and masculinity and men and women in China

Femininity and masculinity in depth psychology

Ideas on femininity and masculinity within psychoanalysis

Since Freud's early discussions on sexuality in psychoanalysis, there have been many debates on how to define and categorise masculinity and femininity. Freud's main critique focuses on the following assertion: The distinction between masculinity and femininity is based on anatomy, and because man possesses a penis and woman lacks it, masculinity has an inborn superiority and domination (Freud, 1924, pp.177–178). Wright listed Freud's, Jones' and Lacan's ideas about femininity and demonstrated that Freud and Lacan both considered the lack of a phallus to be the basis for defining femininity. In this view, therefore, masculinity is the original state and femininity is the derivative, which results in woman being seen as an incomplete man due to her 'failure in relation to the rules defined by the phallus' (Wright, 1992, p.93). Meanwhile, Jones, although she opposed this idea, agreed that the body is the basis of perception of a female's femininity. Along with other scholars whom she lists in her dictionary, she could not avoid citing 'penis envy'[1] in relation to the topic of femininity, despite disagreeing that the masculine is primary. Further, these scholars were unable to relinquish discussing the difference between the female and male bodies, and Wright criticises the fact that many other authors since Freud have 'reduce[d] femininity to feminine sexuality' (p.94). When discussing how a girl develops her own sense of being a woman, they discussed the effect on her development of the mother being without a phallus and the father with a phallus. Thus, the basic issue always centres on the phallus. The boy, who might have different frustrations and identify with the other position to the girl, might share a similar theme of the phallus.

Tyson (1997) pointed out Freud's admission that both man and woman carry 'male parts' and 'female parts', and his attribution of an individual 'sense of masculinity or femininity' partly to 'early identifications' and partly to 'the unconscious fantasies that arise with the recognition of anatomical difference' (p.385). Guarton (1996) studied Freud's statement that 'the end of analysis coincides with the acceptance of femininity', and found that what Freud really meant was that 'men should accept their femininity' under the domination of their masculinity and that women should 'accept their femininity', which 'predates the development of a separate sense of self and precludes the acceptance of desire' (pp.695–696). On the other hand, however, women should 'renounce their masculinity', because masculinity in women is a pathological symptom (ibid.). Tyson (1997) challenged Freud's prejudice against women and argued that sexuality and penis envy were not the exclusive factors in a woman's development. He seemed to share Wright's opinion that 'female psychology is preferred over female sexuality' (p.387). Moreover, Tyson admitted that the development of gender is diverse, but emphasised that the sense of gender identity is built on conflict and eventually settles either on femininity or masculinity, regardless of whether or not it is consistent 'with biological sex'. He ignored the fact that even in a mature individual, gender flexibility exists and conflict might not be necessary if the environment allows someone to choose his/her gender freely, or identify with the father's or mother's sex of his/her own free will. Almost all of these criticisms of Freud highlight his idea of male superiority. While some scholars do disagree with his statement about parental effects on an individual's sense of femininity and masculinity, these scholars share the same premises as Freud – i.e. 1) that femininity and masculinity are very specific ideas and their own characteristics can be distinctly categorised. The development of the sense of femininity and masculinity is based on the conflicts with the mother or father, or on the struggle with both separately; 2) even the feminine and masculine parts can be shared by both woman and man, but a healthy, mature individual should gradually develop one clear gender identity based on solving this inner conflict and the one that is consistent with their biological sex is the better choice. That is to say, a woman should identify with the feminine and a man with the masculine; 3) sexuality, and its representative, the phallus, are at the core of the development of an individual's sense of masculinity and femininity. Some of these premises affect other psychoanalytical scholars' ideas in relation to their own theories on the feminine and masculine.

Instead of the terms 'active' or 'passive', Winnicott (1971) applied the terms 'doing' and 'being' to describe the internal feminine and masculine. Winnicott believed that these two dimensions were universal and distinct in every individual. Igra (1992), who supported Winnicott's view, stated that 'being', the pure female element, 'is related to receptivity, containing, transformation and dependence' and it 'presupposes a tolerance for mutual dependence'. On the other hand, 'doing', the pure male element, 'emerges as a capacity of penetration, linking, ordering-structuring, differentiation and protecting of the mother-baby unit' and it 'expresses the capability of the individual to challenge and use the object in a non-exploiting sense' (p.140). These categorisations focus on the different functions of femininity and masculinity, eliminating Freud's negative judgement of the feminine. Igra also made a clear distinction between passivity, a pathological symptom which 'stifles personal development' and 'being', 'a capacity for receptivity ...', which is 'one of the prerequisites for change and growth' (p.144). However, Winnicott's description of masculinity and femininity is based on emotional states; they are related to another object and have their own contribution in relationships. Jung and his early followers did not think these aspects were related to the masculine, but attributed them solely to the feminine, a view upon which I will expand later.

Further, unlike Freud, Winnicott (1971) stated that 'being' and 'doing' were both experienced through the early interaction with the mother and that 'being' was the primary stage. Boys and girls share the same process of a sense of femininity and masculinity. The mother first expresses the former and then the latter. The individual must recognise the two aspects separately and develop both; this is the foundation of a mature personality. Here, Winnicott discarded the emphasis on the crucial role of the phallus in the development of gender identity and focused instead on the mother's crucial influence, which is progressive. However, like Freud, Igra (1992) claimed that a mature man should carry a leading masculine part while a mature woman should carry a leading feminine part, even if both are equipped with femininity and masculinity. In his opinion, the biological body is still the basis of the development of femininity and masculinity.

Sies (1992) disagreed with Igra's reference to 'being' as the female and 'doing' as the male. Neither should play a leading role in a mature personality, for either a man or woman. The split of attributing 'being' to woman and 'doing' to man would limit both sexes and harm the integration that is emphasised by both Winnicott and Igra as the main achievement of individual development. Sies emphasised that focusing on 'gender differences' or the 'necessary difference of female and male' limits our understanding of what constitutes the real female and male (p.150). She also pointed out that the 'three-sided relationship' (mother-father-child) is an 'organizing factor' for an individual to reach 'his/her position as girl or boy' (p.148); not only do the mother and father both individually play an important role in this process, but they also play a role as a pair – in other words, the relationship between the father and mother affects the process. This is a major development that challenges the dogmatic psychoanalytic understanding of femininity, masculinity and the factors which organise them.

Debates amongst Jungians

Like Freud, Jung also considered both men and women to carry femininity and masculinity. In his theory, the masculine part is in the man's conscious and 'the feminine belongs to man as his own unconscious femininity' (CW5, para. 678), which he named the anima. In parallel, femininity in a woman is represented by consciousness, while her masculinity belongs to her unconscious, called the animus (Harding, 1955/1971, p.29). Jung was passionate about describing the anima, as evidenced by his repeated elaboration of it in his works. As Hillman (1985) concluded, the anima 'remains a portmanteau idea packed thick with other notions – eros, feeling, human relationships, introversion, fantasy, concrete life […] [– and] the development of anima […] continues to mean many things to many men' (p.7). At the same time, Jung had less interest in a woman's animus and while admitting that the animus has both positive and negative aspects, he always discussed its negative effects in a woman, an attitude that also affected his early followers. In Hannah's book *The Animus* (2011), she elaborated the negative influence of the animus on woman and advised them on how to avoid being possessed or controlled by it, before mentioning just briefly that it also has a positive aspect. In a more general way, the early Jungians, who were deeply affected by Jung, referred to anima as a function of relationship and mood, eros and referred to animus as mind and opinions, logos. In the works of these earlier Jungians, the anima covers what Winnicott describes as the state of being and doing, the female and male elements, and the animus has only destructive effects on human relationships. Secretly, Jung and some of his followers shared Freud's attitude towards the superiority of men. They agreed that the response of a woman's unconscious, her thinking function, was that of an inferior man, while man's feeling function was that of an inferior woman. However, they had a more positive attitude toward a man's potential to integrate his own inferior feeling than they did to a woman's potential to integrate her own inferior thinking. Although they all valued the feminine, in fact they valued man's femininity and were suspicious of a woman's masculinity, as Freud was (Jung, 1968; Harding, 1952, 1955/1971; Hannah, 2011). In other words, in their eyes, man would have a greater potential than woman to achieve integration and be complete. Further, when Stevens (1994/2007) explored the stages of life in Jung's theory, he claimed that 'in many cultures there are no female initiation rites, and the tasks of bringing this new feminine consciousness into being falls to the initiated male' (p.76). This assertion reflects a psychoanalytic interpretation and picks up again the old notion that a woman needs a man and his penis to recognise her own femininity, a view criticised by Tyson (1997).

Many scholars in analytical psychology have opposed the original ideas on the anima and animus. Hillman (1985) refuted the notion that the anima is 'the contrasexual side of man', maintaining that this notion is based on 'a fantasy of opposites' (p.9). In other words, its premise is that 'men and women are opposites, conscious and unconscious are opposites, conscious masculinity and unconscious femininity are opposite' (ibid.).

This is an arbitrary statement to put the feminine and masculine into a split, bipolar position, which might be the source of discrimination and wars between them. Further, Hillman emphasised that 'the syndrome of inferior feminine [...] is relative to the dominants of the culture and the *Zeitgeist*' (p.13). It is unfair to say that, today, the anima is still the inferior personality of a man and the man who tries to actively identify with it would be like an inferior woman, not as mature as other men.

Further, Beebe (1989) conceded that both men and women carry anima and animus. Based on his own observation, he inferred that there is 'a more differentiated eros in women and a more differentiated logos in men' (p.xix). (Usually, Jungians appointed eros to the anima and logos to the animus.) Beebe pointed out that 'Jung gradually understood that the masculine and feminine principles are not given; they are built up through experience' (p.xx). Therefore, the different quantity of eros and logos in the inner world of women and men might be the result of different expectations, education and other internal and external experiences which they encounter. The categorisation of the feminine and masculine, and the function of woman and man, are affected by historical, social and cultural elements and would be shifted by the changes in these factors. (Effects from the mother and father are still considered, but they are no longer the exclusive factors.) This idea has been supported by many scholars (Guarton, 1996; Samuels, 1989; Seidenberg, 1991a; Wright, 1992; Young-Eisendrath, 1998). Thus, it is necessary to reconsider the functions of masculinity and femininity in the theory of Jung and his early supporters, and it would be problematic to insist on the categorisation of femininity and masculinity, superiority and inferiority, as Jung originally did.

Hence, it is not that women are born equipped with certain femininity and know how to apply it appropriately, nor that men are naturally familiar with their masculinity. An individual may discard or abuse his/her masculinity or femininity. Both women and men must learn how to balance the feminine and masculine principles, which, as Hillman suggested, might be beyond sexual difference. The idea that it is unnecessary to attribute a dominating gender identity to an individual based on his/her biological sex is also supported by many psychoanalysts (Guarton, 1996; Seidenberg, 1991a; Sies, 1992). Seidenberg (1991b, 1991c) affirmed that, today, woman can pursue achievement, ignore the stereotypical requirement of nurturing and motherhood and become involved with social improvement, as (some) men do. There is no such 'feminine nature' or 'anatomy-destiny' (p.99) that she should worry about. Observation of same sex couples could offer further evidence for this idea. Seidenberg (1991a) suggested that lesbian couples could enjoy 'the warmth and comfort of object relations', which was considered the typical feminine function, and demonstrate 'autonomy and individuation', which were considered the typical masculine characteristics (p.102). The traditionally defined masculinity and femininity could be found in same-sex couples, which together form the foundation of mature relationships. Guarton (1996) also noted that 'both a heterosexual and a homosexual individual' need to bridge the dissociation of the 'masculine and feminine identification', which is split 'in a conventionally polarized society', to 'become engaged in mature relationships' (p.702). This suggestion strongly suggests, again, that regardless of biological sex or sexual orientation, individuals develop masculinity and femininity together. Thus, it is unfair to attribute compensation to one and domination to the other, as Jung and Freud did.

Understanding the feminine and the masculine in the psyche

Samuels (1989), Young-Eisendrath (1998) and Beebe (2011) all agree that the feminine and masculine principles, the anima and animus, might be a metaphor of potential and might link with otherness (a metaphor for alterity). Hillman (1985) suggested that anima may be 'even beyond psyche' (p.55) and he attempted to situate the sexual principle in a much wider context. Colman (1996) was dissatisfied with the proposition that the anima and animus refer to 'difference and otherness' and worried that this 'downgrades the sexual archetypes to a secondary phenomenon, merely a metaphor for the larger archetypal idea of difference' (pp.38–39). It might be true that the notions of the masculine and feminine principles have an auxiliary function, in offering vivid pictures to help people understand more abstruse and intangible dynamics and concepts from daily phenomena. However, this is not a downgrade. On the contrary, it emphasises the importance of femininity and masculinity, which is the basis for a comprehensive understanding of psyche and nature.

A parallel may be found in psychoanalysis. Guarton (1996) applied Yin and Yang in ancient Chinese philosophy and the particle and the wave in quantum physics to illustrate masculinity and femininity. He noted that Yin is related to the feminine, dark and receptive, while Yang is related to the masculine, light and assertive. They reflect the principles of femininity and masculinity, respectively, but are also the principles of nature. On the other hand, the particle, a phenomenon in the universe, is the masculine side 'associated with the sense of I, boundaries, defined, and centered on the separate self', while the wave, another phenomenon in the universe, is the feminine function, demonstrating the 'not-I aspect of the self', which could be illustrated as 'the one who sees the similarities, between self and other [...] and is able to place itself in another's position' (p.692). Yin and Yang, the particle and the wave, cohabit in nature, define each other, and each 'fulfills itself in fulfilling the other' (p.691). This can help us understand femininity and masculinity. They are not concrete, specific sexual certainties, and are beyond the contrasexual position. They illustrate the relation between I and not-I, the tendency for stability and flexibility and the potential of otherness. They are parallel – equally important rather than complementary. Hence, based on what has been discussed, in my opinion, there are three levels of the feminine and masculine both outside and inside clinical settings. The first is the level of the femininity and masculinity of Nature. At this level, anima (and animus), as Hillman suggested, is beyond the psyche and belongs to nature (1985, p.53). Here, femininity and masculinity are abstract. They are two coexisting potentials and parallel flows of energy. For men, Bly (1990/2001) sketched the wild energy of the hairy man, while Estes (1992/2008) portrayed the power of the inner wild woman, and Ma (2010) depicted Xi Wang Mu, a Chinese goddess associated 'with yin-yang duality' (p.92). All of these works provide evidence of these potentials and flows. The psychoanalyst Guarton (1996) referred to Benjamin in assigning the masculine to 'the assertion of the self' and the feminine to 'the recognition [...] of the other' (p.698). This assignment also demonstrates a tendency of interdependency between the nature of the feminine and masculine. The first level of the feminine and masculine is the basic resource of energy and vitality.

The second is the level of the socially/culturally assigned notions of feminine and masculine. At this level, the categories of the feminine and masculine have very specific and usually socially/culturally assigned characteristics. Young-Eisendrath (1984) stated that 'the archetypal feminine is the province of relating and care-giving [...] [and] the archetypal masculine, is the domain of distancing and separating' (p.12). Such categories were supported by Jung and many of his followers, who traditionally put these characteristics, as mood and opinion respectively, into the domain of anima and animus (Colman, 1996; Harding, 1952; Hannah, 2011; Stevens, 1994/2007). However, as Williams (1989) suggested, 'traditional cultural stereotypes' (p.295) bring about this distinction and such categorising of femininity and masculinity is shaped by society and culture and shifts over time. The concrete definitions of femininity and masculinity, however, are hardly cross-cultural and beyond time. Therefore, I would rather refer to the feminine and the masculine within a specific range as 'the culturally/socially assigned feminine and masculine'. On this level, there are a number of derivatives, including the mother and father complexes, and further, 'collusion'[2] in marriage, which lead to the idealisation and devaluation in a mutual relationship. All of these comprise inner experiences, shaped by the culture and society in which we live and projected onto the other and onto our relationship (Williams, 1989, pp.295–297). They are not the same, however, as real external experiences.

The third level is the feminine and masculine in reality: the actual men/women we meet, the actual mother and father we have and the marriage in daily life that we deal with. When psychoanalysts discuss relationships in clinical settings, they usually refer to actual men and women on the third level. Shi and Scharff (2008) have pointed out the effect of social change on couple relationships; when they enter the therapeutic situation, they still focus on the real patients, their actual parents and their personal experiences in the family dynamics. Further, when psychoanalysts relate relationship issues to early personal development, as Clulow (2001) has noted, 'parenting' generally implies 'mothering'. Despite much recent literature on the role of the father in development, this observation of Clulow's still holds today. Most attention focuses on how the relationship between the mother and child affects the child's later relationship with the other. Even Clulow himself, when emphasising the triangular process in the founding of security of attachment, cannot avoid using the term 'the third parties', implying the father. Still, the mother-child relation is the primary one and the father comes later. It could be interpreted that the father's role in the development of the sense of connection is important, but not as crucial as the mother's. Thus, most psychoanalysts continue to focus on 'primitive dyads' (de Varela, 2004, p.234), which originated from the mother-child dyad and were then transferred to the therapist-patient dyad.

Unlike psychoanalysts, Jungians and post-Jungians pay more attention to the second level of femininity and masculinity. They emphasise that in both individual and couple therapy, a mature relationship must pass through the process of distinguishing the real other from one's own projection, and such ideal or devalued projections are usually shaped by our culture or society (Monick, 1987; Sanford, 1980; Williams, 1989; Young-Eisendrath, 1984, 1993). In Sanford's (1980) work with individuals with relationship difficulties, he identifies his patients' 'invisible partners', which are the patients' inner images of female and male. In Young-Eisendrath's (1984) work with couples, when she uses the terms 'the feminine and masculine', she discussed the inner femininity and masculinity that each member of the couple carries, which have specific, separated provinces. Both men and women have a masculine trace and must embrace their repressed feminine. In their work, they work not only with the actual men and women, but also with their patients' images of men, women and relationships, which are what a man/woman/marriage should/could be.In addition, when Jungians and post-Jungians deal with relationship issues in regard to the mother and father, they distinguish the real parent from the mother/father archetype or complex (Colman, 1996; Moore & Gillette, 1992; Young-Eisendrath, 1984). Colman (1996) emphasised that even actual parents carry the contrasexual archetypes, but are not co-terminus with them (p.40). That is to say, even actual experience with the parents would affect our relationship with the other sex, but there are archetypal or, more accurately, social and cultural factors that shape our relationships with the other sex, and with our intimate ones.

Further, in 1984, Young-Eisendrath made the criticism that, in general thinking, the feminine is bonded with motherhood. Particularly in psychoanalysis, psychoanalysts over-emphasise the importance of the mother's role in the child's emotional development and in the maturing of the personality (pp.70–73). However, in her work with couples to that point, she continuously discussed 'the great mother', 'the terrible mother' and 'the negative mother complex', while the father's role was almost entirely absent. However, in her later works, Young-Eisendrath analysed how parental complexes, particularly negative ones, affect or even damage marriages (1993, pp.225–232, 1998, p.210). She started to think that the father played as crucial a role as the mother in children's lives, and there was no reason to make a specific distinction between them.

Colman (1996) analysed the child's paradoxical attitude to incest in the Oedipal phase and stated that through distinguishing the mother and his anima, a man learns how to connect with other women, and a father affects his daughter's relationships with men through the animus. According to him, the mother mainly influences her son's emotional life while the father mainly influences his daughter's emotional life. However, Samuels illustrated that both the internal and external father make the sexual expression of the son move from mother to others (1985b, pp.33–36); Beebe also depicted how the son's emotional attitude might be formed by 'the father's transfer of the anima' (1985, p.109). From these statements, we may infer that both mother and father, on both the second and third levels of the feminine and masculine, influence their children's relationships.

Conclusively, my understanding of the feminine and masculine elements both outside and inside clinical settings is that they are beyond the limit of physical men/women, covering the sexual characteristics shaped by culture and society, but they are not, after all, concrete and cannot be understood by analytical terminology alone; rather, they are potentials and show a tendency to be balanced and integrated. We can find them in each party of a relationship and, more importantly, we must observe the dynamic flow caused by them between any dyadic relationship, in particular, the patient-therapist relationship. This is the key to our work with any individual or couple who seeks a solution to their relationship issues. If the therapist and patient focus solely on each other's concrete biosexuality, the so-called 'erotic transference' cannot be worked through and this will cause the therapy to fail. The second clinical case in Chapter Seven will demonstrate this point.

Women and men in Chinese culture

Basic ideas about femininity and masculinity in China

As mentioned above, in traditional Chinese culture, people use yin and yang to refer to femininity and masculinity respectively. Yin and yang are not isolated notions; one cannot exist without the other and they interact with each other. They exist in the universe with no fixed meaning and consist of the dynamics between things (Brownell & Wasserstrom, 2002, p.26; Ma, 2010, pp.84–87; Mann, 2011, pp.28–31). These notions correspond to the first level of femininity and masculinity in my understanding.

In Chinese medicine, people believe that yin and yang exist in the bodies of both women and men. In the Song dynasty, they even thought that 'prepubescent girls and postmenopausal women' were androgynous, like men at the same age (Mann, 2011, p.87). Therefore, the concepts of femininity and masculinity are not 'categories opposed to each other' and are not 'directly linked to heterosexuality'. They are 'plural categories' which are based on family and society (Brownell & Wasserstrom, 2002, p.34). These ideas are quite different from those of Western thinking, which distinguishes women and men in terms of biological difference and places them in a 'fundamental, immutable opposition' to one another (Brownell & Wasserstrom, 2002, p.26). In other words, in Chinese eyes, anatomy is not destiny. Further, the socially/culturally assigned characteristics of femininity and masculinity are not clearly distinguished or opposite to one another. For example, Chinese people believe that both men and women should be filial, modest and obedient. Although chastity was a requirement of women, men, too, were discouraged from indulging in sexual activities. Sex in itself was not to be enjoyed, but served the purpose of procreation. Apart from that, abstinence was always virtuous for a man (Sommer, 2002, p.68, p.83; Mann, 2011, pp.3–46, p.58). The categorisation of functions and roles of women and men are based on family demands and social requirements. This is the foundation for understanding women and men in China.

The relations between yin and yang, femaleness and maleness, could be within each other, 'and the two are in constant motion relative to each other' (Brownell & Wasserstrom, 2002, p.20). However, in different philosophies of China, they are not equally important. In Taoism, yin is regarded as the primary source, the high value, the foundation of the universe, but in Confucianism, which highlights patriarchy, the importance of yin and yang is reversed (Brownell & Wasserstrom, 2002, p.26; Ma, 2010, pp.85–86). The two incompatible ideas in Taoism and Confucianism contribute to the ambivalent attitudes toward women in China – following the instruction of Confucianism, which was that 'men are superior and women are inferior', but believing the notion of Taoism, which was that the yin/feminine is stronger and the primary force in the universe. In a word, Chinese people value the feminine, but oppress women.

Inferior women and powerful femininity

In imperial China, women were in an inferior position and were oppressed by the patriarchal rules. Therefore, it is easy to reach the conclusion that there was a huge inequality between men and women and women were in a lower, subordinated position. Upon further exploration, however, we might reach a different view.

On the surface, the inequality is obvious. In ancient China, there existed no Chinese character or word to represent women; there were only terms for 'daughter', 'wife' and 'mother'. Furthermore, before a woman married, she had no social identity. Women were tightly bonded with the family: they seemed to be the property of the family and had no individual identity at all at that time. We must observe, however, that people also thought the wife played a central role in 'her marital family' and that 'the regulation and harmony of families was [her] responsibility' (Mann, 1991, pp.208–209). Therefore, women occupied an essential place in Chinese families. Further, the rulers of the Chinese government in every dynasty looked upon families as the basic unit of society. A man without a wife would pose a threat to the government and could cause the collapse of a dynasty (Brownell & Wasserstrom, 2002, p.45; Mann, 2011, p.58; Sommer, 2002). Indirectly, therefore, the contribution of women was also essential for the stability and security of Chinese society. This point will be expanded upon below.

There were three typical features of old Chinese society to prove the inequality between women and men. These coincide with the basic notion in Confucianism of 'superior men and inferior women'. The first feature was foot binding, which had two basic functions. On the one hand, it was the symbol of sex, an erotic and aesthetic taste, a stimulant based on concealment (Ma, 2010, p.34; Mann, 2011, p.168; Xu, 2013, p.94). On the other hand, and more importantly, as Ma's study (2010) reveals, it was a bond to femininity in women. It restricted women's strength, limited their freedom of movement, gave them no choice but to remain in the family and remain loyal to their husbands, and most importantly, it cut off their connection with the earth, the source of feminine power. Behind this restriction and torture, there was the implicit power of femininity and the fear of such power.

The second feature was the requirement for women to maintain their chastity. The best way to ensure this was to keep women cloistered. Working outside and making contact with men outside of the family was considered immoral and threatening to a woman's chastity (Mann, 2011, pp.6–11). There was also a chastity 'package', which not only included sexual chastity, meaning that a woman should not even indulge in sex with her own husband, but also filial piety, obedience and modesty (Theiss, 2002, pp.47–56). The reputation of an old Chinese family was highly reliant upon the performance of the women in this family (Sommer, 2002, p.89) and the effect of a woman's virtue could even extend beyond her own family to the community (Theiss, 2002, p.63).

But why did old Chinese people value women's chastity so greatly? Firstly, as Mann (2011) pointed out, in ancient China, people believed that sexual desire was an 'innate physical need' (p.31) and they did not deny the strength of passion. However, they valued long-term pleasure more and believed that indulging in sex would harm a man's health (pp.39–46). In

Chinese eyes, women were not the passive objects of sexual desire but an active temptation in the sexual realm. There are stories in every dynasty, therefore, of how a 'state-toppler (seductive women)' seduced the emperor and caused a 'female disaster' (Mann, 2011, p.51; Yi, 1998b, pp.25–27). Moreover, Rawski (1991) referred to the common concern among rich families that a young concubine would use the affection of her master to obtain power and destroy the family (p.195). All of these evidence the fear of women's sexual power in the old Chinese dynasties. Besides, the 'unvirtuous, unfeminine women', like a shrew, would also harm a man's masculinity and damage the patriarchal order (Theiss, 2002, pp.61–63). In fact, the rulers of old China realised women's power, resulting in a trend of women being encouraged to be martyrs to retain their fidelity and purity (Mann, 2011, p.124), and even further, to protect the state by devoting their lives to it (Yi, 1998b, pp.25–27). In ancient China, therefore, people consciously valued the power of women and facilitated them to devote themselves for the benefit of the state. At the same time, however, they oppressed women by limiting them to their marital homes in order to eradicate the unconscious fear of the destructive side of feminine power.

The third phenomenon is that of polygamy in imperial China, which is actually a common misunderstanding in relation to Chinese marriage amongst Westerners, and even among young Chinese people. In fact, China has had a monogamous system of marriage since the Han dynasty, which means that a man had just one legal wife, while other sexual partners, including concubines, were the maids of the family. They offered their service to the master and his wife, and both had the power to decide their destiny, even selling them out of the family (Ebrey, 1991, pp.6–8; Rawski, 1991, pp.185–189; Thatcher, 1991, p.47; Watson, 1991, pp.239–246; Yi, 1998b, p.113). There were also patriarchal inequalities in imperial China and Ebrey (1991) considered the basic inequality of marriage to comprise the inequality between men and women (pp.1–24). However, if we explore further, we may reach the conclusion that this was, in fact, the inequality between the classes and social status.

A woman from a poor family was usually treated as an inferior partner, an informal sexual object in relationships, who could be sold, as mentioned above. Even when married, a woman could be 'rented, pawned or sold by [a desperate husband]' because of poverty (Mann, 2011, p.58). In addition, a man from a poor family could never afford to marry a bride and was marginalised, to be referred to as the 'bare stick' (Mann, 2011, pp.4–5; Sommer, 2002, pp.68–74). Thus, both men and women could be the victims of inequality in marriage. However, a wife from the 'matching door' – from a high class background – was almost equal to her husband and sometimes played a dominant role, retaining her own property and her birth family's honour if she was from a powerful family and had a considerable dowry (Chaffee, 1991, pp.159–160; Ebrey, 1991, pp.8–14; Mann, 2011, p.57). Empowered and influential women were not rare in Chinese history (Ma, 2010, p.55). Thus, it is a misconception that only males were valued in ancient Chinese society. On the contrary, women found their own ways to negotiate their position and to hold power.However, this is not to say that women were respected in general. More often, they were treated as the property of the marital family. For example, after the husband died, it was very difficult for them to control their futures and their destiny was usually arranged by the husband's family (Holmgren, 1991, p.63). Mann (2002) used the phrase 'traffic in women' to describe women as objects in the marriage market (pp.55–58) and these words are both vivid and accurate. However, this does not mean that men were free, independent individuals in the same picture.

The man in China: a mother's boy and brother's brother

Compared with the cloistered women in imperial China, men from all classes were encouraged to go outside to pursue their business interests (Mann, 2011, pp.12–13). In addition, a man could have several sexual partners and could even become involved in sexual activities with other men. Unlike in the West, homosexual activity was a widely known phenomenon in China and had never been strictly forbidden. Even rulers in different periods had varying attitudes, from being involved in it themselves to announcing it to be illegal but without severe punishment (Brownell & Wasserstrom, 2002, p.21; Mann, 2011, p.50, p.68, pp.139–150; Sommer, 2002, pp.74–76). However, this does not mean that men were freer, more independent individuals than women at that time.

Yi (1998b) argued that in traditional Chinese culture, a good and respectable man would be abstinent, while sexual desire was not an appreciated masculine characteristic (pp.10–23). In sum, sex should only be in service of reproduction. A good man should not sleep with prostitutes or with men, because these behaviours could not produce offspring. In old Chinese society, people considered homosexuality to be a replacement for heterosexuality, which was regarded to be the correct way for sex to occur (Brownell & Wasserstrom, 2002, p.21; Mann, 2011, p.68, pp.140–149; Sommer, 2002, pp.72–74). Therefore, because of the moral requirement, it was very difficult for a man to really enjoy sexual pleasure.

Further, Yi (1998b) suggested that the typical characteristics attributed to the masculine in Western culture, like aggression, domination and chivalric elements, were not welcome amongst Chinese men. He described how under the Chinese moral system, a man should obey his parents and the emperor. When faced with difficulties in obeying them, such as their demands being ridiculous or exorbitant, he should protest with tears and by falling to his knees. Yi thus concluded that a typical Chinese man should be asexual or woman-like, or more precisely, that he should perform like a child in front of authority – his parents and the emperor (pp.1–24). This is the most radical criticism of traditional Chinese men and proves that, again, at the socially/culturally assigned feminine and masculine levels, there is no clear and opposite distinction in China as exists in the West.

Under such conditions, Yi (1998b) pointed out that the most important relationship for a man in the family was the mother-son relationship (p.36). There is a long custom that a Chinese man is very close with his own mother, for which there are a number of reasons. For women, mother-hood usually offered an important identity. However, in old China, a woman was only recognised by her marital family through giving birth to a son. Before that, she was not fully accepted by her family and would feel inferior, with the risk of being evicted if she only had daughters. When she was getting old or had lost her husband, she could only be dependent on her son (Brownell & Wasserstrom, 2002, p.21; Ma, 2010, pp.64–65; Ownby, 2002, p.243; Yi, 1998b, pp.45–50). Therefore, son-preference was always prominent amongst Chinese women.

On the son's side, in a Chinese family, a father was always strict and distant from his son (Ownby, 2002, p.242), while the mother took responsibility for her son's early education and final achievement (Xu, 2013, pp.101–109; Yi, 1998b, p.50). The mother thus played a more important and approachable role in the son's life. Further, due to the high rate of female infanticide as a result of son-preference (Ma, 2010, p.66; Mann, 2011, p.50; Yi, 1998b, p.57) and the ownership of many women by men from a high class (Ownby, 2002; Yi, 1998, pp.115–116) there was always a skewed sexual ratio in the marriage market. Mann (2011) pointed out that in the nineteenth century, '[n]early 100 percent of females married; up to 20 percent of males never did' (pp.4–5). At the same time, women were required to be secluded and for these men, the only accessible women in their lives were their mothers. In addition, as Ownby (2002) has pointed out, men without a family had a high risk of becoming bandits, leading to social problems and even the collapse of a dynasty. Therefore, encouraging men to be attached to their mothers would be of benefit to the rulers.

Another important relationship for a man in imperial China was comradeship and brotherhood between men (Mann, 2011, pp.142–144; Yi, 1998b, pp.10–18), particularly amongst heroes and bandits, which, on the surface, carries some similarity to Western knights. Ownby (2002) revealed that in the eyes of ordinary people, bandits had a very positive image. He compared the Chinese bandit to Robin Hood, believing them to be quite similar as they both protested against unfair governance; however, on further exploration, they were also quite different. First, Chinese people believed that the masculinity and brotherhood of a hero would be sabotaged by a romantic or sexual relationship with a woman (Mann, 2011, pp.159–160; Yi, 1998b, pp.10–18). Therefore, a real hero must remain abstinent. Secondly, the unfairness of government was not due to the emperor, the highest ruler, but due to his greedy officials (Ownby, 2002, p.235). Therefore, a good bandit would only oppose the officials, while maintaining his loyalty to the emperor and state.[3] Masculinity must be represented in the identity of being the subject of the state.

Marriage and relationships in China from imperial times to Mao's period (1949–1976)

Yi (1998b) suggested that the most distant relationship in a traditional Chinese family was that between a husband and wife (p.364). Other less radical scholars have proposed that the basic emotional tone between a Chinese couple was *enqing* – a Chinese term meaning gratitude and appreciation based on being offered benefits from the other – rather than romantic love (Li, 2007; Li & Chen, 2002; Ng, Peluso & Smith, 2010). It seems that, in a typical Chinese marriage, a strongly emotional connection has never been encouraged. Yi continued that romantic love always existed outside of marriage, between a man and his concubine, a prostitute, in love affairs and in stories of elopement (1998, pp.173–254). Mann studied ancient Chinese literature and discovered many stories on the theme of 'tension between romantic love and arranged marriages' (2011, p.154). Therefore, while romantic love did exist in Chinese culture, it was never encouraged to be present within a marriage.Additionally, there was no equivalent to the Western notions of courtly love in China. In courtly love, the hero and heroine are two individuals, an active man and a respected woman, assigned by their different gender characteristics (Denis, 1983, pp.75–82). In China, however, men, women and even the highest ruler, the emperor, were all servants to the patriarchal order. There was no profoundly mutual relationship between men and women in old China, because both served a common goal.

After the end of the imperial era in China, because of the New Cultural Movement, women were gradually affected by westernisation, which gave them the opportunity to escape from the family and rid themselves of arranged marriages (Ma, 2010, p.58; Mann, 2011). Many new types of female image were invented at that time, including new types of female prostitutes, warriors, students and factory workers. These comprised a group of idealised women – new, pretty and healthy modern girls with attractive and liberated feminine characteristics. They pursued free love, wanted to choose their own husbands and dared to get divorced if they felt unsatisfied in their marriages. Su Qing's autobiography *Marriage for Ten Years* (1944/2009) and *After Ten Years' Marriage* (1946/2009) and Zhang Jung's *Wild Swans: Three daughters of China* (2012) vividly portray women and their attitudes to marriage at that time.

After 1949, in Mao's period, the various new women disappeared. At that time, the Communist Party emphasised gender sameness and pushed women to participate in the workforce and in politics (Brownell & Wasserstrom, 2002, p.31; Mann, 2011, pp.119–120). Wylie (1962) believed that this liberated women from family work and motherhood (pp.7–9). Later, however, scholars of Chinese feminism and marriage observed the political interventions in Chinese marriage at this time (Beijing News Weekly Review, 2015; Croll, 1978, pp.317–323; 1981, pp.1–24; Mann, 2011, p.49). This was not genuine liberation for women's interest. Here, it must be pointed out that in Chinese culture, all men and women and their intimate relationships have been in the service of politics from ancient times to the present day. The interests of the family and state must be placed above individuals' own interests.

However, the Communist Party made this motion explicitly and pushed it in an extreme way. In fact, this extreme tendency led to disasters in Chinese relationships. Evans (2002) described how, in this period, revolution wives were trapped in the tension between serving the family or the state (pp.336–340). Honing (2002) depicted the severe violence against feminine women by the Red Guard, encouraged by the government and the leader, Mao, during the Cultural Revolution. Yuan (2014) illustrated how romantic relationships could cause political persecution and how political interventions led to distrust and intimate difficulties in party couples. In a word, at that time, individuals and their families were trapped in a single mission – obeying the party and devoting themselves to the state. The remnant of these effects still exists today and because of the one-child policy, which is a political intervention, there are new pictures of relationships emerging in China today.

The effects of the one-child policy in China

The one-child policy was implemented in China from 1978 to 2015. The alternative name or a more accurate name for this policy is 'family planning programme'. It aimed to control the growth of the population and to facilitate the development of China's economy (Fong, 2002, p.1100). This policy was not a strict demand that one couple could only have one child, but a decentralised regulation of population, varied by time and region, that was enforced quite strictly in the mid-to-late 1980s and early 1990s; in some provinces, however, a rural couple could have a second child if the first was a girl, while minority ethnic groups could have more than one child, etc. (Johnson, 1993, pp.70–71; Johnson, Huang & Wang, 1998, pp.469–470; Liang & Lee, 2006; Sudbeck, 2012. pp.41–47; Zhu, Lu & Hesketh, 2009). Because of this policy, China is the only country in the world where family planning has been mandated by the government (Fong, 2004).

On the surface, there are three main and direct results of this policy: 1) the effective decline of population growth (Wang, Zhou & Xiao, 1989); 2) the skewed sex ratio (Ebenstein, 2008; Hesketh, Lu & Zhu, 2005; Lee & Liang, 2006; Sudbeck, 2012, p.50); 3) the aging population (Hvistendahl, 2010). However, these effects have been debated.The most radical comments against the one-child policy come from the Chinese scholar Yi Fu Xian. In his book *The Big Country and The Empty Nest*, first published in

Hong Kong in 2007 and subsequently published in mainland China in 2013, Yi argued that the Chinese population would naturally decrease by the development of the economy and education; therefore, the family planning programme had not controlled the population in an effective way, but had, on the contrary, caused a population crisis and labour shortage (2013). However, this argument does not represent mainstream opinion. In 2006, a study on regional difference in fertility demonstrated that, in China, the economy did not affect people's ideal number of children because in some rich provinces, people have more children than in poor provinces (Zhang, 2006). The one-child policy, on the other hand, does control population growth, which would not be automatically decreased by economic circumstances in China as Yi suggested.

Another debate relates to the reason for the imbalanced sex ratio. Because of son-preference, as mentioned above, the imbalanced sex ratio between men and women of reproductive age is not new in China. Female infanticide was recorded during the Han dynasty. After 1949, the number of infanticides was reduced, but since 1979, the numbers of unregistered female girls, abandoned female babies and sex-selective abortions have been phenomenal. These increases are due to the one-child policy (Johnson, Huang & Wang, 1998, p.472; Zhu, Lu, Hesketh, Liu & Zhang, 2009). Compared with other Asian countries like South Korea, India and Taiwan, which all exhibit son-preference and have high levels of sex-selective abortion, researchers believe that the reason for high sex-selective abortion levels in China is the one-child policy (Chen, Xie & Liu, 2007). I will expand upon this point below. On the question of the aging population, Poston, Jr and Walther (2006) do not agree that China is 'a country with an aged population' compared with European countries (p.1). They do admit, however, that there is a dilemma: China is 'providing an important lesson for the demographic transitions of many countries in the developing world', but the one-child policy also violates human rights because of coerced abortions (ibid.) and has harmed many women and girls in China.

'Missing girls' and empowered daughters

As Johnson (1993) noted, the Chinese government often condemns the behaviour of female infanticide and abandonment, but fails to realise that its own policy catalyses such behaviours. Moreover, the government always emphasises gender sameness, but in reality, son-preference still dominates in the Chinese family, particularly in rural areas, where males comprise 70 percent of the population. Therefore, the most severe result of the one-child policy is the skewed sex ratio. If a family can only have one child, they prioritise choosing a son. As Zhang wrote, '[o]ver 40 million girls and women are missing in China, either because of sex-selective abortion, excessive female infant mortality or the under-reporting of female birth' (Zhang, 2006, p.81).

In fact, among all these reasons, the most convincing is sex-selective abortion (Zhu, Lu, Hesketh, Liu & Zhang, 2009). According to a recent article published in the *Economist* magazine, 'half of all abortions world-wide are in China' (Economist, 2015, p.44). Some of these abortions are enforced by the government due to the one-child policy. The Nobel Prize-winning book *The Frog* by Chinese writer Mo (2012) and another book, the Taiwan published *Dark Road* by Ma (2012), vividly portray dark pictures of how government officials captured women who were pregnant with an over-quota child and forced them to abort the foetus, even, on occasion, when the foetus was eight months old. Such operations sometimes threaten the mother's life. Other abortions occur because a single woman cannot obtain permission to give birth to a child due to the one-child policy; while yet other abortions are induced by the woman herself, because she can only have one child and thus aborts a female foetus (Ebenstein, 2008; Wu & Walther, 2006).

Another common reason for 'missing girls' is the abandonment of female babies. According to a study published in 1998, since the implementation of the one-child policy, over 80 percent of abandoned babies have been girls. The age of abandonment does not exceed eight months. Usually, these are girls without brothers and the reason for abandoning them is to avoid penalties and to keep open the possibility of having a boy. Meanwhile, an over-quota boy, even if he already has a brother, is less likely to be abandoned. The parents would rather pay the penalty for him (Johnson, Huang & Wang, 1998). Some abandoned girls are unofficially adopted without registration by families wishing to have a daughter, or are adopted by overseas couples, far away from their natal parents (Johnson, 1993; Zhang, 2006).

As Shen (2015c) has noted, the one-child policy severely harms mothers and women in China. These women who undergo abortions, either by coercion or of their own will, are often traumatised. Women who give up their new-born girls later show self-resentment and remorse and the wound remains for many years. A book published in the UK by Xinran (2011), titled *Messages from an Unknown Chinese Mother* and the TV play *One Child* produced by the BBC, depict the deep pain of these mothers. Further, the American-Chinese scholar Xiao (2015) has revealed that most of the coercive sterility technology that is applied to women's bodies hurts them tremendously. Women and girls are thus the direct victims of the one-child policy.

However, this is just one side of the story. Naftali (2016) has also identi-fied urban Chinese girls as the beneficiaries of the one-child policy. For these single daughters, the policy brings them 'empowerment and individu-ation' (p.71). In fact, in 1985, Croll studied the effects of the one-child policy in Beijing and its suburbs and concluded that people accepted the policy without resistance and did not engage in violent behaviours to mothers and their daughters. Later, Fong (2002, 2004) studied the one-child families in Dalian city and discussed the concept of 'empowered daughters'. Fong pointed out that while most of the literature focuses on the persecution of women by the one-child policy, her own observation and studies counter this assertion (2002, pp.1100–1102). In urban China, a couple accepts that they will only have one child and a daughter is sometimes even more desirable for close emotional bonds (Zhang, Feng & Zhang, 2006).

Further, in a family with siblings, parents prefer to invest in the son's education (Zhai & Gao, 2010), while in rural families, girls may be asked to drop out of school and earn money to support their brothers' education (Fong, 2002, p.1103). However, in a one-child family, the parents have high expectations and direct their full investment into education of the one child, regardless of gender (Fong, 2004, p.107; Naftali, 2016, pp.83–86; Veeck, Flurry & Jiang, 2003). The only child is the parents' only hope upon which they can rely when they get old. The one-child family values education and academic achievement, because they believe that these will bring elite status and a bright future. In addition, in Chinese tradition, a bride's family does not have to prepare a marital house; therefore, a singleton girl can receive more money towards her education than a singleton boy (Fong, 2002, p.1104; 2004, pp.113–114). These daughters outperform boys in the education system because of their 'studious and obedient' gender norm and are successful in their careers (Fong, 2002, pp.1102–1103; Sudbeck, 2012). Thus, Fong offers the conclusion that '[prior] to [the] one-child policy, most girls were raised to be losers', but now these urban daughters are 'all raised to be winners' (2002, p.107).

The results of these high expectations and high level of investment are: 1) an urban daughter can earn money to support her own parents, which was impossible before because a woman could not own her own property; 2) she has the possibility of living with her parents even after she gets married because she and her family might offer better household conditions than her husband does, which would be considered abnormal or degrading; 3) she can ask her husband to share the chores and to take care of their child together, since she also offers a financial contribution to their family (Fong, 2002, 2004, pp.103–135; Sudbeck, 2012, p.52; Pimentel & Liu, 2004). All of these comprise reversals against the traditional role of a daughter and wife and because of these realistic benefits, the prejudices against having a daughter have decreased.

Moreover, as mentioned earlier, in old China, the mother raised her children for her old age and only a son could fulfil the responsibility of taking care of his aging mother. Gates (1993) noted that under such circumstances, a woman could not enjoy the present pleasure of motherhood, because it was a future-oriented task (pp.261–265). However, in a one-child family, because of the close bond between the parent and only child, parents focus more on their current emotional fulfilment, particularly the mother (Chen, 2007).

Chinese people believe that a daughter offers a closer emotional bond than does a son (Johnson, Huang & Wang, 1998, p.489; Sudbeck, 2012, p.52; Zhang, 2006; Zhang, Feng & Zhang, 2006) and that a mother can easily build an intimate connection with her only daughter (Fong, 2004, pp.135–138). All of these challenge traditional family dynamics and mean that daughters are valued more than before.

Further, as Sudbeck (2012) has argued, the low number of children they have frees women from the sole role of motherhood and allows them more time to pursue their social and economic freedom. However, she also mentions that this freedom could be the result of globalisation, not the one-child policy. In this regard, in 2015, when the Chinese government replaced the old one-child policy with a two-child policy, many women protested on online public forums, viewing the new policy as the result of male chauvinism. For women who want to devote time and money to their own interests and have no desire to have more children, the one-child policy can be the best excuse for rejecting their husbands' and parents-in-laws' demands to have a second child (Gates, 1993, p.274). They can use the policy to avoid conflicts and do not need to worry about accusations of being non-filial. Another unintentional result is that due to the skewed sex ratio, for a woman, a second marriage is easier to achieve than previously (Settles, Sheng, Zang & Zhao, 2013). Divorce is no longer an unbearable nightmare for Chinese women and second marriages have become prevalent. Women can extricate themselves from bad or unsatisfying marriages with more freedom and less fear.

This does not mean that these empowered women have no troubles. As Fong points out, there are still obstacles and prejudices in their career development. They have their 'glass ceiling' (2002, p.1102, 2004, p.112), which means that although they have many opportunities to obtain a general job, they are less competitive in achieving elite or professional positions than men due to the gender prejudice that women are less creative and flexible than men (ibid). Fu (2016) noted that this 'glass ceiling' even exists in the marriage market. Despite the excess number of men, it is difficult for a well-educated and empowered woman to find a suitable husband. However, if she chooses to remain single or postpone the age of marriage to await 'Mr. Right', she may be categorised as a 'left-over', reflecting the generally hostile attitude in Chinese society to women who dare to not put family as their first priority.

In general, however, I do not think the one-child policy has wounded or hurt femininity in China, which is a universal resource and energy that cannot be damaged by human activities. To a certain degree, it could be argued that the policy has encouraged the development of feminism in China, albeit at the high price of the pain and blood of rural mothers and girls. As Johnson (1993) argued, these women are a group in silence, who rarely receive protection from feminist groups or a supportive voice from women's magazines.

'Little emperors' or frustrated men?

Compared with the attention given to women and girls, there is little literature about the effects of the one-child policy on Chinese men and boys. Certainly, the policy has not harmed them directly. A common label given to singleton boys is 'little emperors'. (Generally, the term 'little emperors' refers to children of both sexes from one-child families, but nevertheless, no one uses the terms 'little queens' or 'empresses' and this term has its own gender implications.) In the stereotyped impression, 'little emperors' are spoiled and self-centred and it is emphasised that singleton boys are particularly fragile and vulnerable (Naftali, 2016, p.86), with even their parents complaining about these undesirable traits (Fong, 2004, pp.179–182).

This prejudice began from the very outset. In 1993, an expert on adolescent issues, Sun Yunxiao, wrote a popular article titled *A match between Chinese and Japanese students in a summer camp*. He wrote that, compared with the strong, confident and responsible Japanese children, Chinese children from one-child families were weak, selfish and irresponsible babies. This article soon became well known, but after further exploration, it turned out to have been fabricated, full of imaginary, exaggerated and distorted details. Another book, titled *Buy Me the Sky* and written by Xinran, which was published in the UK in 2016, also focused on singleton children in China; it opens with the story of an incapable, rude and childish adolescent boy and suggests that he is representative of the only child in China. In the remaining stories in this book, other singleton children are also portrayed as ruthless, ungrateful and unable to get along with others, including their parents. However, these pictures do not accord with my own experience and observation. Nevertheless, people buy into these stories because they are quite dramatic and accord with their own prejudices. Fong (2004) compared the only child in China with the children from small families in the First World and concluded that there is no significant difference between their personality traits. After synthesising a series of controversial studies on the personalities of children from one-child families, Settles and his colleagues (2013) agreed with Feng's 2000 study, thus countering 'the little emperor hypothesis' and concluded that, 'compared to children with siblings, only children tended to be more advanced in the development of certain cognitive, emotional, and physical domains … [long] term personality outcomes appear favourable to the child' (pp.17–18). This is due to their close bonds and high involvement with their parents.

Fong (2004) pointed out that complaints about the single child, such as that are 'spoiled' and 'unable to adjust', are due to the fact that they are living in the Third World, but are 'born and bred to become part of the

First World' (pp.154–182). Thus, their surroundings continually frustrate them. The single child has full investment from its parents and consequently carries high expectations to be the best in a competitive society in which only a few people can ever be the best; thus, disappointment also comes easily. The only way for a Chinese man to achieve upward mobility is to obtain elite status 'through academic achievement' (p.101)[4] and the gap between the elite and non-elite classes has been gradually increasing over recent years. Therefore, the Chinese man faces a very competitive and narrow journey. Moreover, although men are more likely to achieve an elite or professional position than women, because of the development of light industries and service industries, which prefer young women, the employment markets are not friendly to most men without 'academic credentials or a wealthy powerful family' (pp.113–114). However, such men are the only hope for their parents' old age and it is very easy to imagine the pressure associated with this burden of expectation.

Even today, China has experienced a dramatic growth in its economy and in the early 2000s was getting closer to the developed world in Fong's eyes. However, the pressure has not yet decreased. Most grown-up singles from one-child families face their destined disillusion: they are not the best and they cannot reward their parents (Fu, 2016). *The People's Daily* (2013) made the criticism that young Chinese men lack energy and carry with them an 'old smell'; it seems that in just one night, they turn from being young boys into middle-aged men. However, it is difficult to encourage them because they have to take care of their aging parents and raise their children alone under daily increased financial pressure in a consumerism-oriented society.

Another frustration for Chinese men is that there is an excessive number of men of reproductive age in the marriage market (Poston, Jr & Walther, 2006). Due to the skewed sex ratio, getting married has become difficult and this has even increased the male crime rate because unmarried men are more likely to commit crime (ibid.; Edlund, Li, Yi & Zhang, 2007). Further, a well-educated young woman with a high salary has more choice regarding her own marriage, such as marrying a man from a higher class, or a man from a developed foreign country, or she can even choose to remain single (the latter two options were almost impossible in earlier times). However, an urban man must face the fact that it is difficult to marry a female from the same class, while he might perceive it as unacceptable to marry someone from the countryside and to offer her urban residency (Fong, 2002, p.110; Settles, Sheng, Zhang & Zhao, 2013).

To date, there has been no satisfactory solution for such difficulties. Poston, Jr and Glover (2006) have explored the possible solutions for these bachelors and found that it is impossible for the Chinese government to approve polyandry because this would dangerously violate the traditional Chinese ethic; nor is it possible to encourage bachelors to marry brides from overseas, because they cannot afford it. They suggest, therefore, that it might be a solution for the Chinese government to allow gay marriage. The Jungian analyst, Luigi Zoja, suggested the same to me at a conference in Rome in 2015. However, Xin (2012), who published a book titled *A Study on the Wives of Gay Men in China* tells us that, in China, there are 16 million women married to gay men, most of whom are straight and were cheated into marriage by their husband and his family. One of the main reasons for these marriages is that homosexual men's parents cannot accept that their sons might not have a 'normal' family, with the attendant lost opportunity of having a child, which is considered to be severely non-filial. Therefore, for the only son's parents, it is impossible to accept that their only son will marry another man.

Meanwhile, since 2014, there has been a heated debate on several influential public on-line forums regarding whether Chinese men match Chinese women. Some radical Chinese feminists suggest that urban Chinese women are far smarter and more fashionable than Chinese men, who are still sloppy and unfashionable. Thus, a new prejudice against Chinese men is emerging.

The relationships between young couples in modern times

To sum up, in China, the basic inequality of marriage has never been inequality between men and women. Nowadays, due to the one-child policy and the narrow passage to a successful life through an elite status, the main obvious inequality in relationships is that between the educated and uneducated,[5] and between urban and rural families.[6]

This does not mean that there are no concerns regarding gender inequality. Some scholars believe that many remnants of oppression in relation to women, stemming from Chinese traditional values, still exist and in the post-Mao period, the requirements have returned for women to service the family above their own individual development (Ma, 2010, pp.178–188; Mann, 2011, p.49). However, as Ocko (1991) notes, with equal property rights gradually being given to Chinese women, they will not return to the old days. On the one hand, most public media in China emphasise the importance of marriage, especially for women, and try to push young women to return to the role of wife and mother. On the other hand, a recent study shows that the age of Chinese women at their first marriage has risen steadily (Wei, Dong & Jiang, 2013), while another study shows that on a personal level, good education is the main reason for the postponement of the first marriage (Liu & Gao, 2015). Empowered daughters refuse to give up the power of free choice in their relationships and they only very reluctantly rely on men and marriage as their predecessors did.Certainly, the old traits of Chinese women still exist and the effects from Mao's period have not yet faded. Images of women in contemporary China are various and abundant and the ideal images of wives are no longer fixed (Evans, 2002; Xinran, 2003; Yi, 1998b, pp.68–78). Moreover, the Chinese feminist, Li Xiaojiang, has argued that the development of

Chinese society does not match the progress achieved by Chinese women (Rofel, 2007, pp.71–78). Under such circumstances, 'to recognize sexual difference and identify with one's sexual identity as a woman' remains an as-yet incomplete mission for Chinese women (ibid., p.77). For a young Chinese woman, how to be herself while being a woman brings confusion and conflict.

Meanwhile, the characteristics of Chinese men have also been affected by modernisation and political interventions. Consequently, the relationships between women and men in the younger generations have been diversified and many Chinese people are not yet ready for these changes. The direct result is that marriage instability has increased in recent years, particularly for couples from one-child families (Settle, Sheng, Zhang & Zhao, 2013).Ironically, the one-child policy was the product of a government decision, which was implemented by coercion. However, it has produced generations of single children who value and appreciate individualism. Feng and his colleagues write:

> China's single-child generations are no longer willing acceptors of the country's statist orientation. While many of them are voluntarily postponing marriage and childbearing, and hence form the driving force of today's below replacement fertility, they also increasingly regard it as their right, not the government's, to decide whether and when to have children. To them, population is no longer a number of aggregated subjects, but individual lives that should be respected and cherished.
>
> (2012, p.126)

Therefore, a subtle subversion has occurred at the level of Chinese society and culture. Based on this recognition, young Chinese couples must learn how to develop a mutual relationship between them – with the two individuals not putting external requirements, such as parents' interventions, political concerns, etc., before their own interests in the relationship. This pattern had hardly been seen in China before and begs the question: could we borrow and be inspired by Western patterns or ideas? In the following two chapters, I will discuss the development and applicability of depth psychologies, rooted in Western culture, in a Chinese context.

Notes

1 A typical term of Freud's. The basic idea is that girls feel anxious because they realise that they do not have a penis. Freud thought this to be an important event in female psychosexual development. This stage begins with a girl turning from the mother to the father to ask for love and attention and putting her mother into a competitive position (Freud, 1995, pp.158–163).
2 This is an unconscious transaction whereby one partner 'carries' certain contents for the other as if by agreement (Williams, 1989, p.292).

3 Herein lies another paradox. In Chinese history, a successful bandit could be an emperor. As Ownby (2002) describes, 'such possibilities trouble the collective conscience of orthodox society by suggesting that ordinary people were closer to such liminal groups than many liked to believe' (p.226).

4 A Chinese woman 'can gain upward mobility through hypergamous marriage' if she has a 'lack of education and family connections, but the poorly educated son of powerless parents' does not have such an opportunity and would face unemployment and fall into a lower class (Fong, 2002, pp.1103–1104).

5 For Chinese people, education is an important way to get into the higher classes. For a woman, it is another effective strategy and can even enforce the possibility of marrying an elite man. '[Better-educated] women are moving up the spatial hierarchy; the lesser educated are moving down' (Lavely, 1991, p.299).

6 As White (2006, 2010) has pointed out, the strongest resistance to the one-child policy was from the rural areas and the women and girls from peasant families were the major victims of the policy. However, they had no effective way of negotiating with the Chinese government. Further, the hostility between urban residents and rural peasants has increased, because urban residents think that the peasantry brings excess population while peasants are eager to achieve the high quality of living standards in the city and realise that there are many barriers for them to negotiate (pp.244–265).

Chapter 3

The history of developing psychoanalysis and analytical psychology in China

Psychoanalysis in China

In *The Standard Edition of the Complete Psychological Works of Sigmund Freud*, China and Chinese culture are mentioned just four times. The first mention relates to foot binding, which Freud considered an expression of fetishism and a 'symbolic castration'; the second reference concerns Chinese dream interpretation; and the final two discuss the similarities between understanding Chinese script and language and Freud's interpretive strategies of dreams (Zhang, 1992, pp.7–10). There is no evidence, however, that Freud had any deep communication with someone who knew Chinese culture well, despite several documents recording his correspondence with Zhang Shizhao, a very famous and influential intellectual in Chinese history (Blowers, 1993; Shi, 2014, p.193; Zhang, 1992, p.6). Zhang was an important translator of Freud's work and also translated the works of other Western ideologists. However, although he showed some interest in Freud's works, this interest was part of a general interest in all Western ideas, which were relatively new and striking to Chinese society at that time. Thus, his attitude reflects the initial attitude of many Chinese intellectuals to psychoanalysis, identifying it as just one of many Western ideas that they were eager to learn more about in the early 1900s.

Psychoanalysis in China before 1949

The first of Freud's works to be translated into Chinese was the *Study of Dreams* in 1914 (Shi, 2014). In the following decade, the main interest of translating books and papers in psychoanalysis focused on the interpretation of dreams and free association (Kirsner & Snyder, 2009, p.47). Chinese people's initial interest in psychoanalysis was mainly on these two topics, which is understandable since China is a country with a long history of viewing dreams as meaningful. In the last century, Chinese people wanted to know how people from other countries, particularly from more scientific countries, thought about dreams. On the other hand, by that time, for thousands of years, it had been difficult to imagine that somebody could be encouraged to engage freely in open discussion without censoring. Thus, this topic was quite new to the culture.

In fact, in the early years, behaviourism was the most popular form of psychology in China and behaviourists were against psychoanalysis. At that time, therefore, it was writers who took the most active interest in psychoanalysis. The new generation of Chinese writers applied ideas and concepts in psychoanalysis to create their novels and to write literary criticism. These writers led the public interest in psychoanalysis and in the 1930s this interest reached a climax, with Freud becoming well known among educated Chinese people (Shi, 2014, p.193; Zhang, 1992, pp.25–35). In those years, the main knowledge on Freud and psychoanalysis in China was his sexual theory. Sex-related topics had a long history in China and always caused complicated feelings, which I will discuss in the following chapters.

The severe circumstances surrounding the invasion of the Japanese army and the civil war in China meant that Chinese people paid little attention to Freud or other Western thinkers, whose ideas were unrelated to the ideas of revolution. Furthermore, the main political parties in China had never had positive attitudes towards psychoanalysis (Zhang, 1992, p.34). After 1949, for decades, no one dared to mention Freud without criticising him, or else they simply ignored him and his theories. However, this was no special phenomenon. The only ideas that could safely be learned and spread from the West were those of Marxism-Leninism, which were reinterpreted by the Chinese Communist Party.

In the clinical realm, psychiatry was a totally new subject in China in the early 1900s, while psychotherapy was treated 'as part of Western medicine' (Kirsner & Snyder, 2009, p.47). In 1933, psychoanalysis was launched in the curriculum of Peking Union Medical College Hospital (PUMCH), and the first psychoanalyst in China, Dr. Dai Bingham, took a teaching post at PUMCH to train doctors and treat patients there. Dai was trained by Harry Stack Sullivan, Leon Saul and Karen Honey at the Chicago Institute for Psychoanalysis (Blowers & Wang, 2014, pp.150–151; Kirsner & Snyder, 2009, p.49; Shi, 2014, p.193). In 2011, the first certified member of the International Psychoanalytical Association (IPA), Lin Tao, completed his course and become a recognised psychoanalyst. Thus, 78 years lie between Dai and Lin, the first and second psychoanalysts in China. This long intermediary period demonstrates the difficulties involved in launching psychoanalysis in the clinical realm in China.

After Dai, one of the doctors in Dai's training, Ding Tsan, who was 'a strong supporter of Freud', applied psychoanalytical ideas to his academic writings and clinical practice (Blowers & Wang, 2014, pp.151–154). Along with other pioneers in the areas of psychiatry and psychotherapy, Ding led a miserable and tragic life after 1949. He was forced to stop all his studies and practice due to political intervention (ibid., pp.157–159). The practice of psychoanalysis with patients in China, which had begun in the 1930s, came to a standstill for many years and was not revived again until the 1980s. The whole process was in accordance with the shift of political circumstances and the change of general attitudes towards Western thought in China.

Psychoanalysis in China after 1980

After 1978, due to the Reform and Opening policy, along with other Western ideas, a 'Freud heat' emerged in the 1980s (Shi, 2014, p.193), and in the early years of this decade psychoanalysis began to be applied in the clinical realm. Over time, several main institutes came to carry the task of spreading psychoanalysis in the psychotherapy area.

The first such institute is the Shanghai Mental Health Center (SMHC) where '[t]he German-Chinese psychotherapy training programme led by Adolf Gerlach was established' in 1982 (Kirsner & Snyder, 2009, p.53). This gradually developed into a cumulative course led by the Institute of Germany and SMHC and today it is the most authoritative and influential psychoanalytical training programme in China. The first graduates from the programme are the current leaders amongst communities of psychoanalytically oriented therapies and most psychotherapists in China consider it a great honour to join this programme, regardless of what methods they apply in their practices.

The second such institute is Wuhan 'Chinese-German' Psychology Hospital (WCGPH), which was founded by two of the first graduates from the 'German-Chinese' training programme who received funds from the Misereor Foundation in Germany to build the hospital in the late 1980s. This was the first hospital in China to focus on psychotherapy and to apply it in official therapeutic settings. Most therapists in the hospital claim that they use psychoanalysis, or at least psychoanalytically oriented therapy, to treat their patients. Some have attended the 'German-Chinese' training programme, while others rely on reading books on psychoanalysis which they can obtain in Chinese. Most, however, are 'wild psychoanalysts', who have never received any official training in psychoanalysis, but who gather raw materials to work with Chinese patients in a so-called 'psychoanalytically oriented setting'. Combining what they have read, they develop their own perspectives on psychoanalysis, offer lectures countrywide and have a huge number of followers in China. However, with more and more Western institutions working with Chinese partners and developing more systematic and official training, the influence of WCGPH among Chinese psychotherapists has rapidly decreased. Meanwhile, in 2006, another hospital, Wuhan Hospital for Psychotherapy (WHP), was established in the same city. This hospital is affiliated with the Wuhan Mental Health Centre, the largest psychiatry hospital in Central China that also focuses on psychotherapy. In

2012, WHP developed its own 'Sino-American training program' with a group of psychoanalysts from the US, and this program has rapidly become popular among Chinese therapists, gradually replacing and even outperforming WCGPH in delivering psychoanalysis in China.

Another institute is Beijing, Anding Hospital, where, since 2000, a project called the 'Sino-Norwegian training programme', supported by the Norwegian and Chinese governments, has been running (Shi, 2014, p.194). This has become the second most authoritative training programme on psychoanalysis in China. In 2008, the IPA began its first formal training in Beijing, with four of the nine candidates accepted for training coming from Anding. The first and second certified IPA members are from this group and they now run some 'Sino-British training programmes' to teach infant observation and attachment theory. Because of their work, Chinese therapists have gradually become familiar with these important methods and concepts in psychoanalysis.

The first four institutes are affiliated with hospitals, but the fifth is an online programme without any tangible home. This is the China American Psychoanalytic Alliance (CAPA), the idea for which originated in Dr. Elise Snyder's early communication with a group of Chinese people who were interested in psychoanalysis in 2001 and 2002, and from Dr. Ubaldo Leli's analytic work with Chinese people via Skype that occurred almost simultaneously (Kirsner & Snyder, 2009, p.55). Since 2005, CAPA has offered low-cost online analysis and therapy, and in 2008 they launched a two-year psychoanalytic psychotherapy training programme, which was then expanded to an advanced programme and supervision groups. Compared to the 'German-Chinese' programme and 'Sino-Norwegian' programme, which offer intensive face-to-face courses in a week or nine days once or twice a year, due to the flexibility and accessibility of the online format of CAPA, it can offer a weekly course and supervision for 30 weeks per year. The lecturers, supervisors and analysts, who hail from the United States and other Western countries, do not have to fly to China. Instead, they offer their time to students in China from their own offices, a pattern that is also convenient to the teachers and students and allows ongoing training for Chinese therapists, which was previously quite rare in China. Thus, this programme has expanded rapidly in China and many Western participants are also exploring the availability of such online courses (Fishkin & Fishkin, 2014; Saporta, 2011). The pattern of training provided by CAPA opens a new world for analytical training, and with the gradually maturing technology, more and more on-line platforms have launched similar on-line training programs for psychoanalytic oriented psychotherapy with different Western institutions, such as the Institute of Psychoanalysis (UK), International Psychotherapy Institute (USA), etc. Meanwhile, these platforms also provide on-line treatment to help trainees recruit new on-line clients (China is a large country and for many patients and clients who live in small cities with limited psychotherapy resources, on-line therapy is the only way for them to access psychotherapy. Hence, there is a huge market for such a service). Due to the convenience and low cost of this on-line program, this pattern has become increasingly popular among Chinese psychotherapists.

Another institute, located in Chengdu, is the Department of Philosophy in Sichuan University. The leader, a Lacanian who returned from Paris, built his own training programme to educate so-called 'Lacanian' groups. However, this group is relatively isolated and communicates little with other groups; therefore, its influence is limited to Chengdu, a city in the southwest of China.

Besides the development of these institutes, there have also been some attempts to explore clinical phenomena in China from psychoanalytical perspectives based on the work derived from applying psychoanalysis in the country. Yang (2014), for example, explored trauma in the Chinese family, Plankers (2014) illustrated the intergenerational transition of trauma from the cultural revolution, Wanlass (2014) focused on the inter-generational and cultural transmission of trauma in Chinese couples, Shi and Scharff (2014) discussed projective identification between Chinese couples and Wang and Zachrisson (2014) studied transference and counter-transference in working with Chinese patients. All of these studies show that in clinical practice, people have already been applying psychoanalysis in a Chinese context, and have made some progress.

Indeed, among all psychotherapies, psychoanalysis has been the most popular in China in recent years. Most Chinese therapists proclaim to use dynamic methods to treat their patients and clients. Students from the 'German-Chinese' programme and CAPA are quite proud of their training backgrounds. Since the summer of 2015, several groups of Chinese therapists have visited the Tavistock Centre (now The Tavistock and Portman NHS Foundation Trust) in London and attended short-term intensive courses on psychoanalytically oriented therapy that have been purpose-designed for them. This represents a new attempt. At the same time, as far as I know, only in London many institutes, such as the Tavistock Centre, Anna Freud Centre and Institute of Psychoanalysis, have shown an interest in exploring their training markets in China. Meanwhile, with many therapists demonstrating their desire for IPA membership and with the growing economy in China, an increasing number of Chinese therapists want to be trained in Western countries, which they think can offer full training in psychoanalysis. At the very least, they wish to join a 'shuttle model', inviting Western analysts from certain institutes to China to work regularly with them, while, at the same time, regularly visiting those analysts in their home countries to meet the required number of analysis hours to become an analyst. The founder of CAPA, Dr. Snyder, is positive about this rapidly growing interest in psychoanalysis in China. She thinks that the future of psychoanalysis in China is bright and that it will help Chinese people to understand their own experiences (Osnos, 2011). However, it is necessary to examine these phenomena further in order to support such optimistic assertions.

The growth of analytical psychology in China

Unlike psychoanalysis, analytical psychology received less attention in China before the 1990s. While some of Jung's articles were translated and published in the 1980s and 1990s, this was undertaken for the purpose of literary studies, not for psychological practice. Interestingly, it took much more time for analytical psychology to take hold in China than in Japan and Korea. Despite Jung's great interest in China, its 'psychology', philosophy and religion (Kirsch, 2000, p.220), Chinese people showed interest in Jung later than people in other Asian counties, a phenomenon that Blowers (2000) attributed to politics. As he suggested, 'after the founding of the People's Republic in 1949, by which time Jung's star had risen considerably in the West ... it was no longer possible for students in China to read him. The Communist government severed all ties with non-communist countries' (p.298). Thus, it took a long time for people from mainland China to get in touch with Jungian psychology. It may be the case that when the right time comes and the right person appears, Jungian psychology can be expected to flourish in China.

Analytical psychology in China before 2000

In 1994, Thomas Kirsch and Murray Stein visited China as representatives of the International Association of Analytical Psychology (IAAP) (Stein, 1995). This was the first time representatives of an official Jungian organisation had come to China. They offered presentations and hosted discussions and, during this process, the Chinese demonstrated their interest in Jungian psychology (Kirsch, 2000, p.220). By that time, after a long period of suppression, Chinese psychologists and practitioners had begun to develop great enthusiasm for all Western psychological schools and their treatments. Before Jungian psychology, Freudian ideas and techniques had already spread among Chinese psychological practitioners. This initial interest, however, could not guarantee the now fervent passion for analytical psychology. I will later expand on the difficulties encountered in the flourishing of Jungian psychology in China from the outset.

In 1998, the first International Conference of Jungian Psychology and Chinese Culture, which was a joint IAAP Congress, was held in Guangzhou by Shen Heyong (Kirsch, 2000, p.221). This was the first time Chinese psychologists had organised an academic conference on analytical psychology, featuring both Western and Chinese scholars. By this point,

Chinese scholars were no longer content to be passive listeners; instead, they were active participants in the creation of psychological knowledge. The conference was a first attempt to test the applicability of Jung's concepts and ideas to Chinese culture.

At the same time, some selected works of Jung, such as *Modern Man in Search of a Soul*, *Memories, Dreams, Reflections* and *Man and his Symbols*, were published in Chinese, while some Jungian terms, like 'archetype', 'complex', etc., gradually became familiar to Chinese intellectuals (Blowers, 2000, p.299). Furthermore, the first of the Jungian books, called the *Mandala Series*, were translated into and published in Chinese (ibid.; Kirsch, 2000, p.221). This meant that, besides Jung's own work, the ideas of a number of Jungians also began to appear in China. These translations fostered intellectual interest in Jungian psychology and made Chinese intellectuals reflect on the phenomena and symptoms in Chinese society through a Jungian lens.

Analytical psychology in China after 2003

The rapid spread of analytical psychology and the growth of Jungian institutions occurred after 2003. In this year, Shen received his certification as a Jungian analyst from the IAAP and as a sandplay therapist from the International Society of Sandplay Therapy (ISST) (2015b). He returned to China and has since devoted himself to developing analytical psychology in both academia and clinical practice.

The first academic section for analytical psychology in China was opened in South China Normal University (SCNU), which awarded the first MA and PhD degrees in Jungian psychology in China and which currently has MA students and PhD candidates working under Shen's tutelage. Then, in 2006 and 2009, prompted by Shen's leadership, Fudan University and the City University of Macao launched their own Jungian Studies Centres, while Shen retained his professorship in SCNU. Whilst the institution in Fudan closed once Shen left, the institution in Macao has continued to thrive. These disparate endings reflect the different political circumstances of the respective institutions. Guangzhou, Shanghai and Macao are all governed by the Chinese Communist Party, but each city has different political policies and attitudes. Analytical psychology develops best in the freest cities in China and the low level of political intervention promises to ensure that Macao will be a fertile centre of analytical psychology in the future.

Shen has promoted the application of Jungian psychology in a Chinese context. A review of current dissertations supervised by him shows a concentration on four main themes: 1) explorations of basic concepts in Chinese settings; 2) understanding Chinese literature and culture through a Jungian lens; 3) the application of different therapeutic techniques in analytical psychology; and 4) explorations of new therapeutic techniques based on analytical psychology.

These dissertations reflect the strong interest of Chinese students in analytical psychology. They are attempting to expand their understanding of Jung's basic concepts and to use this Western lens to understand their own cultural and social phenomena. There is, further, an eagerness to apply Jungian techniques to working with Chinese patients. They try to facilitate Jung's ideas and techniques creatively within Chinese settings and have a great passion for integrating Jungian ideas. More importantly, however, they want to contribute to the growth of Jungian studies in their own way and on their own terms. The sheer depth of the scholarship that has been and continues to be conducted evidences the growing acknowledgment amongst the Chinese of the applicability of Jung's ideas. Although the projects differ, they all hypothesise that Jungian psychology can be used to elucidate the Chinese psyche, both in academic and clinical settings.

From my own experience of reading the full texts of some of these theses and attending several vivas and supervisions, my view is that while there is much enthusiasm, there is a general lack of scrupulous academic examination. Furthermore, some studies overemphasise the abstract ideas of 'image', 'psyche' and 'spirit', while neglecting more specific, daily issues. The basic topics of 'sex', 'money', 'relationships', 'power', etc. in daily life are little discussed, and even when these topics do appear, they tend to be discussed on an archetypal or symbolic level. Meanwhile, there is too much focus on classic Jungian work, while the development of analytical psychology beyond Jung has been ignored. Hence, further and more various studies are required to overcome these problems, to bridge archetypal images with conflicts in daily life and to address realistic issues through a Jungian lens.

In addition to academia, both practitioners and the public more generally are interested in Jungian theory. In recent years, more and more translations and publications of Jung's work have been published. A search on DangDang.com[1] shows that there are four different publishing companies now producing editions of Jung's works and a translation of his *Collected Works* is in progress. As one of the translators of his *Collected Works*, many people have approached me, expressing their interest and intent to buy the series upon its completion. Furthermore, translations of books on sandplay are very popular among Chinese therapists, even if they have not used this technique in their own practices. Shen and his students have also published books on analytical psychology. Shen has written two introductory books to analytical psychology and one book to discuss the connection between Jung's thought and Chinese culture, while his students have written works of film criticism and drawing therapy from a Jungian perspective.[2] Moreover, in 2015, two new journals on Jungian psychology, respectively entitled 'Analytical Psychology' and 'Sandplay Therapy', were launched. These are the first Chinese professional journals in this field.

The problem, however, remains that almost all of these translations, except the books on sandplay therapy, are Jung's work, while relatively few of Jung's followers and post-Jungians have had their works translated. Thus, very few people in China are aware of the debates and controversies that have emerged in post-Jungian thought, making it easy to take Jung's original writings as gospel. Most of the translations and publications of his work have been conducted by Shen and his team and they naturally have their own tendencies, which might limit contact with a full view of the world of analytical psychology.

Other important activities charting the growth of analytical psychology in China are the continuous string of conferences that have been held in recent years.[3] Since 1998, Shen has held eight International Conferences of Jungian Psychology and Chinese Culture. Along with Western Jungian scholars, IAAP members and Chinese psychologists, the speakers have also included experts on Buddhism, Taoism and Confucianism and the conferences have even been attended by some influential monks and Taoist priests. This demonstrates the ambitious attempt of Chinese Jungians to develop analytical psychology in a more integrative way, combining Jungian psychology with typical Chinese cultural elements. As I will discuss later, however, this is a creative and risky attempt.

Other activities attract people who are more interested in clinical practice, as evidenced by the various workshops held before the conferences. These workshops are all on techniques originating in analytical psychology. The attending therapists learn from workshops and use these techniques with their patients. They then return, report their cases and discuss the results and difficulties with the teachers. Sandplay therapy is one of the most popular techniques in China. At each of these conferences, I have met therapists from all over the country who wish to discuss their sandplay cases and ask for supervision. That is to say, Chinese therapists are already applying analytical psychology in the practical realm.

Another milestone displaying the salience of Jungian ideas in China is the programme 'Gardens of the Heart-Soul', which commenced in 2008 following the major earthquake in Sichuang (Cai & Shen, 2010). The earthquake occurred on 12th May and Shen's team arrived in the effected regions on 18th May and immediately established a 'Jungian Depth Therapy and Sandplay Therapy Office'. However, it was not easy to work with people who had suffered such serious trauma and at first they were prevented from working in Beichuan middle school: There were too many psychological intervention teams flooding into the earthquake regions and the victims did not welcome psychologists from outside, perceiving such psychological interventions as rude and intrusive. Thus, when Shen and his team arrived at Beichuan and showed their willingness to work there,

Principal Liu Yachun refused their entrance politely but firmly. During their negotiation, however, Gao Lan, Shen's wife, noticed that a young boy playing had a bleeding arm. Gao crouched down, took a cotton swab to wipe away the blood and put some ointment on the wound. This scene touched Liu and he realised that this team would work with his students at a human level. Thus, he finally agreed to allow Shen and his team in. The boy, an earthquake orphan, was the first student to undergo sandplay therapy in the earthquake regions.

As part of this programme, I worked in Beichuan Middle School for two months and then in Shuimo Primary School for a further two months. In the summer of 2008, I was sitting in a tent, waiting behind a sand box and a bunch of figurines. The students came to me and automatically placed these figurines in the sand box; their stories, sadness, fears, expectations and hopes then gradually emerged. During the process, they faced their losses, confronted their mourning and felt the growth inside. In Shuimo Primary School, in addition to sandplay therapy, the students used drawings to express their feelings symbolically. After several months' work, the intensity of their emotions and parakinesia due to the earthquake were alleviated. For example, a 9-year-old girl who had suffered from enuresis due to the earthquake came to me for sandplay therapy. At the beginning, she felt so shy and self-debased that she was unable to say a whole sentence in front of me. Gradually, however, she displayed in the sandtray her horror of the earthquake, her anxiety about daily life and her eagerness to connect with others. One day, she placed a stone in the centre of the sandtray, which I had brought back from the epicentre. The stone, however, looked quite normal and she did not know where it had come from. She then placed several figurines with healing symbols on the stone. This time, she felt very satisfied with her work and actively smiled and talked to me. Following this session, her enuresis disappeared. My colleagues who worked in other locations reported similar results.

During the process of working with victims suffering from serious trauma, we found a) that creative expressions, such as sandtray and pictures based on symbolic language, could help 'victims to find an outlet for their trauma' (ibid.); and b) that group therapy could be very effective in vulnerable communities. This idea also inspired Eva Pattis' work with children from Bogota and Medellin in Columbia (Pattis-Zoja, 2014).

In all this work by Shen and his team, he never emphasised that they were Jungians nor that they used techniques from analytical psychology. The work transcended boundaries and was not labelled 'Jungian psychology' but merely attained the desired results. They helped by working on the ground with people who had suffered from severe trauma and by treating them humanely. This demonstrates how effective Jungian psychology can be without mentioning the Jungian theoretical framework.

Shen and his team worked in the same way with victims of the Yushu earthquake in 2010. By 2019, they had run 86 workstations of 'Gardens of the Heart-Soul' in orphanages around China and recruited volunteers from related backgrounds, including psychologists, psychiatrists and social workers, to work in these stations. What they have done may be the ultimate endorsement for the applicability and efficacy of analytical psychology in China. The main point, however, is that they do not have to say that they are using Jungian ideas and techniques; the results simply speak for themselves.

On the strength of all these studies, publications, conferences, workshops and the project 'Gardens of the Heart-Soul' an Oriental Institution of Analytical Psychology Studies was founded in 2013, which offers a two-year training programme and later, a three-year advanced training programme to foster Chinese Jungian therapists, or at least, Jungian-oriented therapists. This is an independent institute that aims at being the foundation for the future Jungian society to be certified by the IAAP. Each year, more than 200 therapists enrol in the basic training programme and more than 50 students in the advanced training programme for therapeutic training oriented in Jungian psychology. Gradually, Shen has developed a new term for his work on Jungian psychology applied in China – 'the Psychology of the Heart' – and this term is a typical example of the application and contribution to Jungian psychology of the Chinese team, which I will discuss in detail in the next chapter. Based on all of the work listed above, in 2019, during the IAAP Congress in Vienna, it was announced that the first Chinese Jungian Society, the China Society of Analytical Psychology, would be established, and nine days later, at the ISST Congress in Berlin, it was announced that the first Chinese sandplay society – the China Society of Sandplay Therapy – was to be established. For Chinese teams, this was a great achievement, giving them the sense that their work of many years had been officially recognised and that they would have more confidence to deliver ideas and techniques in Jungian psychology in China.

Difficulties of developing Western depth psychologies in China

Despite the rapid development of depth psychologies in China, there are a number of environmental difficulties. The first is due to the political system in China. In 1993, Murray Stein visited China and suggested that the IAAP launch a developing group there. However, his suggestion was met with reluctance. The IAAP had previously attempted to enter Russia and had offered financial support for the translation of Jung's *Collected Works* into Russian; however, this attempt had ultimately failed and there was concern that the same would happen in China (Shen, 2015b). Later, British analysts described how, when they decided to help to train Jungian analysts in Russia, they found that 'although living conditions have since improved considerably, the gap between city and country, rich and poor has enlarged, and the sense of a country recovering from societal, cultural, and personal trauma is never far away' (Crowther & Wiener, 2015, p.276). The exact same words could be used to describe China today. These issues, plus the increased tension between different classes and regions within the country and between the country and the outside world, mirror those in Russia and make 'individuation' difficult to attain.

'Individuation' is one of the core concepts of analytical psychology and is the ultimate aim of analysis. Jung defined 'individuation' as a term 'to denote the process by which a person becomes a psychological "in-dividual," that is, a separate, indivisible unity or "whole"' (CW9i, para. 490). He emphasised that 'it is the process by which individual beings are formed and differentiated [from other human beings]; in particular, it is the development of the psychological individual as being distinct from the general, collective psychology' (CW6, para.757). Samuels describes 'individuation' as 'a person's becoming himself, whole, indivisible and distinct from other people or collective psychology (though also in relation to these)' (1986, p.76). Therefore, individuation includes a process of differentiation, is based on individual freedom and ignores the disturbance from the group and others. In today's China, people are unable to attain these goals spontaneously; rather, they must struggle with the family, society and government.

Further, among psychoanalytic techniques, 'free association' is an important one. However, as was the case when psychoanalysis first came to China in the last century, speaking freely without deliberation is not welcome and is even forbidden by the Chinese government. On this basis, Plankers argues that one reason for the lack of an independent society for psychoanalysis in China is that 'the totalitarianism of a Communist dictatorship has led to a lingering passivization of independent thinking' (2013, p.1012). Thus, psychoanalysis and analytical psychology share the same difficulties.

The strict censorship of the media and internet in China mean that people cannot gain free access to information. Until this year, people in mainland China were not allowed access to Google, Facebook, YouTube, etc., hence they are not able to find or publish inappropriate words on these websites. Under these circumstances, freedom of speech and independent thinking are not encouraged and, as mentioned above, this makes Macao the optimal place in which to develop analytical psychology, as it is a special administrative region in China where the Party intervenes less and people are freer.

Further, over-commercialisation is the main problem facing China today. There is a lack of respect for copyright laws. and pirated software, books and videos are harming the benefits of creators and destroying serious academic study. The strong eagerness to pursue financial gain also makes many Chinese people fear turning inwards, which is harmful to their psyches. In such an atmosphere, they might not really understand depth

psychology and only want to use it to earn money. Indeed, I have witnessed people using self-invented techniques to earn money, while claiming
to be 'Jungian' or 'Freudian'.

Discussion

Compared with Japan, perhaps the Asian country in which Jungian psychology is the most popular (Kawai, 2006), the development of Jungian
psychology in China has some similarities. For example, the first technique
to be introduced in both countries was sandplay therapy. Kawai pointed
out that this is because in Japan people like concrete images that can be
touched (ibid.), a tendency that Chinese people share. As Jung stated, 'in
the archaic world everything has soul' (CW10, para. 136). Jung also noted
that in both countries people have held such a belief for a long time; thus,
they believe that every figurine and every scene in a sandbox expresses
their soul, which is ultimately connected with nature.

When Kawai discusses the difficulties of working with Japanese patients,
one possibility is that 'the Japanese image has its own characteristics and
structure, so the Western style interpretation and self-reflection are not
suitable' (Kawai, 2006, p.437). As a country with a long and continuous
cultural inheritance, Chinese images have the same issue. As Samuels demonstrates, analysts in Japan 'are satisfied with the authenticity and efficacy
of what they do, confident that, far from aping colonial masters, they are
putting down local roots that make their work a genuine hybrid' (Samuels,
2002). This seems to be an endorsement of what Chinese analysts are now
undertaking – developing a localised hybrid, an analytical psychology
based on their own roots.

The difference between China and Japan, however, is that Chinese analysts might go far beyond their Japanese counterparts. Because of their
strong cultural identity, they not only want to localise psychoanalysis and
analytical psychology, but also seek to emphasise the important influence
of Chinese culture on these fields. It is for this reason that there is such
a fever among Chinese therapists in the area of depth psychology.

This fever could be problematic, however. As Plankers argues, 'psychoanalysis cannot be spread and developed by propaganda and money alone'
(2013, p.1012). The strong enthusiasm for psychoanalysis and analytical
psychology is due to the 'unimaginable dynamic of economic and social
development' (ibid.) in China. Most Chinese people want instant achievement and financial success and being a psychotherapist seems to be a new
approach to this. In this sense, the difficulties mentioned above would be
the meaning of applying depth psychology in China. The purpose of Jung's
dialogue with oriental thought was to treat the problem of the Western
psyche, which he believed 'is that it cultivated the extraverted function at
the expense of the introverted' (Clarke, 1994/2005, p.67). China too has

now become trapped by the over-development of extraversion. However, a possible solution does exist. In the process of individuation, 'there is often a movement from dealing with the persona at the start ... to the ego at the second stage, to the shadow as the third stage, to the anima or animus, to the Self as the final stage' (Rowan, 1989a, p.144). This is the process of dealing with external chaos and exploring the inner world, which could offer a possible solution to addressing the current symptoms in China while overcoming difficulties.

Another problem is the overemphasis on 'localisation' and 'integration'. As will be discussed in the next chapter, both Jungian-oriented analysts and psychoanalysts want to add elements from Buddhism, Taoism and Confucianism to psychotherapy. As Samuels (2002) argues, the process of integration is quite difficult, because it 'requires so much responsible commitment on the part of the practitioner, who has thoroughly to familiarise him or herself with the various approaches to be integrated' (p.480). Such integration would be more difficult in a multicultural area. Further, Taoism, Confucianism and Zen Buddhism, which is the form used in China, all have their own systems. The classics in all three were written in old Chinese language, which differs considerably from modern Chinese and is difficult for Chinese people to understand without special education. Further, there exist controversies in understanding these texts even among experts who have devoted their careers to the study of a single text. There have also been debates and conflicts between the basic philosophies and worldviews of the three systems. Thus, a dialogue between depth psychology and these fields is not easy and requires that a practitioner know all three in great depth.

Overemphasising Jung's connection with China might also be problematic. Jung never visited China during his lifetime and his main connection with China was through his friend, the German sinologist, Richard Wilhelm. Beebe (2015) mentions that after he visited China and communicated with Chinese people directly, he felt that some ideas and terms borrowed from Chinese culture and taught in analytical psychology in the Western context were incomplete or even misunderstood (p.262). This is quite true. In the ancient Chinese context, for example, *The Secret of the Golden Flower* was not among the prevalent classics, nor was it in the main research arena; hence, even Chinese scholars found it difficult to claim that they totally understood the book and came to a similar conclusion regarding its meaning: that Jung's interpretation of the book and relevant Chinese terms are more likely to be based on his own thoughts and to have served his own ends. Further, Clarke and Stein both point out Jung's warning regarding approaching the East too closely (Clarke, 1994/2005, p.143; Stein, 2015). As a Westerner, Jung tried to facilitate some Chinese cultural elements to support his own theory; however, all of these were based on his Western roots (or, a Western understanding of the East). The presence of some Chinese pictures and writings in Jung's room might demonstrate his aesthetic appreciation of Chinese culture, but this does not necessarily represent his complete identification with Chinese culture. Shen's Chinese team have overlooked Jung's Western roots and exaggerated the influence of Chinese culture on him. Such claims reached a climax in Shen's recently published book on Jung and Chinese culture (2018a). This might represent a new bias and show the over optimistic connection between Jungian psychology and Chinese culture, a perspective that betrays the true reality. I will discuss this further in the next chapter. In other words, in China, Jung's ideas have rarely been challenged and there has been a tendency to treat all of Jung's work as gospel.

Despite these problems, I remain relatively positive regarding the applicability and efficacy of analytical psychology in China. Samuels demonstrates that to solve the present political issue, we must base our understanding on 'the only world we can be in' while 'the turn to other cultures, or to principles' could be problematic (2015, p.9). As discussed in this chapter, Chinese institutions have tried to heal their own country and people use Jungian psychology in their own way in Chinese settings. Even with the sense of rush and exaggeration, they have made progress, achieved much and contributed to the Jungian realm. However, more could be achieved if they were to give up the attempt at integrating a 'triumphalist psycho-solution', which is quite prevalent in China even if it is not expressed explicitly but is disguised by the emphasis on 'localization' and 'integration' as discussed in the next chapter.

Notes

1 One of the biggest on-line bookstores in China.
2 These books are *Analytical Psychology: Understanding and Experiencing*, by Shen Heyong, 2004; *Analytical Psychology and C.G. Jung*, by Shen Heyong, 2004; *Jung and Chinese Culture* by Shen Heyong, 2018a; *Psychological Allegory in Movies* by Wang Huan, (2011); *The Mirror of Psyche: Drawing Therapy of Mandala*, by Chen Canrui, 2014.
3 The different titles of each conference show the variety and growth of the field in China: the first is 'Psyche: analysis and experience' (1998); the second is ''Psyche: images and synchronicity (2002); the third is 'Ethics and wisdom: East and West' (2006); the fourth is 'The images in Jungian analysis: active imaginations as a transformational function in culture and psychotherapy' (2009); the fifth is 'Dream – the symbolic language of the psyche, nature and culture' (2012); the sixth is 'Wilhelm and I Ching, Jung and the Red Book, dream and active imagination' (2013); the seventh is 'Confronting collected trauma: archetype, culture and healing' (2015); and the eighth is 'Enlightenment and individuation: East and West' (2018). From these topics, we can see a shifting concern towards culture both in the applicability of Jungian ideas to Chinese culture, but also in the influence of Chinese culture on Jung's ideas.

Chapter 4

The applicability of analytical psychology in China

How a Western psychological lens might be adapted in the East

The German psychoanalyst Schlosser (2009), an experienced lecturer on a Chinese-German training programme, asked the question 'Can psychoanalysis be exported to China?' Her Chinese colleagues on the same programme, Xu, Qiu, Chen and Xiao (2014), further asked: 'Is psychoanalysis applicable to Chinese people?' and 'Can Chinese people benefit from psychoanalysis?' Based on their professional experience, they concluded that the answers were yes, yes and yes. If we ask the same three questions in the Jungian psychological arena, based on the work of Shen and his team that I presented in the previous chapter, I believed that the answers will also be three affirmatives.In this chapter, I discuss the current situation regarding the application of psychoanalysis and analytical psychology in Chinese settings and argue in favour of their applicability in this context. My main focus, however, is on the latter, which has more direct connections with Chinese culture.

The application of psychoanalysis in China

As the founder of CAPA, Dr. Snyder, states, 'from the beginning of the twentieth century until the present, a "pure" form of psychoanalysis was never introduced or received in China. There were all always cultural interpretations and adaptions that added Chinese characteristics to the mix' (Kirsner & Snyder, 2009, p.46). This is true in the sense that there has been a long history of assimilating the thoughts imported from other cultures in China, and Chinese people have never been obsessive about the concept of 'purity'. I will expand on this later when discussing the use of analytical psychology in China. Zhang, who explored psychoanalysis in China in the early years, concedes that, 'the Chinese who promoted Freud's ideas turned those ideas to their own purposes' (Zhang, 1992, p.10). Saporta, who offers teaching and supervision in CAPA, also supports this view, claiming that 'the Chinese have always taken what they need from the West and discarded the rest' (Saporta, 2014, p.110). Thus, we can infer that, firstly, from the first day that psychoanalysis arrived in China, the

Chinese began to apply it, and secondly, they have not copied psychoanalysis directly and entirely from the West, but have selected what they need in relation to their own concerns, sometimes even reinterpreting and modifying it. Therefore, we can say that the Chinese use a 'hybrid' form of psychoanalysis.

However, this has caused a number of concerns. Schlosser suggested that psychoanalysis in China 'cannot be expected to be taken over-like a counterfeit-1:1' (2009, p.223); in the same article, however, she also asks, 'Is Chinese psychoanalysis a fake copy?' (ibid., p.220), like a fake copy of an LV purse, or a Burberry coat, which are commonly seen on the streets of China. In addition, many Western teachers from Chinese and Western training programmes have observed (Fishkin & Fishkin, 2014; Haag, 2014; Schlosser, 2009; Snyder, 2014) that their Chinese students and supervisees are difficult to work with in therapeutic settings, that they struggle to maintain neutral and abstinent attitudes and that they have a tendency to challenge these rules with their patients during their training period. One IPA candidate in China, Li (2014), confessed that there are some ethical problems among Chinese therapists, but as Schlosser has argued, after appropriate training, Chinese students will become more deeply involved with the psychoanalytic experience. Based on my own observations, when Chinese students fully understand the rationale behind the settings, they show great willingness to keep them rather than break or contest them. They challenge these settings and encounter ethical problems due to a lack of training and commitment to being analysed. However, these phenomena are declining among young Chinese therapists who have more training opportunities.

Another difficulty that is frequently encountered when trying to apply psychoanalysis in China is the attempt to combine or integrate it with Confucianism, Taoism and Buddhism, which are the basic elements of Chinese culture. Such localisation began when Chinese doctors first applied psychoanalysis and Confucian ideas to treat their patients in the 1930s. Nowadays, Chinese therapists who claim to be psychoanalytically oriented argue that there are many similarities between psychoanalysis and Chinese medicine (Li, 2014), and between psychoanalysis and Buddhism (Xu, 2012). Such ideas are welcomed in China as Chinese people are very proud of their long historical heritage and tend to believe that all ideas and beliefs from other cultures, particularly the 'good' ones, can find a counterpart in their own culture.

The attempt to combine or integrate Chinese beliefs has been termed the 'localisation' of psychoanalysis in China. The first Chinese member of IPA, Lin Tao, argued that Taoism and Confucianism facilitated his understanding of psychoanalysis, and that as psychoanalysis develops in China, efforts should be made to integrate these Chinese cultural elements (Lin, 2014, pp.81–84). He claims that Chinese cultural elements, like *Zhong Yong* in

Confucianism, help him to gain a deeper understanding of the neutral attitude required in psychoanalysis, while 'the actual experience of living' in Tao, helps him 'not be trapped in psychoanalysis concepts', but to explore real feelings and 'the real world' (Lin, 2014, pp.86–88, 2015). A local self-educated therapist, Xu Jun, compares the death instinct with *anitya*[1] and intersubjectivity with *hetupratyaya*[2], and draws parallels between relations in psychoanalysis and in Buddhism. He found similarities between psychoanalysis and Buddhism, and then applied the Buddhist system in psychoanalytical settings (Xu, 2012, pp.60–84).

However, during my interview with Lin, he also cautiously emphasised his belief that 'we shouldn't break the boundaries between' Chinese culture and psychoanalysis. Nevertheless, even when Lin tried to illustrate how to do so, it became apparent that there is no clear and operable way to maintain these boundaries. Wang Xiao, who finished his training as a psychoanalytic therapist at the Tavistock Centre and who has lived in London since 2008 to undertake his training, says that it is not possible to combine such different, even conflicting, elements in Chinese culture and psychoanalysis. This is seen as a 'weird' and characteristically Chinese tendency (Wang, 2015). Li and Xu both attended training programmes in China; most of Lin's IPA training took place in Beijing, while Wang was the first person from the Chinese mainland to be trained in a Western country from the very beginning of his training. It is likely that the more a Chinese person knows about psychoanalysis, the more negative an attitude he/she will have towards combining or integrating Chinese cultural elements with it. The current tendency towards integration may be due to the fact that Chinese therapists do not have sufficient understanding of psychoanalysis and are therefore inclined to rush into the idea of 'localisation'. I will also discuss this tendency in relation to the realm of analytical psychology.Nonetheless, the application of psychoanalysis is unstoppable in China, regardless of whether or not Chinese people understand it well enough. This has given rise to a number of debates which are explored below.

The debate about the differences between applying psychoanalysis in Chinese and Western settings

The strongest point of contention regarding the applicability of psychoanalysis in China is whether therapists should apply psychoanalysis in a different way in Chinese settings, given that psychoanalysis is deeply rooted in Western culture. In general, there are two opposing views.

The first view is that there are huge differences between Chinese people and Westerners. Schlosser (2009), Haag (2014) and Hansen and Pang (2014) have discussed the 'self' in China and the relationship between 'family interests', social requirements and 'individual concerns' and all have reached the same conclusion: namely, that there are no clear boundaries between Chinese people, or, in other words, that in China 'self-boundaries are permeable' (Haag, 2014, p.46). Individualism is seen as negative in Chinese society and so collectivism takes precedence. This gives rise to the concern that it is difficult to maintain boundaries between the analyst and analysand, and to observe psychoanalytical rules and practices. Based on their professional experience in CAPA, Fishkin and Fishkin (2014) expressed the same concern. These discussions are very important in demonstrating the difficulties involved in applying psychoanalysis in clinical practice in China. However, this does not mean that they are impossible to overcome. As pointed out above, all the instances of invasion that they observed occurred during the training process, indicating that immature therapists or those who have not been properly trained have a tendency to make these types of mistakes. This problem can be solved by further training and analysis of trainees by a training analyst. Based on my experience, the younger generation of therapists in China, who have been well trained but are still in the minority, show more tendency to have clear self-boundaries and know how to work within therapeutic settings.

The second view is that 'there is no actual difference between the Chinese mind and the western mind' (Varvin, 2014). In other words, working with patients in a Chinese context is similar to working with patients in a Western context. Some of the experiences of Western lecturers who offer supervisions and analysis support this assertion (Gerlach, 2014b; Scharff, 2014, p.143; Wang & Zachrisson, 2014). Comparing her work in China with that in the US, Snyder pointed out that, 'what is clear is that it is not a difference between East and West, but more like between rural and urban, primitive (in the psychoanalytic sense) and sophisticated, and non-middle class versus middle class' (2014, pp.126–127). She further suggests that if the patients or therapists over-emphasise the cultural differences, this could be interpreted as 'resistance' or 'defensive manoeuvres'. This is quite understandable. In the past 30 years, China has undergone a drastic social shift. Globalisation, also known as Westernisation or Americanisation, has had a profound effect on Chinese people. When young Chinese people grow up exposed to the same commercialism as Western youth, their psyches might come to share common elements with their Western counterparts. Both in a conscious and unconscious sense, they no longer totally identify with their Chinese ancestors. In addition, the basic family structure in modern China is founded on the marriage between a man and a woman who raise children together; this also offers a similar experience of family and personal development to that of Westerners. In this sense, there is no real significant difference between Chinese and Western minds.

However, a more realistic view on the issue of differences, I think, would be that there are some differences between Chinese and Western psyches, but that it is unnecessary to exaggerate these. As Varvin and Rosenbaum state, there are no myths about 'Narcissus' or 'Oedipus' in ancient Chinese narratives. However, even if the contexts appear different at a superficial level, it is possible to find some resonance in their Chinese counterparts, because 'the struggle of the human mind in dealing with transitional processes from the primarily non-verbal pre-Oedipal aspects and Oedipal language-bound experiences' (2014, p.158) are common elements in the mental processes of human beings. However, the appearance of these conflicts and the approaches to solving them vary between contexts.

Therefore, in contemporary China, the otherness coexists with the similarities. If we ignore the otherness, we risk overlooking the uniqueness of the Chinese psyche and misunderstanding our patients, but if we ignore the similarities, this could make us too cautious to apply psychoanalysis effectively in China. Therefore, it is necessary to create a dialogue between Chinese and Western minds and to develop more mutual understanding (Jia, 2016; Lin, 2014, 2015; Saporta, 2014; Snyder, 2014; Varvin, 2014; Wang, 2015; Xu, Qiu, Chen & Xiao, 2014; Zhong, 2014). Zhong Jie, one of the IPA candidates in China, described his dilemma when applying psychoanalysis to treating his patients (2014). He admitted that he encounters some difficulties when attempting to work with his patients in psychoanalytical settings. However, like many other therapists who are interested in psychoanalysis, he and his Chinese and Western colleagues will continue to apply it in the Chinese context and will eventually find the right way to do so.

'The Psychology of the Heart' – the modification of analytical psychology in China

As mentioned in the previous chapter, and as Chinese psychoanalysts have done from the very beginning, the leader of the Chinese team in the analytical psychology realm, Shen Heyong, has tried to apply and develop analytical psychology based on his Chinese roots. His first interest in analytical psychology was from his reading of *The Secret of The Golden Flower*. He enthusiastically wrote:

> I didn't find the secret of the golden flower, but I did find a secret of Jungian psychology, its inner connection with Chinese culture. It seemed as if I got a key to the door of Jungian psychology.
>
> (Shen, 2009, p.7)

Shen believes that Chinese culture is the key to understanding Jungian psychology because of the interconnection between them, and this belief is the foundation of all his work in China. Further, when he tried to introduce analytical psychology into Chinese settings, he modified what he had learnt from Western Jungians and developed his localised ideas based on both analytical psychology and Chinese culture, which he first named 'psy-heart' but later modified to 'the Psychology of the Heart'.

In a presentation at Fudan University, Shen emphasised that there are three steps in his analytical work (2007a). In my interview with him, I asked him what changes should be made when we apply analytical psychology in Chinese settings and he responded along the lines of his previous work (2015b). The modification he made is as follows:

Translating terms in analytical psychology into Chinese is the first step. Translation itself is a cultural exchange. When Chinese people translated Buddhist sutras into Chinese, they had already modified them. Initiation is a two-way thing. The West has its influence on China and China also influences the West. For example, when Gao Juefu translated Freud's works into Chinese in the 1920s, the words he selected already showed his modification and reworking of psychoanalysis, which made it understandable and applicable to Chinese people. When Shen and his team introduced Jung's work to the Chinese, the same thing happened. I will expand on this point below.

Second, Chinese culture has a long history of assimilating other cultures. There is a Chinese archetype, 'Shen nong', which symbolises 'taming and nourishment' (2007a). This is the cultural archetype whereby the Chinese both tamed and nourished Buddhism, which came to China via India (Barrett, 2005; Brook, 1993). Jungian psychology would thus undergo the same process when introduced in China.

Third, timing is crucial for transformation. Here, 'transformation' means integrating Western psychology into Chinese culture. What is fantastic about the *I Ching* is its timing. It offers an effective way to bridge the conscious and unconscious minds. It is 'Jung's Archimedean point' (Jung, 1931, p.141). When Shen and his team translated Jung's *Collected Works*, he examined all the images relating to the *I Ching* in these books and found that Jung had used them entirely appropriately. He found this an incredible feat for a Westerner who had no knowledge of the Chinese language. Thus, if we have sufficient patience and allow time for analytical psychology to flourish, Chinese analysts will find an appropriate way to understand and work with Jung's ideas (Shen, 2015b, 1:26–22:10).Shen continuously emphasises that Chinese analysts should study analytical psychology based on their understanding of Chinese culture, as the latter was crucial to the formulation of the former. As he mentioned in our interview, archetypes on assimilation are common in Chinese culture. These modifications also show that Shen believes the Chinese to have advantages in terms of assimilating and applying analytical psychology and that the Chinese language itself is a wonderful tool for understanding it. After all, it might be easier for a Chinese person to understand the *I Ching*, since it was written in Chinese. Furthermore, the philosophy and logic of the *I Ching* are more understandable for the Chinese psyche, as it is immersed in their cultural unconsciousness.

Based on this trend of assimilation, another core aspect of Shen's modifications is integration. When he trained in Zurich and San Francisco, the first person from mainland China to do so, he received opportunities to work with famous analysts. Moreover, while Samuels pointed out that there are three schools of analytical psychology (Samuels, 1985a, pp.11–21), Shen said that there is also a fourth one – the San Francisco school (2015b).[3] Analysts from all four schools have visited China and offered their lectures and training there. Shen also worked with Gao Juefu, an important translator of Freud's works in the Chinese edition, and studied psychoanalysis from Gao before entering the Jungian frame. Therefore, the Chinese therapists in his team are very open to different schools of analytical psychology and psychoanalysis. This has fuelled Shen's belief that a coalition of analytical psychology will happen in China. His strong ambition to develop an integrative psychology has encouraged him to use his own method of applying analytical psychology in Chinese culture.

Contributions of the Chinese team to analytical psychology

The Chinese team led by Shen have made three main contributions to analytical psychology. The first contribution is to epistemology. For Shen, Chinese characters are 'readable archetypes' (2009) and he regards Chinese language as an 'archetypal formation of character' (1996). In Chinese language, a simple character can express multiple meanings. When he translates terms from analytical psychology into Chinese, he tries to interpret them by combining multiple meanings of Chinese characters and he relates these characters to Chinese classics and old narratives. In other words, he amplifies them and eventually gives these terms meanings that are more comprehensive than their original meanings in Western languages. He also introduces Chinese terms into analytical psychology to describe complicated situations.Shen translates *individuation* as *ZiXing*:

> *Xing* (heart-minded) combined with *Zi* (nature) brings the idea of 'heart' and 'life' together; it gives a word picture of the original psychological image of what we are which we carried from the very beginning of our life and gave it psychological meaning.
>
> (2009, p.6)

From his words, we can see that 'heart' is a very important term for him. In many of his translations, he tries to insert the meaning of heart into the psychological and therapeutic terms he uses. He associates the multiple meanings of 'heart' in Chinese, and for him 'heart' means a) the core centre of the human body, which is beyond the brain; b) thinking, emotion, consciousness, attitude, character and will; and c) the core of the

Tao[4] (1996, 2007a). These meanings of 'heart' are totally based on the Chinese language and rooted in Chinese philosophy, covering several important elements in psychology. I believe that this is why, eventually, Shen named his localised analytical psychology 'the heart of psychology' and named his respective programmes 'psyheart' and 'Gardens of the Heart-Soul'.

In another article, Shen translated the word 'containing' into '*bao chi*'. In Chinese, the two characters have multiple meanings. '*Bao*' can be expanded to mean 'cherishment', 'protection', 'care', 'maintaining', 'giving birth to' and 'hatchment', while '*chi*' can be related to 'holding and control', 'proper limit' and 'companion'. Thus, the meaning of *bao chi* goes beyond the meaning of 'containing'. It comprises an analytical attitude and a basic technique that is used to confront symptoms and the shadows and complexes behind symptoms, and to deal with transference and counter-transference (2015a). Again, his translation is not merely a transposition between languages; it reworks the terms and develops new meanings and applicable methods. In the same way, he translated 'thinking' and 'integrity' (1996), 'happiness' (2007a) and 'love' (Cai & Shen, 2010), reinterpreting these words from Jungian psychological perspectives.

He has also introduced the Chinese term '*gan ying*' into the area of analytical psychology and this term is the foundation of his Psychology of the Heart:

> Since both of the Chinese characters, *gan* (influence) and *ying* (response), are 'heart' characters (i.e., Chinese characters that have heart as the main structure), we could translate this dynamic into English as 'touching by heart and response from heart.' This kind of interaction can be compared with the Western notion stimulus and response. Naturally, because these languages reflect two different systems of psychology, they represent different levels of psyche, even if the dynamic is archetypally, finally, the same.
>
> (Shen, Gao & Cope, 2006, p.71)

Gan ying is a typical Chinese term and Shen uses it to emphasise the importance of his 'heart' and to describe a different level of the psyche that cannot be found in Western languages. At the technique level, *gan ying* could appear in hypnosis, free association and active imagination and, in terms of intervention, it covers transference, projection, empathy and 'resonance'[5] (Shen, 2007b). Again, this is another trial of using a Chinese word to integrate many aspects in psychotherapy. These Chinese characters and words represent a combination of reflections, actions and situations.

Because of Shen's work, the Chinese language could be seen as reworking the terms of analytical psychology and this could represent a unique

Chinese contribution to the field. However, there is also a danger of over-interpretation. If every word in the Chinese language has various meanings, which can cover everything, they might ultimately come to mean nothing. Too many abstract, unidentified meanings in the language will make the proposed terms vague. Thus, the integrative trend in translating terms may lead to greater confusion rather than clarity. This issue became very salient in Shen's speech at the Fey lecture in Huston in 2018 in which he attempted to introduce 'the Psychology of the Heart' to Western audiences. To a certain degree, his presentation was successful: he organised his thoughts on 'the Psychology of the Heart' in a systematic way, established his understanding of psychology based on Chinese culture and brought to the Western audience vivid pictures of the images of relevant Chinese characters and the typical Chinese way of thinking. He amplified the core concept 'the Heart', discussed the meaning of the derived characters and relevant images in depth, but throughout, he failed to provide a clear definition of 'the heart'. Hence, his speech was very rich but vague, perhaps leaving the audience with the feeling that while they seemed to have understood the meanings behind the words, it was very difficult to elucidate what exactly they had learned. Hence, Shen's speech might bring an incomplete understanding or misunderstanding of Chinese culture and his ideas and made it difficult for him to engage in a profound dialogue with his Western audience.

The second contribution is in the realm of practice. Based on Shen and his team's clinical practice and on their understanding of Chinese philosophy, he uses three phrases to describe analytical work. The first phrase is 'settling the unsettled'; the second is 'settling the settled'; and the third is 'settling with destiny' (Shen, 2004, pp.43–50). In my understanding, the first phrase involves understanding the patients and dealing with their symptoms, problems and transference. The second phrase relates to development, with the aim of educating analysands to be better versions of themselves. The third phrase involves individuation, the core and aim of analysis. In *Problems of Modern Therapy* (CW16), Jung developed four stages of analysis – 'confession' (CW16, para. 123), 'elucidation' (CW16, para. 136), 'education' (CW16, para. 150) and 'transformation' (CW16, para. 160). Comparing Shen's phrases with Jung's stages, 'settling the unsettled' is roughly equivalation to 'confession' and 'elucidation', while 'settling the settled' is roughly equivalent to 'education'. However, the third phrase 'settling with destiny' is a typical attitude of Taoism. It is not about 'changing' or 'becoming' (Samuels, 1985a, p.178) who you are, nor is it about adapting actively. It is more like remaining who you are and accepting your fate peacefully. Thus, it is another direction of 'individuation'. This extends the notion of 'individuation' but in clinical practice, this has remained a very obscure idea and hence difficult to convey to trainers.

The third of Shen's contributions is academic in nature. In China, students use sandplay both in their clinical practice and academic studies. Shen's current students study dreams from children, adolescents, old people, prisoners and pregnant mothers and conduct cross-cultural research. China is a large country with 56 ethnic groups; thus, there is much material and many resources available for cross-cultural studies. In recent years, papers have been published on the difference between Tibetan and Han dreamers in an attempt to address the cultural influence on their respective dream images (Li, Yin & Shen, 2015; Yin & Shen, 2015; Yin, Shen, He, Wei & Cao, 2013). Most of these studies concentrate on the images from various groups. Researchers are collecting and studying material from dreams, sandtrays and images, which they think are all very close to the unconscious. However, as Jia (2016) points out, in the realm of psychoanalysis, there continues to be a lack of high quality papers (p.380), with research facing the same problems. Although the volume of theses and papers in analytical psychology has been rapidly increasing year by year and the passion for such research has remained at a high level, the number of international researchers referencing such work is rather low.

Even with its obvious shortcomings, however, all of this work suggests that the application of psychoanalysis and analytical psychology is unstoppable in China. Here, I wish to discuss the crucial concept of the 'Oedipus complex' in the Chinese context. This relates deeply to the topics I will discuss in later chapters where I present the current application of Western-rooted psychologies in Chinese culture.

Oedipus in China – an example of applying depth psychological ideas in the Chinese context

As Parsons (2010) explains, the Oedipus complex is 'a distinctive nuclear complex' in the family structure and there has been a long-standing academic debate on the cross-cultural use of this concept. Simon (1991) believes that, in Freud's opinion, the Oedipus complex is universal, but Silverman (1986), quoting Lessa's study on myths and legends all over the world, points out that stories with Oedipal themes are absent from many countries and regions, including China. Parsons (2010) studied the Oedipus complex in Southern Italy, while Bhugra and Bhui (2002) explored Oedipus in Indian families; both agreed that, first, Oedipus is universal and second, it has its own complexity. It is not cast in 'a rigid manner' in different contexts and, therefore, people in these contexts approach it in a variety of different ways. Hence, it is likely that there are distorted or disguised versions of the Oedipus complex. Consequently, it is possible that in China and in some other cultures, researchers might not immediately recognise Oedipal themes, because they appear in forms which are not familiar to Western researchers.Roll and Abel pointed out that Oedipal stories contain the twin themes of 'patricide' and 'mother/son incest' (1988, p.537). Chinese people are also born into a family with a father and mother and the triangular relationship – 'mother-son-father' – is also the basic element of their families. However, attitudes to the 'mother-son' and 'father-son' relationship in China are dominated by filial piety. In my interview with Wang (2015), I asked about the difficulties he had encountered during his training. In response, he took the Oedipus complex as an example. He said that it was difficult to imagine having sex with the opposite-sex parent and competing with the same-sex parent, and furthermore, that it was difficult to understand the castration anxiety associated with this complex. This view is not uncommon among Chinese people. Oedipal themes seem to totally conflict with the requirements of being good sons and daughters in Confucian society, which are based on respecting and obeying one's parents. Respecting one's parents means keeping a distance, while obeying them means never challenging them, let alone competing with them. On the other hand, Chinese people have a great interest in the Oedipus complex, even if they feel it is unacceptable and discuss it passionately, regardless of whether their attitudes are for or against it.

Since Freud's ideas first began to arrive in China, the Oedipus complex has featured among the three main psychoanalytic themes[6] in Chinese literature (Zhang, 1992, p.57). Writers at that time drew on the Oedipus conflict directly to create their own novels and plays. They depicted competition between fathers and sons and the sexual tension between mothers and sons and between daughters and fathers.

Later, the scholars who were influenced by psychoanalysis made some attempts to identify the Oedipal complex in Chinese literature. Cai (2009) explored the well-known Chinese romantic tragedy 'Liang-Zhu' and came to the conclusion that Zhu's love for Liang is rooted in the fact that he is 'a desirable Oedipal substitute'. In addition, the gap between them in terms of socioeconomic class makes each of them 'a forbidden object' to the other, which is also a basic element in the Oedipus complex. Gu (2009) analysed the 'filial piety complex' in Chinese literature from ancient times to the present day and assumed that it represented 'an Oedipus disfigured'. However, the outcomes of these Chinese stories are quite different from the original Greek tragedy: these stories end with the death of the child who is either killed by the father or commits suicide.

In the clinical realm, there is a typical kind of Chinese hysteria known as *Koro*, a psychotic symptom that was first reported by Chinese doctors. Koro means that a young male patient is pathologically worried that his penis will withdraw into his body with fatal consequences (Gerlach, 2014a; Snyder, 2014). Gerlach studied Koro and concluded that this symptom is caused by the 'fear of castration' among young Chinese men. He further claims that: 'Koro embodies a regression to orality with ... defense derived from unconscious aggressive and libidinous desires towards mothers and avoidance of the Oedipal conflict with the father' (Gerlach, 2014a, p.140). This provides clinical evidence to support the existence of the Oedipus complex in the Chinese psyche. Instead of being castrated by the father, the child castrates himself. In this way, he avoids both defeating his father and challenging the dominant principle of 'filial piety'.

However, in Chinese culture, there is another triangle, namely that of 'mother – son – daughter-in-law'. Chinese literature features stories about this typical Chinese conflict, the competition between mothers-in-law and daughters-in-law. In many such stories, the father is absent for business reasons or because he is carrying out government duties. Therefore, 'the hatred of the father disappears ... the love for the mother, or a surrogate mother is intensified' (Gu, 2009, p.129). We could infer that in Chinese culture, the son's excessive obedience to the mother is a disguised form of the sexual tension that exists between them, particularly when the father is away. Therefore, when the son marries another woman, there will inevitably be competition and jealousy between the mother-in-law and daughter-in-law. Such stories invariably end up with the daughters-in-law giving up their marriages or even taking their own lives (ibid., pp.123–130; Zhang, 1992, pp.68–84). To summarise, in all of these Chinese stories, the children are ultimately defeated by their parents' wills. From these stories, we can infer that in Chinese culture, the younger generations are not encouraged to win any kind of competition with their elders and if they attempt to challenge their parents, they are doomed to failure. Real incest rarely occurs, but sexual tensions are concealed behind sons' obedience to their mothers' demands in order to maintain a distance from their wives.

A close bond between mother and son is encouraged by Chinese society under the guise of filial duty. In a family without a father's physical presence, this might serve as a useful strategy for keeping both mother and son loyal to the wider family, or the community, which is always privileged over the demands of the individual. On the other hand, from a psychoanalytic perspective, it is possible that showing excessive respect to the parent may be a reaction formation, which is a common defence mechanism in China. The hatred exists, but instead of killing the parent, the child kills himself, or ejects his wife from the family. Killing the offspring, or reducing the possibility of propagation in a family, is a severe punishment. Therefore, in China, the Oedipus conflict leads in another direction – the child destroys himself to punish his parents.

Furthermore, Jung's concept of the 'mother complex' might offer some more accurate insights into Chinese family dynamics. Jung claims that 'the mother ... cannot help playing, overtly or covertly, consciously or unconsciously, upon the son's masculinity, just as the son in his turn grows increasingly aware of his mother's femininity, or unconsciously responds to it by instinct' (CW9i, para. 162). During this process, the mother and son identify with each other. Jung points out that some 'typical effects on the son' due to his mother complex are 'homosexuality and Don Juanism, and sometimes also impotence'. In other words, a son with a powerful mother complex cannot have a mature, stable relationship with another woman, such as his wife. This theme is very common in Chinese literature. The widowed mother encourages her son to be a hero, and in return, the son gives up his own chance of emotional fulfilment.

Leichty (1978) argues that the only way to resolve the Oedipus complex is for the son to identify with the father and to give up his desire for the mother as the object of choice. From a psychoanalytic perspective, only when they overcome the Oedipus conflict can people achieve a state of adult maturity. Jung claims that 'an individual is infantile because he has freed himself insufficiently … from his childish environment and his adaption to his parents' (CW5, para. 431). However, in Chinese culture, identifying with the father would mean disrespecting him, which is why in ancient China a child would avoid writing his/her father's name or pronouncing a syllable that sounded the same as that name. Children are also encouraged to bond with the mother and to place her in an exalted position over other women. Obedience to parents has been the most important principle in Chinese society for thousands of years, but it would be unfair and inaccurate to say that no mature Chinese adults have existed during this time. Since the Oedipus complex performs a different drama in Chinese culture, there must be some way of dealing with it that is particular to the Chinese and which needs to be explored further.

Discussion

When psychoanalysis came to China, Western therapists showed much concern about whether it could be successfully applied to Chinese patients, while their Chinese colleagues took a more positive approach. Ng (1985) claimed that psychoanalysis could be better understood by Chinese people, and through his empirical studies, showed that non-directive and exploratory therapies are effective with Chinese patients. This view is shared by Lin (2014, 2015). Comparing his work with Western patients in London to his work with Chinese patients in Shanghai, Wang (2015) came to the conclusion that there are no significant differences between the two groups in psychoanalytic therapy. Chinese therapists likely believe that psychoanalysis can definitely be successfully applied in China and the only problem that concerns them is how to 'localise' it; that is, to integrate it effectively with Chinese cultural elements. In the world of analytical psychology, there is little discussion about its applicability in China. Because Jungian psychology contains some Chinese elements and quotes Chinese terms, and since some studies have been conducted on these aspects, both Western analysts and their Chinese colleagues tacitly agree that it can be effectively applied to the Chinese psyche.

In fact, many studies have been conducted on therapeutic work in cross-cultural and cross-racial settings, in other words, on working with patients from non-Western cultures in Western countries, including looking at Western therapists working with non-Western patients, or therapists and patients who both come from non-Western cultures (Akhtar, 1995; Layton, 2006; Roland, 1996a, 1996b; Yi, 1995). None of these studies are completely negative about the applicability of psychoanalysis to non-Western patients. Instead, some researchers state that emphasising racial or cultural differences might act as a tool for transference (Holmes, 1992), or that it demonstrates non-Western therapists' sense of inferiority as a minority group and white therapists' sense of superiority as the majority group (Yi, 1998b) and that it creates a distance between the therapist and patient and provokes racially-based prejudices (Bradshaw, 1978; Evans, 1985). As mentioned previously, when Western analysts work in China with Chinese patients and students, the arguments focus on whether they should apply psychoanalysis differently with Chinese patients[7]; however, the premise of its applicability is undeniable.

In analytical psychology, in the final chapter of *From Traditional to Innovation: Jungian Analysts Working in Different Cultural Settings*, Crowther and Wiener concluded, after reading about their colleagues' work with analysands and trainees in intercultural settings, particularly in countries without a culture of analytical psychology, that despite the challenges and disagreement on certain issues, such work is valuable and benefits both sides – both the deliverers and receivers. Finally, 'working in different cultural settings permits practice to make a greater impact on theory' (2015, pp.209–293). It validates the applicability of analytical psychology in China. Further, in the same book, Beebe shares his experience of applying Chinese philosophy to understanding the dreams and images of his analysts and himself. Furthermore, from his experience of working with patients in China, he not only confirms that analytical psychology is applicable there, but also foresees that engaging with Chinese Jungians will enrich and enliven Western Jungians and help 'Chinese therapists become freer to use their own self-experience in their work as counsellors and healers' (2015, p.269). As discussed in the previous chapter, the groundwork laid by Shen and the achievement of his team are endorsements of its applicability in China and its use in that context is unstoppable.

The dilemma of 'colonialism'

When we talk about 'difference', we are confronted with a complex issue. All therapists working with patients from non-Western backgrounds in Western settings must discuss the differences, regardless of whether they come from Western or non-Western cultures. Cushman criticises the idea of ignoring the cultural difference as a form of 'psychological imperialism' (1996, p.479). However, overemphasising differences, or encouraging Western psychotherapists to follow an 'emphatic-introspective approach' (Yi, 1995, p.380) in order to adapt to their Asian patients seems to place Westerners and non-Westerners in unequal positions. It makes Western culture appear more mature, sophisticated and stronger, or in other words, it represents Western superiority. Haag compared American 'guilt culture' with Eastern (including China and Japan) 'shame culture', claiming that '"guilt" … was seen on a more developed, namely Oedipal, level, deriving from an internalized moral standard or superego' (2014, p.47). She also asserted that Chinese people lack curiosity and find it difficult to be abstinent in therapeutic settings. This kind of Western superiority is very common among Western analysts and, though they may not recognise it consciously, it is often concealed under the guise of sympathy, encouragement and careful adaption to Chinese people.

Even Jung could not avoid succumbing to Western superiority when he talked about the difference between the Eastern and Western psyches. As Clarke (1994, 1995) and Blowers (2015) point out with reference to Jung's description of the one-sidedness of the East and West, he automatically placed the West on the 'high developed intellectual' side (Blowers, 2015, p.281) with the natural inference that the Eastern psyche is, conversely, undeveloped and unintellectual. However, I think this assessment is unfair and can be disproved given sufficient knowledge of Chinese history.

Herein lies a dilemma. If a Western analyst ignores the cultural difference, he might be accused of 'psychological imperialism', or there is a danger that he will use his values, which are based on 'Euro-American culture', to diagnose his non-Western patients, and consequently reach the wrong conclusions in terms of the psychopathology. However, if a Westerner tries to adapt his approach to take account of the patient's background, this would suggest that the patient is not intelligent or developed enough to 'fit' the original tenets of Western psychology. Therefore, the treatment would still be Western ethnocentric.

Because of this dilemma, further exploration is required of how to 'adjust' Western-rooted psychotherapy in China to make it more adaptive without putting the two parties in an unequal position explicitly or implicitly. Some Chinese therapists have shown their interest and concern with this topic. For example, the Chinese psychoanalyst, Jia Xiaoming, wrote a paper *Psychoanalytic Training in China: Cultural Colonialism or Acculturation* (2016), in which she warned Chinese therapists to be careful about absorbing Western teachings without thinking. She suggested that training psychoanalysis in China should be based on dialogue not on monologue and encouraged Chinese therapists to be more creative based on integrating their own cultural rooting, such as relying more on self-experience (a special term for Chinese psychotherapists' own therapy or analysis) with local psychoanalysts even if these analysts are not qualified by inter-national standards, and reducing the frequency of analysis. This is the first paper to discuss this issue in a direct way and it reflects a common concern and further thoughts of the first generation of psychanalysts in China after having learned, applied and taught psychoanalysis in China for many years. At the second Asia Pacific Conference of the International Psycho-analytical Association in Tokyo, Wang Xiao, one of the younger generation of Chinese psychoanalysts, gave a presentation that showed a different atti-tude. In his speech, he emphasised that, in China, psychoanalysis is at the beginning stage of development and has quietly challenged traditional Chinese values, with many misunderstandings and assumptions. Therefore, at this stage, as beginners, Chinese psychotherapists should, like little babies, rely on their Western teachers who offer a 'holding environment' to teach and correct them so that they may learn more original psychoanaly-sis rather than a modified or adapted edition thereof (Wang, 2018). This speech caused a hot debate amongst his Chinese and Western colleagues, with the main argument revolving around how much Chinese therapists should absorb from Western masters in the realm of depth psychology and how much independence they should retain.

In my opinion, Shen's work in China might offer a solution to this dis-agreement. As a Chinese man brought up in Shandong province (the hometown of Confucius), he is equipped with in-depth knowledge of Chin-ese culture. As the first person from mainland China to complete the full training in both Jungian psychology and sandplay therapy and to qualify as an IAAP member and ISST member, Shen completed his training in Zurich and San Francisco and as such gained rich experience and know-ledge of analytical psychology in the Western setting. Furthermore, having undertaken clinical groundwork with Chinese people from all over the country, he and his team have a comprehensive understanding of the con-temporary Chinese psyche. In the past few years, they have built a bridge designed to facilitate a dialogue between East and West. He offers a more egalitarian perspective which can help Westerners understand the Eastern psyche and, more importantly, he makes Western psychological ideas and concepts accessible, coherent and applicable to Chinese people.Further-more, Shen also offers the possibility of a new, integrative school of Jung-ian psychology. Samuels revised his classification of the schools of analytical psychology, so that the four new schools 'could be presented as a simple spectrum: fundamentalist-classical-developmental-psychoanalytic' (2011, p.10). In some ways, the new classification is based on the different attitudes that exist towards psychoanalysis, from rejecting it completely, to warmly embracing it. In China, people do not make the same distinctions between psychoanalysis and analytical psychology as do Westerners. They are interested in both and focus on the similarities between them, tending to regard them as different levels of interpreting human nature. As such, they do not see the two psychologies as in any way contradictory. Shen is a great believer in hypnosis and Winnicott, and he always emphasises the importance of Chinese cultural elements in the human psyche. Therefore, in his claim that there is also a 'San Francisco' school of analytical psychology, there could be a hint that he intends to develop his own 'Chinese school' which would not necessarily integrate all of the schools within analytical psychology, but would offer a more integrative perspective with which to understand and work with the human psyche.

Nowadays, Taoism and Buddhism are no longer unfamiliar and exotic to Westerners, and in fact, have an influence on the Western psyche (Plankers, 2013). There have already been discussions about how ideas and methods from Buddhism can be applied within psychoanalytic therapy in Western countries (Epstein, 1988, 1990, 1995, 2013). In studies of analytical psychology, many Western analysts and scholars use Chinese cultural elements, particularly the *I Ching*, to enrich their understanding of Jungian ideas and phenomena in relation to the human psyche, like synchronicity and individuation (Beebe, 2008; Cambray, 2005; Coward, 1996; Stein, 2005; Zabriskie, 2005). In recent years, Chinese Jungians have also contributed to offering new ways of understanding dreams, the unconscious and feminine aspects in human beings (Ma, 2010; Shen, 2011). However, in this reciprocal process, challenges and problems could not be ignored, for Chinese teams in particular, and these require more examination and further discussion.

Problems and challenges of applying depth psychology in China for Chinese teams

The first problem of applying depth psychology in China is the tendency to idealise Western masters, such as Freud, Jung, Winnicott, etc., due to the long history of authoritarianism there. Jia (2016) points out that Chinese people have put Freud in a very high and authoritative position, taken his writings as the truth and treated IPA members as his preachers (p.379). Amongst Jungians in China, the situation is almost identical. They have remained stuck to Jung's classic works and treat his words as gospel, ignoring the fact that Jung and his theory were rooted in Jung's own time and culture. Some of Jung's thinking and writing is limited and outdated in today's world, particularly his perspective from a superior white male stance, which may have been normal during his time in Zurich, but could be seen as racist and sexist in a broader context today. Among post-Jungians today, these issues are debated and Jung's thinking and works are criticised; however, dissenting voices have rarely been heard in China and instead, the Chinese team prefers to treat Jung as a wise man who was highly influenced by Chinese culture and who adeptly adapted the Chinese lens to understand the deepest layer of the human psyche (this tendency is very obvious, for example, in Shen's book *Jung and Chinese Culture*). Hence, even with the emphasis on being integrative, the delivery and development of Jungian psychology have remained monocultural until now.

Secondly, when discussing 'integrating' or 'localising' depth psychology in China, in both the realms of psychoanalysis and Jungian psychology, Chinese teams all focus on interpreting such Western-rooted ideas and notions by their understandings from Chinese culture. In other words, they assume an a priori sameness and similarity between them and never mention the differences. Particularly in quoting Jung, the Chinese team highlights places where Jung mentioned Chinese elements to prove how important Chinese culture was to Jung but neglects the context or tone of these words, rarely mentions that Jung also used many terms, perhaps even more, from Indian and African culture, and never challenges Jung's understanding of Chinese culture. On the other hand, at most international conferences that I have attended, Chinese speakers use special Chinese terms that are unfamiliar to audiences from other cultures and combine these terms with those from Western psychology to interpret their case or establish their understanding of the psyche. However, they rarely make any real comparison between the two groups of terms, which would mean evaluating both the similarities and differences, not to mention discussing the possibility of a mismatch and inadequate relevance. Although this approach might enrich the perspectives of depth psychology, sticking to the one-sided approach might make the presentation into a monologue, giving the audience a 'crash course' on Chinese culture but hindering further communication.

Due to these two main problems, the current fever of depth psychology in China might imply the possibility of narcissistic idealisation. On the surface, people seem to be very open, curious and flexible and to admire their Western masters and teachers very much, but underneath people only value one voice, that of their counterparts in other worlds, while ignoring or discarding voices which are less harmonious with their own. This attitude brings three challenges for the further development of depth psychology. First, different Chinese teams, without idealisation and tolerance of differences, are quite sensitive to competition and do not know how to prompt authentic and deep cooperation. Second, in Russia, during the process of delivery of analytical psychology, it was noticed that there had always been 'a disjunction between [the] sophisticated understanding of theory' and the method of practice with patients (Crowther & Wiener, 2015, p.278). In China, because of the rush to integrate Chinese elements, this phenomenon could be even worse. The ideas and notions from Buddhism, Taoism and Confucianism are very obscure, ambiguous and even controversial, as I mentioned in the last chapter. Hence, the attempt to combine these elements with clinical practice would be less friendly for new therapists. During the process, without clear definition and specific instruction, many therapists simply copy their teacher's words rigorously without full understanding, and this brings confusion and frustration to both themselves and their patients. Third, the real dialogue between East and West has not been fully engaged by either side. The current main approach for Chinese therapists to express themselves in international communication brings obstacles to mutual understanding, because specific Chinese terms are overly quoted without deep examination and adequate comparison. As a result, Western audiences require time to follow the meaning and it is difficult to challenge or criticise the ideas, as well as difficult to reference. Therefore, although such presentations bring fresh and extended materials to the field, the delivery of such voices from Chinese therapists has been very limited and they have not been heard by a broader audience.

The core of these three challenges is how to promote dialogue between Chinese teams, between therapists and patients and between East and West. People who have devoted themselves to the delivery and development of depth psychology in other cultures are aware of the importance of dialogue and emphasise that the foundation of such dialogue is putting the two parties in equal positions, having mutual curiosity, recognition and respect and developing a negotiated relationship (Beebe, 2015, p.267; ibid, p.277; Jia, 2016). The next question is how to promote such dialogue. Cushman points out that the only way 'to understand others and live with others in peace and with respect' is to have a 'genuine conversation' based on 'conceptualiz[ing] the dialogic meeting and mutual cultural exploration' (1996, p.489). Hence, for Chinese teams, this means, in the first place, initiating real curiosity about other cultures by putting aside their cultural pride for a while, carefully listening to what their Western masters and colleagues are trying to express, noticing and understanding the differences between the various cultures, not being in a rush to recognise the similarities or integrate what they have just learnt with what they already know and, most importantly, providing space for disagreement. The key to 'authentic dialogue' is accepting the fact that the dialogue could fail and the two parties may never reach agreement.

Further, beyond their own internal problems, all Chinese teams also encounter other challenges which are quite unique for China and for this era. The first is the prevalence of on-line training programmes and therapy. Cyber work is still new in the realm of depth psychology and further research should be conducted on its applicability and validation. In China, as a large country with a large population and with a huge gap between different regions, for many people, their only option is to obtain services over the internet. The positive side of this is that it makes depth psychology more available to more people in a cheaper and more convenient way; the negative side is that such on-line work has gained immediate popularity in China without scrutiny. No one can guarantee the long-term results of such work.

Further, heavy reliance on cyber work also carries a high risk of breaking confidentiality and Chinese therapists and their patients' work being exposed through monitoring and intervention from the government. The second aspect is that because of the prevalence of on-line work, accompanied by the increased market and lower costs, investment companies are also demonstrating an interest in depth psychology in China. Many on-line platforms for training and therapy oriented in depth psychology have received support from investment companies. However, work in this area requires patience and a slow pace for the growth of the psyche, and a focus on immediate profit, which is the only aim of such companies, is totally contrary to this aim and likely to damage the area. However, resisting the enchantment of hot money has always been a challenge for humanity.

Nevertheless, even with the problems and challenges discussed above, from all the work that the Chinese team has already done, we can conclude that applying psychoanalysis and Jungian psychology in China is reciprocal. This process will reshape the ideas and techniques used in both psychoanalysis and Jungian psychology and make resources for understanding the human psyche more abundant and comprehensive. Furthermore, as Varvin suggests, 'this process may change not only our scientific perspectives and viewpoints but also [our] view of ourselves' (2014, p.116). This will in turn affect the Western psyche. After all, according to the concept of the 'collective unconscious', we all share the same vast psychological space.

Conclusion

It is apparent that China has been through a great shift in recent years. This has presented many new issues, while the old problems have emerged into consciousness. 'Individualisation' has arisen in the younger generations and we have gradually had to face our traumatic history, maintain a distance from our long traditions and learn to mourn the separation and loss during the process. In this context, psychoanalysis can be very helpful. Furthermore, materialism and an eagerness for achievement and money cast heavy shadows over Chinese people today. The Jungian idea of 'individuation' might be a good remedy for this condition.

In my eyes, the modifications that have been made to psychoanalysis and analytical psychology in China are not too few but too many. Most Chinese therapists are still only on the first step and need to learn more, undertake more training and develop a better understanding of the real meanings of Western ideas. Thus, modification and integration are the next step. This will happen spontaneously, however, and there is no need to force the process.

As Cushman suggests, 'analyst and patients might be better served by confronting what a dialogue with others reveals about one's own culture frame' (1996, p.487). This could also be put into practice by applying Western psychological approaches in Chinese settings. Both the West and the East would be affected by so doing and would benefit from the process. In this book, I attempt to apply Western concepts to confront and explore Chinese culture and to identify new approaches to understand and resolve intimate issues in relationships between couples. Such an attempt will be shown in my interviews with young Chinese couples in the next chapter.

I would like to end this chapter with a story. In 2013, I went to Laoshan with Shen and a group of analysts from the Institute of Jungian Studies in Zurich. These analysts were sitting around a circular stone table. Paul Brutsche[8] began to imitate Jung's way of speaking. Shen asked him whether Jung would come back to this world and build another tower like his building in Bollingen near Kusnacht – but in China. Just as Brutsche was saying, 'YES, I will ...', a sudden gust of wind whipped up around the group. Jungians would probably call this 'synchronicity'.

Notes

1 A term in Buddhism, meaning nothing can last forever and everything is in the process from birth to death.
2 A term in Buddhism, meaning inter-dependent origination.
3 Samuels classified Jungian analytical psychology into three different schools – the 'Classical School', the 'Development School' and the 'Archetypal School' (1985a, p.15). However, he later revised his classification, as I will present later.
4 A term in Taoism and one of the central concepts of Chinese philosophy, symbolising the principle of the world.
5 Amman, (2004, pp.245–246).
6 The three main themes are the interpretation of creativity, the Oedipus complex and the interpretation of dreams.
7 Scharff (2014) wrote an article named 'Five things western therapists need to know for working with Chinese therapists and patients'. Apparently, in his opinion, Chinese people should be treated specially and carefully.
8 A Jungian analyst from Basel, Jung's hometown, who played Jung in the play *The Red Book*.

Chapter 5

Experiences, disappointments and expectations
Interviews with young urban Chinese couples

This chapter is based on materials collected and analysed from eight couples I interviewed in three cities – Beijing, Shanghai and Wuhan. The interviewees were recommended to me by therapists in these cities. They comprised patients, students and friends of these therapists, who demonstrated interest and curiosity in couple therapy as a means to solve their marital problems or better understand their marriage. In choosing couples, I also applied a certain criteria: four of the couples comprised husbands and wives without siblings (henceforth, one-child family couples), while four comprised husbands and wives with siblings (henceforth, non-one child family couples). My hope was that this distinction between one-child and non-one-child family couples would allow me to see whether couples from the two family types would differ when they establish intimate relationships with spouses from the same background. As this was a pioneer study, I did not examine mixed couples, comprising one partner without siblings and one with siblings, which are also common in China, because when the effect of gender roles and prevalent misunderstandings and bias between these two different kinds of families were added, studying them would be much more complicated and would require further and deeper examination, which could be the topic of a whole other book.

Through these interviews, as both the interviewer and researcher who had been raised in the same cultural and social circumstances, I identified a number of facts regarding the relationships between young Chinese couples who wished to remain in long-term relationships, and interpreted these facts from depth-psychological perspectives. While eight couples is a small sample, some degree of diversity was observed between them. First, their hometowns covered eight provinces in China, including the east, north, middle, south, southeast, northeast, northwest and southeast parts of China. They thus represented the variation in customs and traditions associated with different regions. Second, while most couples were in their thirties, some were in their early forties, while one husband was 47. They had all been born and raised in China and had thus experienced the modification and transition of Chinese society since 1978 and had been affected by these changes.

Below, I will give more details about these couples, to depict their respective backgrounds and situations more clearly. The four couples from one-child families are Mr. and Mrs. Zhao, Mr. and Mrs. Qian, Mr. and Mrs. Sun and Mr. and Mrs. Li; the four couples from non-one-child families are Mr. and Mrs. Chou, Mr. and Mrs. Wu, Mr. and Mrs. Zeng and Mr. and Mrs. Wang.

One-child family couples

Mr. and Mrs. Zhao had been married for 16 years when they arrived for interview. Mr. Zhao was 43 and Mrs. Zhao was 42. Both had baby faces and a lively demeanour. Mrs. Zhao was very open and showed a strong curiosity about my work. She had studied psychology for one year and she had been the one to contact me and initiate the interview because the topic had piqued her interest. They had a seven-year-old son and lived locally with Mrs. Zhao's parents who helped with childcare. They had begun dating when they worked in the same company approximately 18 years previously. When they came to me, they said that despite having a terrible experience in the first few years of marriage, to the extent that they had almost filed for divorce, they were now basically satisfied with their marriage.

Mr. and Mrs. Qian had been college classmates and now worked in different departments in the same university. They looked like typical intellectuals – elegant and polite. Both were 38 when they came to me and had been married for 12 years. They had a seven-year-old son and had lived for a time with Mr. Qian's parents for childcare reasons. However, because of the severe conflicts between Mrs. Qian and her parents-in-law, they eventually moved out, but stayed in the same neighbourhood and visited the grandparents' apartment almost every day. Mrs. Qian had had psychotherapy for a couple of years because of emotional issues after the birth of their child. She was now seeking help from a couple therapist because they had encountered a new difficulty in their marriage: with the new two-children policy, her husband had a strong desire to have a second child, but Mrs. Qian was very opposed to this idea and worried that it would cause the same nightmare – interruption of her career and more conflicts between her and her parents-in-law – as her first child had brought.

When *Mr. and Mrs. Sun.* came to me, Mrs. Sun was seven months' pregnant with their first child. She was a very pretty, blooming young women. Mr. Sun was sitting very close to her and seemed slightly protective of her at first. Mrs. Sun's parents took it in turns to come to Beijing to take care of her. Both Mr. and Mrs. Sun were immigrants to the city. Mr. Sun was 32 and Mrs. Sun was 31. They used to be colleagues in the same company and had been married for two years, after first living together for two years. Their intention in seeking couple therapy was that, while they thought their relationship was basically OK, they worried about possible issues in the future due to the addition of a newborn baby.

Mr. and Mrs. Li had been living together for two years and planned to marry ten days after the interview. They began dating following a recommendation by mutual friends. They were also immigrants to Beijing. Both were 31 and they had no child at the time of interview, but planned to have one in the future. They were generally satisfied with their current relationship, but as new, young immigrants in a big city who did not own property, they worried about the uncertainty of the future but were also quite looking forward to finding their position and fortune in the city.

Non-one-child family couples

Mr and Mrs Chou. Mr. Chou was the oldest interviewee at 47 and was also the oldest child in his family. Of all the husbands I interviewed, he seemed to be the most typically conservative, traditional, middle-aged Chinese man. He had a sister and brother, while Mrs. Chou, who was 39, had a younger brother. She seemed much younger, more open and livelier than her husband. They began dating after being introduced to each other by mutual friends. When they came to me, they had been married for 13 years. They voluntarily elected not to have children but had several dogs. They had had major issues at the beginning of the marriage, mainly because, as Mrs. Chou described, Mr. Chou was a very traditional Chinese man; hence, he was unwilling to get involved in housework and relevant family affairs and always put his parents' issues prior to the issues of their own small family, which caused Mrs. Chou frustration and upset. Now, however, he had changed a lot and the greatest difficulty had been solved. At the time of the interview, they were relatively satisfied with their marriage.

Mr. and Mrs. Wu. Mrs. Wu gave birth to her first child one month after our interview. She was 37 and had an older sister. She had suffered from her relationship with her mother, whom she considered to have a personality disorder, and who had been in psychotherapy for her depressive disorder for many years. Mr. and Mrs Wu had been married for 11 years. He was 38 and had a younger brother. Mr. and Mrs. Wu had been high school classmates and he knew her situation quite well and supported her therapy. He was a very open and honest man and admitted that their marriage used to be terrible and that they had attended couple therapy sessions more than ten times. Their relationship was now improving because of couple therapy and they were quite looking forward to the new child. They were living with Mr. Wu's parents.

Mr. and Mrs. Zeng were 32 and 33 respectively and both had an older sister. For work reasons, they lived in two different cities which were not far from each other and only spent weekends together. They had been married for four years and had no children. Mrs. Zeng had once had an abortion because she had thought they were not ready to become parents. They did not have any clear plan to have a child in the future. Between the ages of 14 and 15, both of Mrs. Zeng's parents had died and Mrs. Zeng suspected that her mother had committed suicide. She had been raised by her mother's family and had felt both lonely and closed with this family. A common friend had introduced Mr. Zeng to her and they had had a relationship since then. However, they were having severe conflicts and claimed to suffer a lot in their relationship. Therefore, they planned to try couple therapy. During our interview, they showed that there were many disagreements between them.

Both *Mr. and Mrs. Wang* were in their second marriage when they came for interview. Mr. Wang was 43 and Mrs. Wang was 39. Both seemed very depressive and lacked energy. Mrs. Wang was the only one of the eight wives who complained about her husband from the beginning to the end of our interview, while Mr. Wang was the only husband who sighed throughout the process. Mr. Wang had a younger sister, while Mrs. Wang had an older brother. They were introduced by common friends and neither had children from their first marriages. They had been married for three years and had a daughter who was almost three years old. Mrs. Wang's parents lived with them and helped take care of the child. Mr. Wang was the only one of the husbands who showed an active desire to participate in my interview, while among the other seven couples, it was the wife who contacted me and initiated the interview. He emphasised that it would be very difficult for him to accept a second failed marriage, but he and Mrs. Wang reported irreconcilable problems in their marriage and Mrs. Wang kept saying that she thought divorce would be the only solution.

As mentioned, while the sample was small, the descriptions above demonstrate the diverse situations of these couples in the basic structure of small families among young Chinese people and they also represent the diversity of stages and scales of conflict among young Chinese couples.

I held the eight interviews in three therapeutic rooms, one in each of the three cities. The interviews were based on 20 questions: two questions for both members of the couple, asking them to describe their marriage/relationship from the beginning to the present, and in particular to elaborate on the main difficulties or problems they had encountered or were dealing with, their future expectations for the marriage, or the goal of their couple therapy if they planned to undertake it; nine questions each for the wives and husbands, the contents of which were basically the same for both parties. These questions covered their current relationships, their evaluations of their spouse's behaviour patterns and their own behaviour in the marriage, the effects of their natal families and other people on their behaviours and expectations in the marriage, the romantic stories that they found most impressive and their own opinions on the ideal Chinese husband/wife.

In formulating these questions, I sought to address the expectations of these couples regarding femininity and masculinity in relationships, what they were experiencing at the time of the interview and the causes of disappointments and problems. These questions were not read out to them but were organised in a facilitatory and conversational way to prompt them into dialogue. The interviews lasted between approximately 50 and 90 minutes each, with the average length of interview being approximately 75 minutes. All interviews were recorded using audio equipment with their consent.

I used Thematic Analysis (TA) to analyse the interview data. TA is a 'foundational method for qualitative analysis' and 'a method for identifying, analysing and reporting patterns (themes) within data', which 'interprets various aspects of the research topic' (Braun & Clarke, 2006, pp.4–6). It is flexible and 'independent of theory and epistemology, and can be applied across a range of theoretical and epistemological approaches' (ibid., p.5). Furthermore, it does not regard 'researcher subjectivity ... as a problem to be managed', but values the 'unique standpoint of the researcher' and appreciates 'the researcher's evolving engagement with their data' (Clarke, Braun & Hayfield, 2015, p.223). Thus, it was deemed suitable for analysing the interview data and providing some clues to understanding Chinese couples by analysing themes in the narrative accounts of their relationships. The function and benefits of TA are quite essential for the study in this chapter, which is a pioneering study in couple relationships without a well-constructed theoretical frame. Through this study, I explore the possible theories that can be used to interpret the collective consciousness on this topic. Further, as mentioned at the beginning of this chapter, as a researcher who shares the same background as the research subjects, I preferred to treat my own experiences and feelings, in other words, my subjectivity, as a tool to understand my Chinese compatriots, rather than treating this subjectivity as a problem to be 'controlled' or 'eliminated', which is not possible if we treat the unconscious as a reality.

According to the responses given in the interview, I identified themes based on the various questions. I also recorded the interactions between the couples, their body language and the times at which they smiled or cried during the interview. All the themes were derived from the data and covered categories based on the interviewees' own words. I provided the frequency of categories used in the interviews and reported the difference between the responses from one-child family couples and non-one-child family couples. Through thematic analysis, I identified 12 key themes – relationships in flux, interaction in the narratives, spouse expectation, characteristics, emotional behaviours and performances, attractiveness, attitudes to the child, relationship with the spouse's parents, relationship with the natal family, influence of the natal family, explicit Western stories and figures in the narratives and impacting factors related to Chinese culture. These themes are organised into the following five frameworks: 1) the current situation; 2) personal characteristics and desirable characteristics of relationships; 3) effects of and relations with extended family; 4) impact factors of Chinese culture; and 5) Western factors in their narratives. Below, I will discuss each of these separately.

The current situation

In this section, I focus on the themes: 1) relationships in flux; and 2) interaction. From the results of the questions put to these couples to describe their current situation, I wanted to explore how they evaluated their current relationships, what difficulties they had previously experienced or were experiencing now and how they interacted with each other in reality at the moment.

Relationships in flux

All the couples demonstrated a tendency to treat their relationships as a process of modification rather than as a fixed result. Three couples (Qian, Sun and Li) described their relationships as currently in 'balance'. Mrs. Qian reported her current relationship with her husband as 'harmonious', while Mr. Qian described his relationship with his wife as 'affectionate'. Mrs. Sun described her marriage as 'stable' and 'peaceful', while Mrs. Li said that she and her husband were 'close'. Both Mr. and Mrs. Zeng agreed that their relationship was very unstable. Mrs. Zeng described her and her husband as 'romantic lovers' and 'hateful enemies' and said that the relationship vacillated between 'passion' and 'aloofness'. Mr. Zeng agreed and said that sometimes they were close, while at other times there was a huge distance between them.

Three couples (Zhao, Chou and Wu) who had been married for more than 10 years described how their relationships had been improving in recent years. Two (Zhao and Chou) reported that in the early years of their marriage, their relationship had been 'terrible' and 'difficult', but was now 'satisfactory'. Mr. Chou described his current relationship as 'sweet' and 'perfect', while Mr. Zhao said that he and his wife were very close at the moment. Even so, both couples agreed that problems might emerge later and improvements could be made. Mr. Wu attributed the improvement in their relationship to his wife's individual therapy for her depressive disorder which had lasted for some years, as well as to 10 sessions of couple therapy that they had received. Mr. Wu reported that they could now trust each other and he was quite confident in their future. Mrs. Wu said that she could now feel the equality between her and her husband, but that the relationship was still changing.

These three couples largely credited the improvement in their relationships to a change in one of the partners. Mr. Zhao and Mr. Wu considered that the 'reflections' and 'growth' of their wives had improved their marriage. In another couple, Mrs. Chou pointed out that her husband's 'transition from the role of the son to the role of the husband'[1] had improved their relationship.

In one relationship that was obviously deteriorating, Mrs. Wang felt that her husband should take the main responsibility for their 'terrible' situation. Both Mr. and Mrs. Wang were in their second marriage; Mrs. Wang said that she had thought her current husband would be different from her first husband, but it turned out they were the same. (There seemed to be a repeated pattern in both of her marriages.)

These comments on their marriages challenge the traditional Chinese attitude, whereby the wife should be responsible for the harmony of her marital family and the couple's relationship, while the husband has, historically, rarely been blamed for the failure of couples' relationships (Mann, 2002, pp.101–105; 2011, p.34; Yi, 1998b, p.45). In contrast, the young generations have gradually come to believe that husbands also have a duty to maintain and improve their relationships. For example, Mrs. Wu had undergone her own therapy for a depressive disorder and she and her husband had had couple therapy together. For them, it was not sufficient to treat the wife alone and it was deemed necessary for the husband to also take responsibility. Such couples demonstrate the possibility of finding equal positions for each spouse in their marriage. However, this is just the beginning and their old attitudes have not reversed or disappeared completely.

When discussing the difficulties and improvements in their relationships, they showed a tendency to consider one spouse to be chiefly responsible for the situation. This resembles Jung's idea of marriage where one spouse is the container and the other the contained (CW17, para. 31–34). (The word 'containing' was also repeatedly mentioned by interviewees as a positive and ideal characteristic in couple relationships. Although these couples were not familiar with Jung's term, they used the exact word used by Jung.) In Jung's work, he did not assign the role of 'container' and 'contained' to specific genders; rather, he thought each party in a couple could play either role, but each could mainly either 'contain' or 'be contained' (CW17, para. 40). In the work of post-Jungians (Young-Eisendrath, 1984, p.12; Zweig & Wolf, 1997, p.26), 'containing' is chiefly characterised as the feminine aspect in relationships. Like Jung, the couples interviewed did not consider the function of 'containing' to be gender specific; either wife or husband could be responsible for the relationship, but if the role of container was assigned to one person, this person would be expected to take this role most of the time. The stereotype here is not gender-related, but relates to the rigidly assigned role of one spouse in the relationship.

Interaction in the narratives

The interactions that occur between two people in a relationship were emphasised by the interviewees. A relationship involves the process of 'adjustment' and 'adaptation', while the two spouses 'tolerate' and 'contain' each other and offer each other 'support' and 'comfort'. In the least stable relationship among the eight couples, Mr. Wang repeatedly said that he could no longer 'tolerate his wife's nagging'.

'Communication' was also emphasised. Mr. and Mrs. Zhao who were satisfied with their current relationship both agreed that 'communication' was the key. Mr. Zhao said that he had considered getting a divorce in the first difficult years of the marriage because his wife had refused to communicate with him. Mrs. Zhao conceded that since making an effort to communicate, although they sometimes have arguments, their relationship has improved. Again, Mr. Wang reported an inability to 'communicate' and 'a subsequent estrangement between them'.

Mr. and Mrs. Wu, who had had couple therapy, both agreed that they had learned how to communicate in therapy and that communication used to be the main difficulty between them. In the two couples who were planning to do couple therapy, Mr. Qian and Mr. Zeng hoped it would 'facilitate their communication'. Mrs. Qian said the goal of attending couple therapy was to make her husband 'understand' her. Mrs. Zeng said her goal was to be treated as an equal partner by her husband in their communication. Therefore, for them, 'communication' was the key to solving most marital difficulties.

In terms of communication, Mrs. Sun and Mr. Li emphasised the importance of similarity between a couple, such as 'having a common language', 'sharing the same interests' and 'watching a movie together'. Mr. and Mrs. Zeng and Mrs. Wang reported being different from their spouses and resenting this difference. Mr. Zeng said, 'It is difficult to communicate with my wife because of this difference'.

'Complementarity' was also emphasised in couples' relationships in these interviews, and it was said to serve for cooperation. 'Cooperation' was cited as a positive aspect of the relationships, including 'sharing the housework' and 'handling the family affairs together'.Unlike the traditional requirement for Chinese couples (Pan, 1999, pp.4–8; Yi, 1998b, pp.45–51), for the younger generations, communication and interaction are essential ingredients of matrimonial satisfaction and happiness. As Farrer says, for them, 'togetherness', 'frequent communication' and 'companionship' are important means to increase and maintain intimacy (2014, pp.73–74). Further, they placed a high value on complementarity, which corresponds with Clulow's emphasis of this in Western marriages (1989, pp.53–55), as well as the high value placed on similarities.

However, I found these couples were unable to tolerate differences and separation. Hence, for them, 'complementarity' and 'cooperation' meant that they could reach the same position and share similar attitudes without any disagreement or conflicts. From Jungian and post-Jungian works, similarity and togetherness are typical feminine aspects that foster relations, while difference is a typically masculine aspect that could harm relations (Giegerich, 2008, p.120; Young-Eisendrath, 1984, p.12). Chinese couples embrace similarity and togetherness and struggle with difference, which could cause conflicts. On the surface, they support Young-Eisendrath's emphasis on the importance of the feminine principle in her work with couples, but they do not share the same stereotype in terms of the socially/culturally-assigned feminine/masculine principles.

On 'sharing the housework', differences exist between one-child family couples and their non-one-child family counterparts. Four one-child family couples mentioned that they did the housework together, while three wives from non-one-child family couples complained that their husbands were 'lazy'. In the least stable relationship, Mrs. Wang said, 'I do all the housework and take care of our baby, but he cannot take care of himself', while Mr. Wang said that they were unable to share any activity and that his wife rejected all proposals by him to do things together. The two other wives, Mrs. Chou and Mrs. Zeng, also mentioned their husbands' inability to manage their own lives, while Mrs. Zeng expressed the hope that her husband could have 'more active interaction' with her and that they could 'go shopping' and 'decorate their house' together.

Unlike traditional requirements for husbands, the younger generation, including both men and women, think husbands should also be involved in family affairs and that it is no longer plausible for husbands to be absent from the household. For one-child family wives in particular, they asked their husbands to share the housework with them, while one-child family husbands, who may have been affected by culturally-assigned femininity due to a close bond with the mother, took this responsibility for granted.

Personal characteristics and desirable characteristics in the relationship

In this section, I discuss four themes: 1) spouse expectations; 2) characteristics; 3) emotional behaviours and performance; and 4) attractiveness. From questions regarding how interviewees express their opinions to their spouses and their reflections on their own performances as husband/wife, in addition to their ideal images of a good husband/wife, I address the personal characteristics they valued or disliked in their relationships and the desirable characteristics they expected to find in a husband and wife.

Spouse expectations

In terms of spouse's abilities, the wives described their husbands as 'knowledgeable', 'intelligent', 'rational', 'fond of reading', 'humorous' and 'hard-working'. The husbands described their wives as 'capable', 'practical', 'hard-working', 'funny', 'smart', 'independent' and 'managing home affairs'. Mr. Qian said that his wife was 'not capable in her career', while Mr. Wu said that his wife was 'unstable in her job'.

When the interviewees discussed the abilities of the ideal spouse and their expectations of their spouses, the wives cited the following characteristics: 'ambitious in career', 'earning money', 'knowledgeable', 'talented', 'could handle all external affairs' and 'managed family affairs'. Mrs. Wang said that a husband should make sacrifices for his family, while two of the one-child family wives, Mrs. Sun and Mrs. Li, emphasised that husbands should share the housework. The husbands cited the following characteristics to describe their ideal wives: 'focus on family affairs' and 'sacrificing for and devotion to the family'.

The wives said that to be a good wife, one should 'manage the family affairs', be 'independent' (two younger one-child family wives, who were in their early thirties, Mrs. Sun and Mrs. Li, said that this meant 'being independent in their career', while two non-one-child family wives, Mrs. Wu and Mrs. Zeng, said it meant 'being financially independent'). The four one-child wives also emphasised that a good wife should 'have her own career', 'balance between career and family' and 'assist her husband's career'. When husbands described a good husband, they said he should 'have a good career', 'earn money', 'get involved in family affairs' and 'balance his career and family'.

Shi and Scharff (2014) have proposed that modern Chinese men are retaining the old values and priorities while Chinese women are demanding more equal rights (p.341). Based on the small sample in this study, this assertion is partially true. When couples described their abilities both within and outside of relationships, descriptions related to intelligence and external achievements were mainly applied to husbands. Both husbands and wives thought wives' abilities should be used first and foremost to serve the family. Also, as Steinfeld points out, a common belief still exists in China that men should devote themselves more to work than women (2015, p.127). However, both husbands and wives agreed that the husband should become involved in family affairs and even Mr. Chou and Mr. Wang, who did not really do so, agreed with this premise in principle. Furthermore, while conceding that a wife should focus on her family, one-child family wives tried to retain their careers and emphasised career achievement, traits that once reflected culturally-assigned masculinity. They were determined to find a way to maintain a balance between their families and careers. The young generations have begun to challenge the old family assignment whereby the husband is the breadwinner and the wife is the homemaker.

Another difference between interviewees from one-child families and non-one-child families was that when discussing external achievements, non-one-child family couples mainly emphasised 'financial or economic achievement', while one-child family couples mainly referred to 'career achievement' or 'career development'. One young couple, Mr. and Mrs. Li, who confessed that their main current difficulty was financial pressure, still focused more on career than on money. This conflicts with the common concern that young couples from one-child families have a greater economic burden because they have to support four elderly parents and at least one child (Wang, Zhou & Xiao, 1989). Based on my observation, besides the full investment parents place on an only child, once that child grows up, s/he can attain all the economic assistance of the parents as well as inheriting their fortune. Moreover, due to traditional Chinese values, parents are expected to save every penny of their inheritance, meaning that only children can benefit greatly from their parents' support. Therefore, such children have more opportunity to focus on self-realisation rather than on practical issues, particularly one-child family wives who are less bonded with traditional requirements for girls and have more financial security than their counterparts with siblings.

Characteristics

With regard to their spouses' characteristics, wives described their husbands as 'kind', 'confident', 'reliable', 'stable', 'responsible', 'sincere', 'arrogant' and 'self-centred'. Mrs. Wang called her husband 'irresponsible' because he could not take any pressure, while Mrs. Zeng called her husband 'irresponsible' and 'selfish' because he always broke his promises. Husbands described their wives as 'kind', 'reasonable', 'honest', 'reliable', 'straightforward', 'unselfish' and 'virtuous'. On the characteristics of their ideal spouse and expectations of a spouse, the wives used the words 'responsible' and 'loyal', while the husbands used the words 'kind', 'virtuous' and 'loyal'.

In the wives' opinions, a good wife should be 'virtuous' and 'loyal'. In husbands' opinions, a good husband should be 'loyal' and 'responsible'.

Emotional behaviours and performances

Wives used the following words to describe their husbands' emotional behaviours and performances: 'nice', 'listening to me', 'affectionate', 'easy-going', 'caring for me', 'considerate', 'positive', 'emotional', 'reluctant' and 'insensitive'. Husbands used the following words to describe their wives' emotional behaviours and performances: 'nice', 'gentle', 'warm', 'caring', 'considerate', 'sensitive and fragile', 'defensive', 'affirmative' and 'demanding'.

On the ideal spouse and expectations of the spouse, wives wanted their husbands to be 'understanding' and to be 'gentle', 'careful', 'considerate', 'supportive', 'respectful', 'containing' and 'caring'. Two wives from one-child family couples expressed their wish directly: Mrs. Qian said that a good husband should treat his wife like a cherished baby, while Mrs. Sun said that a husband should express his love to his wife directly. The husbands desired their wives to be 'kind', 'nice', 'gentle', 'considerate' and 'to comfort me' and 'to contain me'.

The wives said a good wife should be 'supportive', 'containing', 'mediative' and 'comforting' and should 'listen to her husband', and 'keep the boundary for the family'. The husbands said a good husband should be 'warm', 'supportive' and should 'make his wife happy'. Two one-child family husbands, Mr. Zhao and Mr. Li, said that a good husband should 'love his wife and children', 'spend time with the wife' and 'be in the company of his wife and children'.

Overlap exists in the descriptions and expectations related to character and emotional functions. Words such as 'virtuous', 'loyal', 'gentle', 'considerate' and 'caring', which used to feature only amongst requirements for wives, now also appear in relation to husbands. Both wives and husbands share a common view on this point. For one-child family couples in particular, both wives and husbands expressed the importance of a husband loving his wife and directly expressing his feelings. (Nevertheless, for Jungians, relating with feeling is typically associated with culturally-assigned femininity [Young-Eisendrath, 1984, p.12; Zweig & Wolf, 1997, p.26]). This result contradicts Scharff and Scharff's affirmation that intimacy and passion are less important in Chinese than in Western couples (2014, p.329).

This modification might be due to the following: 1) the effect of 'Westernisation', as the romantic stories of Western literature and Hollywood films idealise the virtues of male lovers and the ability to express love directly; and 2) the prohibition of concubinage and prostitution under Chinese Marriage Law (Woo, 2006, p.92; Yu, 2015, p.41), which has changed the traditional relationship in which Chinese men situated their feelings in extramarital relationships (Pan, 1999, pp.5–8). Instead, Chinese men must now turn to their wives to find their feelings and thus connect with 'the feminine' in their marriages.

Body language can also show the emotional ability and connection between the couples. During the interview, two one-child family couples (Zhao and Sun) sat very close to each other. In another one-child family couple, even during a severe argument between them in the interview, Mr. Qian patted his wife when she cried. In the four non-one-child family couples, I did not observe any body contact.

In the interviews, the wives smiled 65 times in total, while two non-one-child family wives, Mrs. Zeng and Mrs. Wang, did not smile at any stage of the process. Three non-one-child family wives, Mrs. Wu, Mrs Zeng and Mrs. Wang, cried in the interviews, 13 times in total. Mrs. Zeng cried over memories of her dead parents. The other instances of laughter and tears were all related to interactions and relations with their husbands. All the husbands smiled in the interviews, 26 times in total. None of the husbands cried. These wives were more open to expressing their current feelings directly than their husbands. This accords with the common stereotype of the feminine and masculine.

I also counted the active interactions in the interviews. These comprised positive interactions, such as joking together, showing support for each other's speech, etc.; negative interactions, such as blaming, refuting, denying, etc.; and neutral interactions, such as adding new information, reminding, asking for details, etc. In the four one-child family couples, the ratios of active interaction between wives and husbands respectively were: 5:8; 14:24; 7:9; 4:0. In the four non-one-child family couples, the ratios were: 10:4; 33:6; 5:1; 5:4.

Again, in one-child families, males showed more willingness to actively contact their intimate female others and to engage in more physical touch, presenting more attachment – in other words, more socially/culturally-assigned feminine aspects – because, as will be shown later, they have closer bonds with their mothers in the natal families.

Attractiveness

Some of these couples mentioned the importance of appearance and attractiveness in an intimate relationship. Mrs. Qian said her husband was 'handsome', while Mr. Qian said his wife was 'beautiful' and 'shapely', while Mr. Zhao said his wife was 'lovely'. None of the non-one-child family interviewees commented on their spouses' appearance. Four wives said they were attracted by 'handsome' men, while two husbands (Mr. Chou and Mr. Qian) said the ideal wife is 'beautiful' and 'shapely', but Mr. Chou said his wife's appearance was just OK while Mr. Qian said his wife met such criteria.

As Buss suggested (2015, pp.138–141), for men, appearance is an important element when choosing a spouse; however, in these interviews, women expressed their interest in men's appearance more openly. This may be due to a): the development of feminism in China, which encourages women to express their desires; b): the active role of women as a subject of desire rather than an object of desire in forming relationships in the Chinese collective consciousness, as will be expanded on in the next chapters; or c): traditional attitudes whereby men avoid indulging in beauty and sex. We should observe, however, that one-child family husbands compliment their wives' attractiveness more. Again, this is evidence of their likelihood to express affection to their wives.

Effects of and relations with extended family

In this section, I address the questions concerning how interviewees were raised by their parents, how they were affected by their parents and their current living situation. I discuss: 1) attitudes to the child; 2) relationship with the spouse's parents; 3) relations with the natal family; and 4) influence of the natal family. As mentioned in Chapter 1, extended family is important for Chinese couples, the relationships between parents-in-law and daughters/sons-in-law have always been considered key elements in couples' relationships and parenthood and childrearing have always been the main issue between a couple.

Attitudes to the child

For all these couples, being a good mother is included in the standard of a good wife, and being a good father is included in the standard of a good husband. Even Mr. and Mrs. Chou, who did not plan to have a child, shared this idea. Two wives from one-child families, Mrs. Zhao and Mrs. Sun, directly expressed that a mother takes the main responsibility for childcare, but that the father should also be involved.

Sometimes, children caused worries and conflicts between the couples. Three one-child family wives, Mrs. Qian, Mrs. Sun and Mrs. Li, showed concern about the interference of a new baby. During the first pregnancy, Mr. and Mrs. Sun expressed their severe concerns regarding the future days with their child; Mr. Sun was worried about financial pressure and said that their life would be 'modified greatly' by the baby, while Mrs. Sun was worried that her husband would be unable to assist her and would avoid difficult tasks after the birth. The childless couple (Li), who were due to marry soon after, focused on the financial pressure if they had a child in the future, while Mr. Li was more worried about the interference of a baby in their career development.

In the three couples with a child, Mrs. Zhao said that husbands should spend more time with the child, and Mrs. Wang said that her husband ignored the child and should make more effort as a father. However, neither of the husbands considered their parenting problematic. Mr. Qian said he was dissatisfied with the way his wife treated their child. Mr. and Mrs. Qian had had severe conflict regarding whether they should have a second child and this was their motivation for seeking couple therapy. Mr. Qian insisted that they should have a second and claimed that the birth of a second child would bring 'manageable problems' rather than 'huge interruptions', while Mrs. Qian was strongly resistant and said a second baby would destroy her life. Two one-child family wives, Mrs. Qian and Mrs. Sun, expressed their concerns about the conflicts between childcare and their career development. None of the non-one-child family wives mentioned this.

The idea of low fertility is popular among young Chinese women. Among the wives interviewed, despite marrying in their early 20s, they chose to postpone having their first child. The one-child policy gave young wives a good excuse to have fewer children, while the new two-child policy has caused resistance in young wives and conflict with their husbands. Mr. and Mrs. Qian were an example of this. Some one-child family daughters had benefited from the one-child policy and identified deeply with it.

Nevertheless, the topic of children was important to Chinese couples, to the wives in particular; during the interviews, even Mrs. Chou, who had chosen not to have children, and Mrs. Li, who was due to marry soon and did not yet have a child, emphasised the value of motherhood for a wife. For young Chinese wives, the traditional requirement to be a good wife still conflicts with the need for self-realisation; therefore, they show great anxiety about the birth of a baby. However, for Chinese husbands, such conflicts do not exist.

Relationship with the spouse's parents

Six wives mentioned difficulties in getting along with their husbands' parents. Three (Mrs. Qian, Mrs. Wu and Mrs. Chou) said that they had had major problems with their parents-in-law and that the conflict had almost damaged their couple relationships; Mrs. Sun, whose parents took it in turns to take care of her during her pregnancy, was worried that severe problems would occur between her and her parents-in-law in the future. Four wives said that the difficulties between them and their parents-in-law made them feel inadequate in their role as wives.

In the three couples with difficult relationships between wives and parents-in-law, Mr. Qian clearly expressed his dissatisfaction with the 'impolite' way his wife treated his parents; Mr. Wu could not understand why his wife took these conflicts so seriously and considered her 'over-sensitive'; Mr. Chou appreciated his wife for the efforts she made for his parents. Of the remaining five husbands, Mr. Zhao clearly expressed that the couple relationship was more important than the parent-child relationship and that a husband should always take the side of his wife and argue with his parents on her behalf.

None of the husbands considered themselves bad sons-in-law or mentioned difficulties with their parents-in-law, even if they were living together. Mr. Sun said he had felt quite relieved when his wife's parents came to live with them to look after his pregnant wife. Two husbands, Mr. Zhao and Mr. Chou, mentioned that their own parents had suggested that they be filial to their parents-in-law.

During the interviews, five interviewees discussed their opinions of the couple relationship between their parents-in-law, while Mr. Zeng discussed other couple relationships in his wife's family, because Mrs. Zeng had lost both her parents in her teens and hence he had no direct information on their marriage. All five showed a certain degree of knowledge about their spouses' families.

As Sun (1983) points out, in the Chinese value system, a person only exists in terms of their social relationships, and without a social context, a person can have no meaning. Unlike Western society, the boundaries between individuals are not clear in Chinese families (p.11). Thus, in Chinese marriages, no couple relationships can exist exclusively beyond the relationships in the extended family. For this reason, when young Chinese couples discuss the standards of a good wife or husband, they always include the role of a good mother and a good father, and even that of a good daughter-in-law, in their description. However, for young Chinese wives, the traditional conflicts between daughter-in-law and parents-in-law still exist, while the aim of becoming a mother has decreased in importance.

Relations with the natal family

I noticed that of the 16 interviewees, six had been raised by their parents; seven had been raised by their parents and maternal grandparents, which meant that when their parents had been busy, they had been sent to the maternal grandparents' home; one had lived with the parents and paternal grandfather together; one had lived with the maternal grandmother and the family of the mother's sister because her parents had lived in a barren place and could not feed her; and one had lost her parents in her teenage years and had spent her pre-marriage days with her mother's family. For them, the maternal families played an important role during the growth of a child.

The three couples with children and two pregnant couples lived with either the husband's or wife's parents, while the three childless couples lived by themselves. In China, for generations, it has been difficult for couples to be separated from the extended family (Teng, 2014, pp.358–359) and it is common for retired parents to look after their grandchildren (Yu, 2015, p.39). These interviewees and their parents shared this point in common. Relying on parents for childcare has not changed over time, nor with modifications to society and family structure.

I also discovered that none of the interviewees' parents were divorced. Eight interviewees said their parents' relationships had been terrible; three interviewees said their parents' relationships used to be terrible but had improved as they got older; four interviewees said their parents' relationships were not bad; and Mrs. Zeng said that before her mother's suicide, her father had treated her mother well but her mother had still suffered in the marriage.

At the same time, none of the interviewees reported appreciating or admiring their parents' marriage or took it as a role model. In the past, many Chinese wives and husbands did not file for divorce, but instead complained about their spouses and felt dissatisfied with their marriages throughout their lives. Therefore, the high divorce rate in the new generation may be due to less external control over marriage and more individual and free choice regarding one's spouse and the life pattern among the young Chinese (Woo, 2006, p.95; Jeffreys & Yu, 2015, pp.43–47). Hence, the increased divorce rate among the younger generations does not equal a decrease in satisfaction with marriage; young Chinese couples, such as the interviewees in this study, make efforts to improve the quality of their marriages when they choose to remain in long-term relationships.

All eight wives elaborated on the relationships of other family members, including the following: relationship between maternal grandparents, couple relationships of mother's siblings and couple relationships of own siblings. Four husbands discussed the relationships of other family numbers, including the relationship between maternal grandparents and couple relationships of siblings.

Again, extended family is important to young Chinese; they care about not only their own parents, but also their relatives in the extended family. Although the younger generations show a tendency to separate from the extended family and create individual space, they are interested in others' relationships and try to connect with others in the extended family. In China, such relations are important for both sexes.

Influence of the natal family

Seven wives said that their own performance as a wife was affected by their own mothers, both in wanting to be like their mother and not wanting to be like their mother. Among the wives who wanted to be like their mothers, two one-child family wives, Mrs. Sun and Mrs. Li, identified that their mothers had had their own careers; one non-one-child family wife, Mrs. Zeng, identified with the mother's financial independence; Mrs. Sun also identified her mother as being quite traditional and as having taken care of the paternal grandfather who had had a severe illness; and Mrs. Wang said she wished she could be as gentle as her mother, but she could not do so within her marriage because of her disappointment with her husband.

The wives who did not want to be like their mothers were both from one-child families: Mrs. Zhao said she could not fail in her marriage as her mother had done, but she identified with some of her mother's characteristics, such as being 'organised' and 'capable' in housework; Mrs. Qian said she did not want to be as 'sensitive' and 'fragile' as her mother, but while she felt that this trait had repeated in her own marriage, her mother's marriage and her maternal grandmother's marriage, nevertheless, the 'couple relationship has improved in every marriage'.

Three wives had received advice on couple relationships from their own mothers, including 'do not choose a husband like your father' (Mrs. Zhao) and 'do not trust your husband's family' (Mrs. Wu). Four one-child family wives had experience of their own mothers speaking openly with them about their own marriages and husbands. No non-one-child family wives mentioned such an experience. Two one-child family wives, Mrs. Sun and Mrs. Li, emphasised their mother's career; no non-one-child family wives mentioned this.Four husbands, Mr. Sun, Mr. Li, Mr. Chou and Mr. Wu, considered their mothers to be models of the ideal wife. Mr. Chou added that his maternal grandmother was also a representative of the good wife and the most diligent woman in China. Mr. Wu also mentioned his paternal grandmother. Three of the four husbands, Mr. Sun, Mr. Chou and Mr. Wu, clearly expressed their wish for their wives to learn from their mothers. One one-child family husband, Mr. Sun, had no impression of romantic stories and all the stories that touched him were about great mothers and a deep connection between mother and son.

These young Chinese wives spoke out about their negative judgements of their mothers' marriages and some were critical of their mothers' roles as wives, while young Chinese husbands had rather positive appraisals of their mothers' roles as wives. These husbands had close bonds with their mothers and were likely to identify their mothers as great women and ideal wives.

This difference could be due to 1) the competition and jealousy between mother and daughter; or 2) the adoration and admiration between mother and son. In other words, there are different Oedipal dynamics between mother-daughter and mother-son relationships. However, as discussed in chapter 2, the mother-son relationship has been valued and idealised while the mother-daughter relationship has been outside of ethical attention and hence has had more possibilities. In chapter 4, it was also shown that the mother complex is more applicable to Chinese people, in particular to Chinese men; thus, the difference may be due to the fact that girls have a more realistic and objective observation of their mothers.Three one-child family wives described the effect of the father during the process of choosing a husband. Mrs. Zhao clearly expressed that she had decided before she got married not to choose a husband like her father; Mrs. Sun and Mrs. Li said they wanted to find a husband somewhat like their fathers. Aspects of disappointment in the father included 'no ability to express his feelings' and 'alcohol addiction'; aspects of the father they admired included 'protecting his family', 'sharing the housework with my mother' and 'negotiating with us'. No wife had received advice from her father and no non-one-child family wife mentioned the effects of her father on her own marriage.

Three husbands, Mr. Zhao, Mr. Chou and Mr. Wu, said that they wanted to learn from their fathers, such as being 'responsible' and 'caring for our family', but they also mentioned that their fathers had not been perfect husbands and they were trying to avoid the defects of the father, such as being 'bad tempered'. Two one-child family husbands, Mr. Qian and Mr. Sun, said their fathers had been terrible husbands, because they were 'selfish', 'bad at work', or 'gambled too much'. Three husbands, Mr. Zhao, Mr. Li and Mr. Chou, had received advice from their fathers on couple relationships, including 'how to choose a wife', 'how to get along with the wife' and 'being filial to the wife's parents'.

Chinese women show no strong adoration or admiration for their fathers and, as with their attitudes to their mothers, they criticise their fathers' role as husband. Chinese men, on the other hand, shared the same attitudes toward their own fathers. Most of their judgements and criticisms of their fathers regarded their emotional capability and relations with the family. Here, again, the Western pattern of Oedipal complex might not be applicable to Chinese boys and girls.

Differences existed between the one-child couples and non-one-child couples. One-child family wives reported having more interaction with their parents. Mothers were more likely to share their own stories and feelings about their marriage with an only daughter than with a daughter with siblings. Only daughters tended to have close bonds with their mothers and identified with their mothers' career achievements (mothers with one child have more time and energy to invest in their careers). Further, only daughters mentioned the effects of their fathers on their couple relationships, while daughters with siblings rarely mentioned the effects of the father alone.

One-child family husbands had great passion in terms of mother-son connections and rarely mentioned their mothers' defects. However, one-child family husbands mentioned their fathers more than non-one-child family husbands, even describing them as 'terrible', because they had more frequent interactions with their fathers. The 'absent father' was not as common in one-child families as in families with several children, because there is less financial pressure in small families and more attention is given to the only child.

Compared with boys from one-child families, girls in one-child families had less tendency to idealise either parent. One-child family wives always discussed both the positive and negative aspects of both parents. These wives had a rational view of their relationships with their parents and such rationality can be identified with culturally-assigned masculinity.

Explicit Western stories and figures in narratives

In order to identify the effect of westernisation on Chinese couple relationships, I address the explicit elements, stories and figures relevant to Western culture in the interviewees' narratives. I noticed that when they discussed the romantic stories that were most impressive for them, three interviewees mentioned three typical Western romantic stories that had taken place in Asian regions. Mr. Wang said the miserable but beautiful ending of *The Sorrows of Young Werther* had impressed him most.

When they described the figure of ideal husband and wife, Mr. Sun cited David Beckham as an ideal husband because of his achievement in his career and the devotion of his time to his family, while Mrs. Wu said her ideal wife and ideal husband were Song Mei Ling (due to her elegance, independence and confidence) and Hu Shi (due to his intelligence, gentleness and loyalty to his wife) respectively. Both figures are US-educated members of the Chinese elite. In fact, both the female and male figures they mentioned were a combination of the socially/culturally-assigned notions of feminine and masculine in the West, as I discussed above.

Impact factors relating to Chinese culture

I also tried to identify how these couples had been affected by Chinese culture. I noticed that all the interviewees showed a tendency to be conservative in choosing a spouse, rather than remaining on the dating market, which reflects quite traditional Chinese values. Seven couples were in their first marriage. Four couples had been matched up by friends or relatives, while four couples had been classmates or colleagues for a while before starting to date. All of them began dating their potential spouses with certain knowledge of the other, which is quite common and traditional in China and none of these relationships started from dating random people or strangers.

Before their marriage, two wives had never had other boyfriends; three had had one ex-boyfriend; and two had dated more than one man. Three husbands had never had other girlfriends; two had had one ex-girlfriend; and two had dated more than one woman. Three wives said they had had no expectation regarding a husband and had tried their best to keep the first relationship they had. Mrs. Wang said that although her first husband had been terrible, she had wanted to continue her marriage before her parents broke it up, because she was trying to be a loyal wife in a traditional Chinese marriage. Mrs. Chou mentioned that, at the beginning of their dating period, her husband's conservative attitude toward sex made her consider him a good man. Four husbands also said that they had had no expectations regarding their future wives before the marriage and had tried their best to adjust to the girls they were dating. They emphasised adaptation to the other rather than opening up new dating options.

Three non-one-child family wives said that the 'traditional requirements' of a wife had a huge influence on them, such as being 'gentle', 'virtuous' and 'devoted to the family'. One one-child family wife, Mrs. Zhao, shared this opinion, saying, 'an ideal wife should do the housework and cook for the family', even though she admitted she was bad at these things.

Five husbands said that traditional Chinese females are the ideal wives. These wives are 'gentle and virtuous', 'sacrificing and devoted to the family'. The typical female images they mentioned were the fox ladies in *Liao Zhai Zhi Yi*[2] and *Bai Su Zhen*[3] (all of these female figures are quite prevalent in ancient Chinese legend as I mentioned in Chapter 1: they are fairy ladies with magic power, who actively court the nice but poor men, help these men to overcome difficulties and establish their careers, or even sacrifice themselves for the benefit of the men they have chosen. In a certain way, they play roles partly as wives and partly as mothers to these men) and their own mothers.

Mr. and Mrs. Wu mentioned that the most impressive romantic stories for them were *Liang Zhu* and *Niu Lang Zhi Nv*. (Both are well-known romantic stories in China of young lovers who are forced apart because of their parents' objection to the match.) Mrs. Wang said that the most impressive romantic story for her was *The Dream of Red Chamber*, a famous novel written in the *Qing* dynasty, and she felt pity for the two leading characters, a pair of young lovers who could not marry despite being suitable for each other and deeply in love. Three interviewees said that the most impressive romantic stories were in *Jing Yong*'s new chivalry novels, which are influenced by both Western chivalric romance and traditional Chinese legends.

On the surface, interviewees mentioned fewer Western stories and figures than Chinese ones and did not directly discuss the Western influence, but I found that they were deeply impressed by the content and quality of Western romantic stories.

Further, in these interviews, I also noticed that idealised wives were all Chinese female figures, while idealised husbands were almost all Western type males. Two husbands, Mr. Sun and Mr. Wu, even said that there were no images of good husbands in the Chinese tradition. Zhang (2011) said that in China, a common belief exists that '[W]estern men are superior to Chinese men in their masculinity and sexuality' (p.193). Idealised Western male figures in Hollywood movies are quite popular in China today, but a traditional Chinese wife is still preferred by Chinese families.

On the other hand, young people pursuing long-term relationships continue to have rather conservative attitudes toward finding a long-term spouse. This is quite traditional in China. While arranged marriages are now illegal in China, semi-arranged marriages are commonplace (Kam, 2014, pp.76–80). Therefore, young couples are not encouraged to date too much and attempt to remain with the first person with whom they have a relationship, especially when that relationship has already been recognised by their natal family.

Discussion and conclusion

As mentioned at the beginning of the chapter, in seven of the couples that were interviewed, the wives initiated the interview, and during the interview process, women were more open to expressing their immediate feelings, smiling and crying than men. It was easier for men to express positive feelings than negative ones in front of the interviewer. The Chinese men's attitudes to discussing couple issues were more defensive than those of their wives. This corroborated an observation I had previously made regarding the motivation for couple therapy from my initial conversations with couple therapists in China.

In general, however, young Chinese couples can be seen to show a tendency to muddy the traditional role requirements and functions of husbands and wives. The requirements for husbands in the new generation, such as getting involved in household and family affairs and expressing their affections openly, are approaching the aspects deemed feminine in the traditional Chinese value system, but young husbands still want their wives to be more traditional. On the other hand, young Chinese women are pursuing more equality with their husbands in their marriage relationships. In their relationships, both husbands and wives show a tendency to embrace culturally/socially-assigned notions of femininity (similarity, togetherness and relationship) and to give less welcome to culturally/socially assigned notions of masculinity (difference and separation) from the depth-psychological perspective. This accords with most Jungian and post-Jungian attitudes that value the feminine principle, as discussed in Chapter 2. The Chinese writer Wu (2016), who claimed to be deeply affected by psychoanalysis, made the same observation and criticised both Chinese men and women for trying to project the caring mother onto the other spouse and of enjoying the security brought by the relationship (pp.56–59).

However, the notions of femininity and masculinity in China have never been the same as in the West. A Chinese historian Sun Longji, who got his PhD and became a professor in history in the US, points out that in American culture, activeness is assigned to individuation, which is categorised as the masculine principle, while passiveness means relying on a relationship, which is categorised as feminine. Thus, in the American stereotype, both men and women in the East are feminine (2010, pp.375–383). After comparing Japanese legends with Western ones, Kawai (1982/2007) also reached the conclusion that in the West, men have been encouraged to pursue the truth actively and to engage in fighting, while women have been encouraged to passively accept the reality and to engage in waiting. In Japan, however, both men and women adopted the latter as the principle of survival (p.162). Therefore, the qualities attributed to the feminine and masculine, respectively, in the West are not universal. In China, some qualities deemed feminine in the West, such as valuing relationships, are important for both sexes. Further, as discussed in Chapter 2, the typical Western masculine aspect – being the subject of desire, and sexual desire in particular – does not necessarily belong to the masculine and, further, is not a quality for a good man in the traditional Chinese system.

In depth psychology, stereotypes always exist in the field of the feminine and masculine. Rowland (2002) criticises Jung's idea regarding the Logos domination of males and the Eros domination of females and comments that there is no 'permanent assignment of Logos to male consciousness, Eros to women' and that these principles should not be confined by 'bodily sex' (p.42). Nevertheless, she took the Logos and Eros, or masculine and feminine, as divisible and opposite entities.

In the East, people do not share the same attitude to the feminine and masculine. Kawai (1982/2007) criticises Neumann's absolute division between patriarchal ideology and matriarchal ideology and viewed this division as the product of a Western patriarchal ideology. He assumed that the feminine ideology carries both activeness and passiveness, that they are not exclusive concepts and that they are difficult to define absolutely (pp.211–214). In China, people share this opinion, insofar as they have a flexible attitude to the notions of feminine and masculine. As discussed in Chapter 2, on the surface, the male has been superior to the female in China for many years, but in the Chinese system, the mother's position has always been supreme and the power of the feminine has never been ignored. Further, Chinese people do not treat the female and male as opposites, or as mutually exclusive. As mentioned above, for one-child families in particular, this ambiguity between femininity and masculinity is obvious.

The stereotype in Chinese culture is in another direction. For many years, in China, collectivism has been dominant in the social system and the concept of individualism has only come to be known by the Chinese in the last century since the new cultural movement. Therefore, Chinese people have admired the concepts of 'relationship', 'connection' and 'harmony among everything' and have been unable to tolerate 'difference' and 'separation'. They tended to emphasise 'adjustment' and 'adaption' to remain in a relationship, rather than keeping one's options open for new relationships. Further, in Chinese tradition, marriage and couple relationships have never been personal issues, but are, rather, always affairs of extended families and communities; therefore, the relations of a couple have always been attached to a larger net of relations. This explains why, in these interviews, all interviewees mentioned that a good wife/husband has to be a good parent and must get along with her/his own parents and parents-in-law. However, as discussed in Chapter 2 and here, young people from one-child families value their individuality more than their companions who have siblings. This difference is particularly obvious for only-daughters and daughters with siblings.

In the new generation of Chinese, the mother-son relationship has not changed greatly, but the father-child relationship and mother-daughter relationship have changed due to the one-child policy. Hence, the mother complex remains dominant and prevalent today, but only daughters receive attention from both parents and such attention has not been indicated in the Chinese tradition. As a result, on the one hand, only-daughters have been empowered and have more financial security and their own voices (which is why they show a tendency to advocate the one-child policy); on the other hand, they face more conflicts between the old Chinese values and their desire for self-realisation than their male counterparts.

When Faludi (1991) criticised the backlash of anti-feminism in the 1980s and 1990s in the US, she described the bias and hostility towards independent women and the popular belief that equality and independence made women 'unloved', 'unhappy', 'dehumanized' and 'uncertain of their gender identity' (p.4). In China today, women face the same criticism. In my interviews, no husband appreciated the independence of his wife in her career and her capability beyond family affairs. Thus, these only-daughters have to challenge and sometimes also negotiate with their husbands and the cultural requirements that lie behind these husbands. On this point, they share the same dilemma as their Western counterparts.

Nowadays, clearly distinguishing which qualities young Chinese people derive from Western influences and which qualities derive from Chinese culture is difficult to accomplish. The Westernisation of Chinese literature, movies and TV programmes has lasted almost a century, since the New Culture Movement began in 1919, and even since Marxism and Communism originated in the West. Thus, a number of generations in China have been raised in a hybrid culture; in other words, for many years, some Western elements have been integrated with Chinese traditions. As discussed in Chapter 4, China is relatively good at absorbing elements of other cultures and making its own localisation. This can be seen in *Jin Yong*'s novels, which are Chinese stories with implicit elements from the West. Today in China, if you ask people in the public media and in their daily lives, what is purely from the West and what is exclusively Chinese, you may get very different and confusing answers that contradict each other. Therefore, when Chinese people talk about the West, they might talk about the Western world of their fantasy, which is the opposite of their sense of their surroundings. There is a tendency for young Chinese people to idealise the typical Western relationship, in terms of Western masculinity and relating to individuality in particular, as shown in my interviews. This is a rebellion against the dominant collectivism.

Thus, to understand relationships between young Chinese couples, their respective feminine and masculine aspects and the impact of the West and traditional Chinese elements in their relations, ambivalence is the key. As Steinfeld (2015) points out, while one could assume that the trajectory of development in China 'will follow a Western model. Yet China's history and culture is unique and is shaping the country in its own way' (p.13). The relationships of young Chinese couples have also been shaped and have developed in a unique way during this process.

I have to confess, as a pioneer study, my interviews have many limitations. First, it was confined to couples living in cities. Couple therapy is relatively new in China and, to date, couples in rural China have had no access to it. Therefore, it was difficult to approach couples living in rural areas during this period. Second, during the process of recruiting couples who were interested in or who intended to try couple therapy, on many occasions, wives approached me showing interest in being interviewed, but then cancelled at the last minute because their husbands refused to attend. Volunteer bias means these results cannot be generalised to all young urban Chinese couples, and eight couples is a small sample. Third, while I had been informed prior to the interviews that some couples had clashed over the husband's love affairs, none of the couples mentioned this during the interviews when discussing their difficulties. Major secrets and events that bring pain and shame are difficult to raise in a one-time interview. Some of these couples were experiencing crisis and were suffering in their marriages at the moment of interview, such as Mr. and Mrs. Qian, Mr. and Mrs. Zeng and Mr. and Mrs. Wang, and they needed further professional assistance.

Nevertheless, the results have raised some preliminary facts about relationships and intimate images of young Chinese couples who wish to remain in long-term relationships and turned to assistance from clinical professionals. This study focuses on the collective consciousness among these Chinese couples – what they expect and what is unwanted in their couple relationship, and what are considered to be good and bad features of husbands/wives. However, I cannot say that the interview results will predict the future relationship between the couples nor can they show the diversity and complexity of behaviour patterns among young Chinese couples. More in-depth exploration will be conducted in the following chapters.

Notes

1 She means that at the beginning of their marriage, the husband identified him as the son of his parents more than as the husband in his small family, and now he takes his first identification within his family as the husband.
2 A collection of fairy tales and legends recorded during the Qing dynasty.
3 The heroine in a famous legend named *The Legend of White Snake* in China.

Chapter 6

The Peony Pavilion as a picture of sexual individuation

In the previous chapter, by analysing the data from interviews with young Chinese couples, I argued that, in China, the requirements of women and men are different, but the attitudes towards femininity and masculinity are not as divided as in the West. Moreover, culturally/socially-assigned femininity and masculinity in China are not opposite to each other, as they are in the West. For example, both the feminine and masculine carry the qualities of activeness and passivity, and further, in relationships, females are more active than males. On the other hand, Western ideas and attitudes towards both sexes have affected Chinese people, in particular regarding idealised male images. In contemporary China, the notions of femininity and masculinity are ambivalent. The one-child policy has aggravated this ambivalence, and for the children of one-child families, the requirements of women and men have been muddied, particularly for daughters. These conclusions stem from analysing the narratives of young Chinese couples and reflect the collective consciousness in relation to intimate relationships in China. In this chapter, I address the unconscious perspectives on this topic in Chinese culture by amplifying and critically assessing a story central to Chinese identity; one that has shifted depending on what purpose it was required to serve through different historical periods.

Teleology and amplification

Such an approach to interpreting literature within the context of China is not new. As early as the 1920s to 1940s, the years in which the People's Republic of China was founded, a number of Chinese scholars adopted psychoanalytic perspectives to understand Chinese literature and cultural phenomena (Feng, 1925/2009; Guo, 1921/2009; Hong, 1935/2009; Pan, 1924/2009; Su, 1935/2009; Zhao, 1927/2009; Zhou, 1923/2009). Such scholars mainly focused on the theory of libido and all agreed that erotic passion existed in Chinese culture, but that the mainstream of Chinese society oppressed sexual desire, particularly in women. Today's scholars follow the same path when identifying cultural issues in China. Ye (1997), for example, considered the core of Chinese culture to be an anti-Oedipal complex, which means that filial piety is a kind of superego with which to suppress the Oedipal compulsion. Sun (2006, pp.4–5; 1983, pp.111–116) argued that the typical Chinese personality is fixed on the oral phase and thus, co-dependence between the mother and baby is the foundation of Chinese relationships. Such arguments have been carried and exaggerated by the well-known psychological author Wu Zhihong in his book *The Nation of the Giant Baby* (2016). These scholars mainly facilitate psychoanalytic perspectives to criticise Chinese culture and to address the problems therein. However, Ye claims that this approach might be inappropriate, because Freud's theories were based on his observation of individual cases and problems would exist if they were applied to understanding collective phenomena. He argues, however, that it is fair to say that the Oedipal complex affects the Chinese psyche in an opposite direction to that in the West (1997, pp.525–532). From these arguments, we may conclude that, previously, Freudian theories on sexuality were the main tools used by Chinese scholars to facilitate analysis of the Chinese psyche.

However, in psychoanalysis, as Papadopoulos (2006) points out, the lack of 'shared unconscious structures' (p.26) means that this method ignores the 'social-cultural influences' (p.32) of unconscious interaction between people. This corresponds with Ye's doubts with regard to directly applying Freud's ideas to the Chinese psyche. Further, this method is only one of the 'two basic methods in approaching psychological phenomena', i.e. the 'causal-reductive' method (ibid., p.29). Jung considered this to be 'oriented backwards' and that it 'has a disintegrative effect on the real signification of the unconscious product' (CW6, para. 788). However, this view of the psyche is one-sided. Compared to this approach, Papadopoulos (2006) identified Jung's method as constructive, being 'based on teleology', meaning that phenomena can be understood 'in terms of their purpose and final cause – their goal' (p.30). He emphasised that 'teleology is unfolding as a lived experience' and that more attention should be paid to the process rather than the final product (ibid., p.31). In a more comprehensive sense, Papadopoulos described Jung's approach as 'an epistemology of archetypal teleology', 'offering a bridge between the personal realm and the wider collective structures'. This approach 'includes a constructive process that would take into account the archetypal organizing influence [...] that affect not only the individuals [...] but also their interpersonal exchanges and unconscious mutual projections [...] as well as each person's interaction with own personal history [...] and the social-cultural influences' (ibid., pp.31–32). Hence, it offers a deep understanding on people and their relationships within their context, both consciously and unconsciously. Papadopoulos continued that, under this approach 'it is not only the past that shapes the present, but also the present that shapes the past [...] in a reciprocal manner' (ibid., pp.32–33). In other words, our history and culture shape our current actions, but 'we', at this moment, also choose how we read our history and understand our culture.

Due to the historical continuity with localisation and assimilating elements from other cultures of China, this archetypal teleology gives us a more complete picture of the Chinese psyche with which to understand Chinese people and their relationships.

In this chapter, amplification is applied as the main technique of a Jungian approach. As Papadopoulos described it, the archetype and its influence cannot be analysed, translated or interpreted, but must be related and connected 'in a constructive, purposive and teleological way' (ibid., p.35). Amplification is the precise way to relate and connect personal contents with the cultural psyche. Samuels (2005) defines amplification as 'the use of mythic, historical, and cultural parallels in order to clarify, make more ample and, so to speak, turn up the volume on material that may be obscure, thin, and difficult to attend to' (p.67). This is a method by which our materials may make our psychic resources richer and more understandable. Jung applied this method to interpreting patients' dreams and treated it as an approach to connect personal clinical materials with the collective unconscious in order to facilitate comprehension. Gradually, post-Jungians extended the fields of Jung's intention on this concept and used it to conjoin subjectivity with external objectivity and to fit cultural knowledge to the personalities of people within a given culture (Cambray, 2001; Hubback, 1984). Thus, it 'is a kind of "natural thinking," proceeding by way of analogy, parallel and imaginative elaboration' (Samuels, 2005, p.67), which can be applied to explore the results from the last chapter within a broad cultural context and to gain a deeper understanding of them. Hence, in this chapter, I make an attempt to undertake an amplificatory description while maintaining a more historical and contextual approach to my analysis. The two main risks of amplification are over-intellectualisation and inflation of meaning (Samuels, 1986, p.22; 2005, p.67). Thus, this research must stick to concrete facts while honouring the feeling tone of the materials. Further, cautious examination of the materials should be kept in mind throughout the process.

The story of *The Peony Pavilion*

All Chinese romance stories mentioned by the interview participants share a common element – the active role of women in love relationships. This means that, in these stories, the female character actively approaches the male character and shows her interest in him. The Ming dynasty story of *The Peony Pavilion* by Tang Xianzu vividly portrays this automatic arousal of female desire for love and sex.

Du Liniang was the teenage daughter of the city mayor, Du Bao. As the only child in her family, her parents raised her very strictly and wanted her to become a virtuous lady. One day, however, her maid told her about a large garden in her home with a beautiful vista, which she was forbidden to visit alone (at that time, ladies were expected to remain in their chambers and spending time outdoors, even in the garden of their own homes, was considered disrespectful). However, when her father was out, Liniang snuck into the garden and became infatuated with the spring scene there – the flowers blossomed and butterflies and birds flew in pairs. She felt something inside her move deeply and emerged with a strong desire to have a romantic relationship with a man. She then dreamt of a handsome young man, a graduate, and made love to him in the dream. Upon waking, she missed the man and lamented that it had been merely a dream. Her parents invited her tutor, Chen Zuiliang, who was also a doctor, and a nun named Sister Stone to treat her, but both of them failed. Eventually, her lovesickness and sadness killed her. After Liniang's death, her father was promoted to be a provincial official and had to move with his family to another location to defend against an intrusive enemy. He buried his daughter in the garden and built a temple near the tomb. He then invited Sister Stone to live in the temple and to guard Liniang's tomb.

Liniang's ghost was sentenced in the underworld. However, the judge in the underworld discovered the reason for her death and was touched by her beauty and vivacity. Hence, he decided to keep her body fresh and asked her to come back to life at the appropriate time. Meanwhile, Liu Mengmei, the man in Liniang's dream, was on his way to the imperial examination. He fell ill in the city where the garden was located but Chen Zuiliang saved him and sent him to live in the temple for his recovery. Mengmei visited the garden and found a portrait of Liniang. He immediately fell in love with her and gazed at her portrait from day until night. Mengmei called upon the ghost of Liniang and they met night after night. After Mengmei proposed to Liniang, she told him she was a ghost and asked him to open her tomb and help restore her to life. With the assistance of Sister Stone, Mengmei opened Liniang's tomb and she came back to life.

Mengmei then went to the capital with Liniang where he completed his examination. Usually, it would take a long time for the result of the examination to be revealed. During this waiting period, Liniang ask Mengmei to meet her father, hoping to gain his blessing for their marriage. However, Zuiliang had already reported that the tomb of Liniang had been opened by Mengmei and he was accused of being a grave robber. Du Bao, Liniang's father, accepted this accusation against Mengmei, refused to accept his daughter's resurrection and accused Mengmei of robbing his daughter's tomb before placing him in prison for this crime. At that time, the result of the examination came out and Mengmei was recognised by the government as the 'number one scholar' and soon released. The couple then proved to Liniang's father that she really was his resurrected daughter. Even at the end, however, when the emperor hears this story and gives his blessing to the marriage of Mengmei and Liniang, the father remains quite upset. He begs Liniang to choose her natal family over her husband, but she refuses to do so.

The story described above first appeared as an opera. The author, Tang Xianzu, was a famous playwright who lived in the late-Ming dynasty. Since the Middle-Ming dynasty, Chinese people had not only watched the opera on stage but had also read the scripts at home. In the years after *The Peony Pavilion* was published, it became a bestseller. All literate families in the late Ming and Qing dynasties kept a copy. Further, many scholars produced commentaries and reviews of it (Hua, 2015, pp.107–108; Liang, 2017a). Thus, by the late days of imperial China, its popularity had prevailed for many years.

The story had a very strong and profound effect on its readers and traces of the story were evident everywhere in subsequent years, in other plays and novels. In particular, female readers in the Ming and Qing dynasties were deeply moved by the story. Some reports even suggested that some female readers tried to court the author, Tang, to become his wife or even his concubine because of his deep understanding of women. Some women felt that they were the embodiment of Liniang when they felt erotic desire but had to face disappointment in their own marriages, and even mimicked her death. Finally, a female actress died of a broken heart when playing Liniang on stage. Furthermore, in those years, female writers published commentaries and reviews and tried to interpret the story from their own perspectives, which was quite rare at that time in China (Li, 2007; Liang, 2017a; Xie, 2008, pp.19–25, p.43; Xu, 1987, pp.213–217). Thus, this story has resonated greatly with Chinese women since its first public performance.

However, we must observe that Liniang's story was the idealised pattern for these women. Her experience deeply touched them because few of them had the opportunity to be her. Liniang was an only child whose father was a government official with no concubine or other children. Hence, he valued her greatly, which was quite unusual in China. Usually, because of the son preference and the emphasis on the number of offspring, a man in Liniang's father's position would have had several wives and children. Further, Liniang was educated and had her own tutor, while many girls, even those born to rich families, were illiterate due to the common belief that 'innocence is a virtue for women' and that reading would damage that innocence. Therefore, even Liniang and her family had to follow certain mainstream rules of the time; however, under further examination, her characteristics and her relationships with others, in particular with her father, were quite modern. Liniang represented the idealised image for Chinese women of the period while her self-awareness and behaviour resemble more a modern woman, in particular the only daughter in contemporary China.

Sexual individuation

Women's active role in romantic relationships

The most important scene in the opera is Scene 10: The Interrupted Dream. This is the scene that has been performed most frequently on stage (Hua, 2015, p.45). (Because *The Peony Pavilion* is quite a long opera, people usually choose to perform just a few of its scenes.) Scene 10 vividly depicts how Liniang automatically realised her own beauty and sexual desire. When she walks in the garden and exclaims of its beauty in spring, she spontaneously finds the same beauty inside herself, a girl in her prime. In her singing in Scene 10, she expresses that the love of beauty is in her nature and she is very confident that her inborn beauty can affect the environment around her, such as the birds and fish being amazed and the flowers and the moon being moved by her beauty.

She discovers her own attractiveness and laments that it cannot be seen, reflected or appreciated by others, in particular by a real man. She emphasises her nature from an aesthetic perspective and believes her beauty can defeat that of other beautiful things in nature. We can find in this young lady a strong sense of self-awareness and confidence. She discovers the power of the feminine in herself and also demonstrates a strong aspiration to be seen. Usually, a woman is seen due to a man's desire for her and, in this sense, she is treated as an object of desire. Berger (1972) claimed that in the aesthetic tradition, a woman cared about being seen by men. She split herself into the surveyor and the surveyed. She first surveyed herself from inside and judged herself from the male perspective and then adjusted her appearance, her gestures and behaviour according to the attitude of external men (pp.45–57). This way of being seen serves to fulfil men's desire, which is problematic from the perspective of today.

However, in *The Peony Pavilion*, the beauty and sexual attractiveness of the feminine are not created or discovered by men; they already exist in nature, in a garden. Liniang first realises her own beauty, then wants somebody, a proper object, to reflect that beauty; hence, her desire to be seen is quite active and she has no intention of changing herself to adopt others'/men's perspectives. She falls asleep and dreams of a young man, Liu Mengmei. In the dream, he announces his love to her and exclaims her beauty.

At this moment, it is not the real man, the real Mengmei, who is announcing his love to her and exclaiming her beauty, but the man in her dream. In other words, he is her own creation. She needs a man to see her, to appreciate her beauty, to understand her loneliness and be attracted to her. She thus creates such a man, an object, to reflect her and to fulfil her desire to be loved. All these admiring words for her come not from the man, but from herself.

This process, as Hua (2015, p.231) and Liang (2017b) suggest, shows a 'feminine awareness'. Her beauty is not discovered or appreciated by a man, but by herself in the first instance. Further, her sexual desire is not aroused by a man; it is in her nature and she feels this nature suddenly, without ever having had real contact with a man, and then expresses her sexuality automatically. Thus, she is not a passive receiver of sexual desire, but a subject of it. There is a further small detail in the opera after Liniang's revival: Mengmei wants to have sex with her because he thinks they already had physical relations when Liniang was a ghost. However, Liniang refuses this proposal and suggests that they can only sleep together again after they have received permission and a blessing from her parents. According to Liang (2017b), this seems to be a regression: Liniang becomes a conservative girl and obeys the patriarchal requirements of chastity once more. However, if this was the case, she would not dare to fight for her husband in front of her father and choose him over her family in the final scene. Here, her rejection of his proposition is not a negative regression but shows, rather, her sense of being the subject of desire. She has a strong self-awareness and self-assertiveness; thus, despite having recognised Mengmei as her husband, she retains the right to say no to him when she is not ready. She is the one who owns her body, not her father, or her husband. Being the subject of desire not only means that she can initiate her own desire, but also that she has the right to say no to another's desire for her; otherwise, she will always be in danger of being objectivised by others. (In the youth edition of *The Peony Pavilion*, it is worth observing that the butterflies are embroidered on Liniang's dress and the flowering branches are embroidered on Mengmei's gown; these imply the active and passive roles respectively in their relationship. In Chinese literature, butterflies are always the ones to court flowers, and not vice-versa.)

Later, in the Qing dynasty, another book called *Caizi Mudan ting* was published. This book offers many interpretative comments on *The Peony Pavilion*. The book was authored by a couple, of whom researchers believe the main commentator was the wife (Xu, 1987, p.100; Yu, 2015, p.26; Hua, 1998). This female commentator applied symbolic sexuality to interpret every scene, detail and even the most innocent parts of the script of *The Peony Pavilion*. Shang (2005) suggested that this occurred 200 years earlier than Freud's psychoanalytic approach. However, there is a long tradition of sexual symbolism in Chinese culture which may not be very psychological in the modern sense. Thus, I prefer to say that Cheng Qiong, the female commentator, applied an almost proto-psychoanalytic method to interpret the story of Liniang and thus to validate women's sexual desire. She pointed out that just like young boys, young girls also have a natural impulse to sexuality and that this desire should be recognised and not forbidden. Further, women should have the right to fulfil their sexual desires (Hua, 2006). At first glimpse, Cheng's ideas seem subversive; however, in Chinese culture, it is a given that sexuality is 'an innate physical need' for both men and women (Mann, 2011, p.31). Just like boys, when girls enter puberty, they can feel it directly.

This is the opposite direction to that taken by typical Western stories, in which men are always assigned the role of the suitors who actively approach the women with whom they have fallen in love. Shakespeare's *Romeo and Juliet*, which was written in the same period as *The Peony Pavilion* was published, is one example of this Western pattern. Jung wrote, '[m]en are rarely split off from sexuality, because it is too evident for them'

(2008, p.313). It seems that sexual desire is bonded with men's nature and it is evident and does not need to be aroused by others. Jung rarely mentioned women's sexuality, but we can discern that, in his opinion, women's sexuality is implicit and can be separated from her; thus, it is a secondary product. Stevens agreed with Jung's idea on the sexuality of men and women and concluded that a young woman needed either a ritual or an initiated man to assist her to 'enter the productive phase of her life' and to bring her to 'the new feminine consciousness'. As such, she is the Sleeping Beauty awaiting a man's kiss to arouse her sexuality (1994/2007, p.76). However, such ideas are inherently essentialist and are not suitable in Liniang's case.

Freud and his followers were of the same opinion. Bonaparte's work *Female Sexuality* uses the same Sleeping Beauty metaphor to describe the passive state of women's sexual desire (cited by Mitchell, 1971, p.164). This idea shows a common belief regarding the difference in sexuality in the West: men carry their innate sexual nature actively, while women's passive sexual desire needs to be awakened. Idema (2005) compared Liniang with Sleeping Beauty and concluded that the two stories shared a common theme insofar as both girls enter a forbidden place where they have their first sexual experience. They then experience a period of sleep and achieve rebirth because of a young man (p.293). However, Idema ignored the main difference between the two girls, which is that Liniang 'summons' the young man into her dream and approaches him actively as a ghost. She is not a real Sleeping Beauty without consciousness but knows her sexuality automatically.

Hence, Sleeping Beauty is not the counterpart of Liniang in the West. However, we can find female images that do try to pursue love actively in the West. In the story of 'The Lady of Shalott', the image of the heroine has some similarities with Liniang. In Tennyson's poem (1832), Lady Shalott was a cursed girl who was unable to leave the little isle on which she lived in a tower, spending all of her time waving but only able to see the world of the isle through a mirror. After seeing the reflection of a pair of young lovers, she laments, 'I'm half sick of shadows'. Later, she sees the reflection of Sir Lancelot, a young, handsome knight of Camelot and immediately falls in love with him. Her mirror cracks and she chants her death song, takes a small boat to leave the isle for Sir Lancelot and dies on her way to find him. Her journey ends with the knight and his companions seeing her corpse in the boat. They read her name on the boat and appraise her beauty but without knowing of her experience and her passion for Sir Lancelot. (There is a well-known painting of the Lady of Shallot by Waterhouse [1888] in the Tate Britain. In the painting, the Lady of Shallot is ready to leave the isle and to seek her love and her death. She seems to be sad and alone but determined, while the plants around her are withered, foreshadowing her unfortunate ending.)

The similarities between the Lady of Shallot and Liniang are that, at the beginning, Liniang is trapped in her chamber, while the Lady of Shallot is trapped in a tower on an isle, and neither are allowed to leave. The chamber and the isle can be seen firstly as symbols of the social requirements for a virtuous lady, in which movement is limited and remaining innocent paramount. Then, both heroines gain access to the external world. Liniang finds the garden in her home and her sexuality is awakened by the flowers, birds and butterflies, while the Lady of Shallot has a mirror and is unable to bear the loneliness any longer when she sees the reflection of a pair of young lovers. Neither of the girls' initial sexual desires are directly aroused by a real man. However, the men in their fantasy, in a dream or in the mirror, motivate them to leave the places in which they are trapped, to take action and to break the limits that have been placed upon them. Hence, the two girls demonstrate their activeness in pursuing love. However, their stories end differently. *The Peony Pavilion* is a story of rebirth, while *The Lady of Shallot* is a story clouded by death. Thus, further examination of what caused the different directions of the two stories is required.

The process of sexual individuation

Zhang (2005) applied perspectives from Campbell's archetypal mythology to analyse the story of *The Peony Pavilion* and concluded that this was a complete circle of a heroine's journey, an adventure from departure to return, covering the themes of enlightenment, suffering, death and rebirth (pp.259–288). It can thus be viewed as the process of individuation. The call to adventure was Liniang's sexual desire, while her journey ended with her marriage to Mengmei. Thus, the journey begins with her awakening sexuality and the ultimate aim is to attain authentic unification with a real man. I call this process sexual individuation, because in this process, sexuality is the key word and the main task is to develop a mature sexual relationship with the other and to find a way to establish one's own life based on such a relationship.

Stein (2006) described the process of female individuation in four steps: 1) shedding of her persona; 2) turning to the inner world; 3) rejecting the eagerness for security and dependence and uniting with the animus; and 4) making a commitment to a relationship and never abandoning her spouse (pp.98–99). However, Liniang's process of individuation differs in some respects from Stein's pattern. In Stein's fairy tale, the start of a woman's individuation is quite passive; she loses her persona and identity, but does so involuntarily (ibid., p.94). However, Liniang turns first to her inner desire and then actively gives up her persona as a virtuous lady and as her father's daughter and becomes a ghost. In *The Peony Pavilion*, Tang noted that Liniang's 'passionate longings brought about her death' (1598, p.130) and that these passionate longings are an expression of her self-realisation (Hua, 2015, pp.48–49). Her death is an active protest against the oppression of her passion, a choice she makes after discovering her self-awareness. This is a common theme in Chinese romantic stories. Eventually, such death serves for rebirth, a new way of living. Hence, it is different from the death instinct, which leads to destruction.

Xu (2007) studied the literature of the Ming and Qing dynasties and concluded that there were many stories in this period about females fighting to attain freedom and an independent personality. These fights were mainly in pursuit of the right to love and marry freely. Many of these stories occur between a female ghost and a human male and they show the determination of these women who prefer to fight to the death and for whom even death cannot prevent their love. Xu further emphasised that these women were usually smart and intelligent, as well as brave and faithful (pp.94–115). Hence, their fidelity does not stem from some social requirement but from their own choice and they have clear self-awareness.

This suggests a conflict between individual will and social requirement in the period of the Ming and Qing dynasties, in which the oppression of women was most severe in China. However, the literature is replete with female figures like Liniang, who recognise their sexual desire, actively court a romantic relationship and fight against the standards of the social requirement for chastity. These images show an authentic autonomy and consistency between their inner desire and outer behaviour. The cost of this autonomy and consistency is death and such death comprises both a literal and symbolic separation from the world. As Jung said, 'the development of the psychological individual' involves 'being distinct from general, collective psychology. Individuation ... is a process of differentiation' (CW6, para. 757). Liniang must distinguish her own desires from the requirements of her parents and society, and separate from her natal family to rid herself of her persona as a lady, to leave her former identified object, the collective patriarchy, and give up the security and dependence she gleans from her family. This is the first half of her individuation.

However, this is not enough. As Stein (2006) noted, the first half of the hero's journey comprises separating and maintaining awareness, while the second half comprises uniting potentials with the theme of Eros (p.89). If Liniang only has intercourse with Mengmei in ghost form, this is not a solid unification, not a real marriage, and her Eros cannot be authentic. As Jung observed, 'you can only individuate in your concrete life' (1932, p.757) and 'you cannot individuate if you are a spirit ... so if you speak of individuation at all, it necessarily means the individuation of beings who are in the flesh, in the living body. It is of course meant to become a reality ...' (1934, p.202). Here, Jung emphasised the importance of body in the process of individuation. Nevertheless, Saban (2011) criticised Jung for focusing too much on the interior aspects of individuation and 'radically apart from embodied others, or even the otherness of our own body'.

He pointed out that self had to be embodied and 'entwined with the world' (pp.115–116). Therefore, Liniang must come back to life, face the real world and interact with others as living flesh; otherwise, her process of individuation will not be complete. To attain freedom as a ghost in the realm of death is not sufficient and freedom in the world of fantasy is not real freedom.

Hua (2015) also points out that the first half of *The Peony Pavilion* is romantic, while the second half is realistic. The second part is as important as the first (pp.331–332). Their relationship, which was established in the realm of fantasy, eventually returns to the real world of daily life. Therefore, after Liniang comes back to life, she asks Mengmei to meet her father with her. This also demonstrates her activeness and makes their unification more official and grounded. Moreover, in China, there are several stories that depict the father-daughter relationship, of which *The Peony Pavilion* is just one example. Here, the father is not only her biological father, but also a symbol of the patriarchy. She has rebelled against all the rules in the patriarchal world and now chooses to confront what she opposes. This could be seen as an effort at reconciliation, a wish to be forgiven and accepted by her family. However, it is, in fact, a challenge. She must face her father's anger and disagreement, which is evident from the fact that her father wants her to be a virtuous lady and did not allow her to play in their own garden in the first place. To die in protest is brave, but to confront the patriarchy is even braver. She challenges the collective requirements placed on women, overcomes her shame and expresses her feelings honestly. This shows a higher level of autonomy.

The female commentator, Cheng, also noted that women have the right to have 'passionate longings', but at the same time, they must take responsibility, which means finding the right man, appreciating him and fighting the father, the patriarchal system, for him (Hua, 2006, p.271). In this way, a woman can really achieve sexual individuation and utilise her female power for her own sake. By the end of the story, the father says he can forgive Liniang only if she abandons Mengmei and returns to her natal family once more. However, she refuses to do so; she chooses her husband over her father, thus rejecting the principle of filial piety, which has been the dominant value in China for thousands of years, and fighting against patriarchal regulation, which is central to Chinese tradition and culture. Therefore, the core of the story of *The Peony Pavilion* is about how an individual stands up for herself, faces conflicts and does not submit to the collective expectations. As mentioned above, Liniang, like her other female counterparts in Chinese romance stories, has a modern consciousness of the self.[1]

On the surface, Lady Shallot shares the same stage as Liniang, who also felt the inner call to rid herself of her persona as a virtuous lady. When she left her weaving work and took a boat to leave, she had the courage to discard security and dependence and followed her longing to unite with her animus. In a certain way, she almost finished the first half of individuation in a similar way to Liniang. However, for her, her sexuality was not as conscious as it was for Liniang. In other words, she was driven by her passion unconsciously and dared not make a clear appeal to physically unite with a real man. Thus, she died on the way to Sir Lancelot. As Poulson (1996) said, 'in death [she] has become a Sleeping Beauty who can never be wakened, symbols of perfect feminine passivity' (p.190). Hence, when Sir Lancelot, the man upon whom she had projected her longings, encounters her, he sees only a Sleeping Beauty with a 'lovely face'. Her activeness was only maintained for a short period before she succumbed to a still, passive end. Her death preserved her innocence and cut off her connection with the real, external world when she had the opportunity to unite with a real man. In other words, she was only able to connect with the man in her fantasy and was unable to enter the second half of sexual individuation, to really fulfil her sexuality. In short, her journey to self-awareness was not completed. Her activeness terminated in the middle of her path to the real world and turned into passivity. Hence, her love remained in the realm of fantasy and she was unable to make herself a living person. Compared to Liniang, she only had a half modern consciousness of self.

In his own preface *to The Peony Pavilion*, Tang wrote,

> Love is of source unknown, yet it grows ever deeper. The living may die of it, by its power the dead live again. Love is not love at its fullest if one who lives is unwilling to die for it, or if it cannot restore to life one who has so died.
>
> (Tang, 1598/2002, p.ix)

Tang believed that love could conquer death, and in his story, love transcends the principle of patriarchy. In other words, the individual appealing to love triumphs over the moral requirement of collectivism. From the experience of Liniang and the Lady of Shallot, it is demonstrated that: 1) there are certain obstacles in the path of sexual individuation; and 2) overcoming obstacles requires that individuals be active and have a determination to overcome difficulties or aggression.

Obstacles to the path to individuation

Stein noted that the core of female individuation is for a woman to rid herself of her identification with the controlling inner mother (2006, p.97). In this Chinese story, what I discussed above is how the heroine fights against the patriarchal system. On the surface, they go in different directions. However,

Neumann (1951) points out that even when experienced as a patriarchal Uroboros,[2] the phallic-chthonic gods still belong to the realm of the Great Mother (p.12). Hence, beyond the biologically assigned roles of the mother and father, the patriarchal principle might be the conscious order of a society, but beneath this, in the deep unconscious realm, the power of the Great Mother cannot be neglected and it has secretly dominated people's psychological lives. In China, such power is very obvious. As discussed in Chapter 2, Taoism believes 'Yin' to be the primary power in the universe. Chinese scholars think that although Chinese women have not had political power in our long period of traditional patriarchal society, mothering has been highly valued and pregnancy and fertility are the most important family issues. Hence, it is often the mother who takes charge in her son's family and her son must be filial to her, admire her and obey her will (Sun, 2010, pp.351–354; Wu, 2016, p.23; Ye, 1997, pp.40–55, p.202; Yi, 1998b, p.364). The dominating Great Mother is the foundation of a traditional Chinese family and further, the deep root of Chinese ethics.

The mother figure in China is quite one-sided, however; in other words, only the good mother exists. In many cultures which refer to the Great Mother, there are two typical figures: the good and the bad mother. Sometimes, the most important Great Mother can be both nurturing and destructive. However, there is rarely an image of an evil or terrible mother in Chinese culture. Almost every mother in Chinese myths and legends is good, nurturing and inspiring. Some provide moral models and enlightened figures for their sons. Sometimes they cause damage, but they do so for good reason, not out of malevolence. Although there are some well-known mothers-in-law who have treated their daughters-in-law badly, they are still good mothers to their sons and all their actions are for their son's benefits. This one-sided mother is difficult to protest against and fight because she is so nice to her children on the surface, but she does have the power to secretly devour her children's wills and to prevent them from gaining independence.

Therefore, on the one hand, Liniang stands against her father's will and challenges the patriarchal system for which her father stands; on the other hand, if we explore the story in more depth, beneath this system, Liniang must also struggle with and separate from her identification with the devouring mother who has unconsciously constellated her image in Chinese culture.

The oppression of sexuality

As discussed in Chapter 2, Chinese people recognise the primacy and power of female sexuality but they also adopt strategies to limit this feminine power and to control women's sexual desire. In the Ming and Qing dynasties, a common way to do so was to confine women within a very limited space. Idema considered the garden in *The Peony Pavilion* to be a symbol of sexuality (2005, pp.291–297). Liniang, who was forbidden from entering the garden and had to remain within her chamber, was not only cut off metaphorically from her connection with her sexual nature, but was also literally confined, which was a requirement for young ladies at the time.

As Mann (2011) points out, there occurred at this time segregation of the sexes within the household while, at the same time, the practice of foot binding cloistered women within their own chambers to limit their inter-action with others and from outside men in particular (pp.7–12). Therefore, Liniang and other young ladies of her era had to remain indoors and shut off their feminine awareness, a primary and latent factor in women's nature, which, ironically, cannot be shut off.

A deep chamber looks like a deep well. Liang (2017a) describes how such chambers were usually on the second floor of buildings and had just one window high up on the wall, which was solely for ventilation and lighting. The position of the window guaranteed that young ladies would not be seen by others, nor could they look outside. Thus, such chambers were a kind of prison. Chinese people thought that if a woman's beauty was seen by a man, he would be seduced, or even conquered, by following the woman's sexual power. Therefore, the best way to avoid such a situation was to cloister women in deep chambers.

When Miles (1988/2001) discussed 'the body politic', she said, 'Since women were seen as reproductive beings, any and every disorder they experienced was treated by treatment of the reproductive organs'. She further mentioned the practice of 'female circumcision, the excision of the clitoris and external genitalia' to cure women's disease (pp.244–245). In Chinese culture, there is no record of female circumcision, but there is a long history of foot binding. Both practices are attempts to control and objectivise women by torturing their bodies. Nevertheless, the aim of excising the clitoris is to eliminate women's sexual pleasure, while foot binding limits women's mobility and confines their power to within the household. Ironically, in the sense of Chinese aesthetics, foot binding increased a woman's sexual attractiveness as an object.

Further, Chinese people understood that controlling feminine power, either through confinement in a deep chamber or through foot binding, was not sufficient. Besides literal and physical confinement, their minds were also confined. Luxun (1918) pointed out that in China, women were encouraged to be 'Jie' and 'Lie'. 'Jie' means that a woman maintains fidelity to her dead betrothed or husband, while 'Lie' means that a woman commits suicide after her betrothed or husband has died, or if she is raped. In sum, women should maintain their chastity and sexual purity. Mann (2011) named such women 'faithful maidens' (p.122). Liang (2017a) noted that in the record of *History of Ming* the number of such 'faithful maidens' was four times the total number in the records of previous history. He explains this increase as stemming from the increased population in the Ming and Qing dynasties, which also increased the risk of damage in society. Women were the core and foundation of the family; thus, if women could be stable in the family and had a high level of morality, they could manage their husbands and sons well.

In contemporary China, people face another round of issues related to the vast population and skewed sex ratio. The terms 'Jie' and 'Lie' are no longer used, but emphasis on the importance of women's chastity and purity has returned. In 2015, a university in Xi'an asked its female students to sign a pledge not to have sex before or outside of marriage (xinhua.net, 2015). In 2017, a female lecturer aroused a huge debate in China for offering lectures on 'female morality', in which she taught women how to be 'faithful maidens' and to maintain their love for their husbands even if they encountered domestic violence. She recruited many students and her lecture can be found on YouTube[3]. In the same year, the BBC reported on the 'Chinese virginity debate', triggered by the popular TV show *Ode to Joy 2*. In this show, a girl was dumped by her boyfriend when he discovered that she was not a virgin. These voices, which should have disappeared from modern society, continue to haunt China. Such strategies are effective, making many Chinese women hide their sexual desires and forming a stereotype of their passive sexuality.

This oppression of sexuality does not just pertain to women, however. After all, if most women must value their chastity and retain their virginity, then, due to the skewed male/female gender ratio, it would also be difficult for men to fulfil their sexual desires. Further, in traditional values, sexual activity for pleasure has not been welcomed and it has been believed that a man's sperm is his vital essence and that he should keep his sperm within his body to maintain his health; hence, sexual activity which is not for the goal of reproduction would harm his vitality. A man of noble character should be abstinent and fulfil his desires through aesthetic activities (Mann, 2011, pp.39–46, p.58; Ye, 1997, p.204). Hence, in a typical Chinese romance, the hero is always a young, innocent graduate, like Mengmei. While before meeting Juliet, Romeo had had a physical relationship with another woman, there is no evidence that Mengmei had been intimate with a woman before meeting Liniang. Despite meeting several young nuns in the temple, those relationships were innocent.

Not only has the sexuality of young men and women been oppressed, parental figures also demonstrate no overtly sexual activities. In *The Peony Pavilion*, a story initiated by a girl's sexual desire, no sexual trace is found in the mother and father figures. Liniang's parents only had one daughter and they were a typical Chinese couple of the elite class, whose relationship was respectful and remote. Following Liniang's death, her mother suggested that her father take a young concubine to bear him a son. Her father, however, rejects this suggestion and focuses entirely on his work to defeat the invaders. Mengmei was raised by an old male servant, who was single and devoted all his life to Mengmei's family. Liniang's tutor, who saved Mengmei's life, was a single, pedantic old man, who seemed entirely removed from sexuality. Another mother figure, Sister Stone, the old nun who protected Liniang's tomb and assisted Mengmei to open her tomb, became a nun and was named Stone because she had no vagina and could not have sex. Hence, the sexual hormones are absent from these parental figures. This is ironic, because as mentioned above, this is a story full of sexual symbols. However, this is both common and understandable. In a typical Chinese family, once a couple has finished their task of reproduction, they should focus on their roles of father and mother and their sexual interaction is no longer important. In Chinese stories, it is very difficult to imagine that a mother and father have a sexual life.

'Giant Babies' without mature sexuality

It is a very prevalent phenomenon that in Chinese literature, young people of reproductive age have an obvious desire for sex. However, a decent lady should retain her chastity until she meets the right man, while a virtuous gentleman should preferably not have sexual experience beyond the aim of reproduction. Sun (1983) concluded that in China, sexual activity only serves for reproduction and marriage, since reproduction was not regarded as being for the pleasure of sexuality; hence, the individual's sexual desires and pleasure are entirely removed from marriage and reproduction activities (pp.238–242). He further pointed out an exception to this, however; another aim of sexual activity is to nourish life.[4] He considered this to be another way of feeding, whereby sexuality is not a genital desire but a replacement of the oral desire (ibid., pp.111–115). In sum, traditionally, when sexuality has been allowed, it occurs in forms which do not involve a mature intimacy between two individuals.

Influenced by Sun, Wu (2016) studied the national character of Chinese people and concluded that China is a nation of Giant Babies. According to him, all Chinese people remain at the oral stage, with a mental age of less than one year old. Moreover, symbiosis with the mother is a pattern that is both common and encouraged in Chinese culture (pp.8–15). Both Sun and Wu adopted Freud's and Klein's ideas to make a direct interpretation of Chinese culture. Applying a Western-rooted pattern to examine the Chinese psyche brings an ineluctable result: Chinese people are less mature than Western people. Further, both scholars applied extreme cases or part of the picture to Chinese culture to represent all Chinese people and the whole picture in China. However, Liniang and other female figures in literature, as mentioned above, demonstrate a higher level of sexual maturity and have characteristics of a high developmental phase. These figures also form part of Chinese culture and have been highly valued. Hence, both Sun's and Wu's arguments are limited by their one-sided assertions and ignore the complexity of Chinese culture. Nevertheless, their ideas remain valuable for understanding the problems in China and the conflicts between modernisation and traditional Chinese values. The image of the Giant Baby, a grown-up face with a baby's mental stage, paints a vivid picture to facilitate our understanding of certain issues specific to Chinese culture and the reasons for certain difficulties in Chinese marriage.

In this sense, when we look at the picture of the deep chamber, a dark, narrow and sometimes humid place, it seems to be a symbol of a womb. The foot binding, which limits movement, and the brainwashing of 'Jie' and 'Lie', in which women were asked to obey moral rules unquestioningly, can be considered to demand of women that they be dependent on others and the patriarchal system and that they forgo their independence and self-awareness. Wu says that, from his observation, although some young Western girls date sugar daddies, the phenomenon of young girls dating or marrying a man of almost their father's age is more common in China. After interviewing these girls, he found that their attraction to older men is not necessarily related to their money and power and sometimes has nothing to do with these factors, but is rather due to the girls' eagerness to be taken care of and their seeking for love and attention. Thus, they are looking for maternal care from an old man (ibid., pp.57–58). Obviously, Liniang is not such a girl. She is the only child in her family and is valued and cherished by her parents (her family hire a tutor and a maid for her, and during the period of her illness, her mother is quite sensitive to the reason for her illness and shows her understanding and sympathy, while her father denies his daughter's sense of sexuality and tries his best to save her. Following her death, her parents are very sad and her father even builds a temple to memorialise her and guard her tomb). In studying a number of well-known Chinese romance stories, I observed that most heroines who dare to find an appropriate lover by themselves are only children, a few have just one sibling and a very small number have several siblings. In all cases, however, the heroine is the youngest and the spoiled child. Hence, one of the conditions for separating from the primary care of the mother is to have received enough love. This fits with attachment theory, which states that a secure base with love and attention facilitates the developmental phase of 'separation-individuation' (Bowlby, 1973, pp.360–362).

Not only are women under pressure to remain at the early stage of development, it is also preferable for men to remain Giant Babies. In romance stories, Mengmei is a typical male who is pretty and fragile without a moustache or muscles, the signs of a mature man. Apparently in *The Peony Pavilion*, the figure of Mengmei is not as vivid or lively as the figure of Liniang. He is attractive to women and can easily secure the help of a mother figure. However, he seems unable to defend or protect himself when faced with an accusation from a man. Sun (1983/2011) argues that Chinese men are very feminine in the eyes of Western people, because they are too close with the mother and the mother always stands between the father and son; hence, they identify more with the mother (pp.215–219). However, this conclusion is due to Sun's application of the Western culturally assigned models of femininity and masculinity to his analysis of Chinese people. Further, only in romance stories is Mengmei a typical male figure; in stories of political events and novels about brotherhood in China, the leading figures can be strong and aggressive, with heavy hair. Hence, Mengmei's type does not represent all male images of China. However, a man of his type does have the advantage of attracting Chinese women. A study on sexual preference in China demonstrates that, for many years and even today, Chinese women have preferred pretty boys with narrow shoulders and light hair, while men with muscles are less attractive (Dixson, Dixson, Li & Anderson, 2007). Such boys are not necessarily feminine, however, as such descriptions are culturally dependent; more precisely, they seem immature and their sexuality seems undeveloped, like a child or even a baby. Further, they demonstrate a certain passivity in a relationship compared with their female partners. It was Liniang who visited Mengmei, led him to open her tomb and guided him to confront her father. In a word, he is less mature than her and hence his action was motivated by her.

Moreover, Wu's most inspiring idea about the term 'Giant Baby' is that the parents of these Babies – the passive boys and dependent girls – are also Giant Babies and the over-emphasis on filial piety – asking children to obey all their parents' orders unconditionally and placing the parents in the most important positions in their lives – is an attempt to treat parents as such (2016, pp.370–373). This idea has similar counterparts in both relational psychoanalytic and post-Jungian theories. Benjamin (1995) points out that the mother must have the ability to distinguish the real baby from her fantasy, 'to set clear boundaries for her child and to recognise the child's will, both to insist on her own independence and to respect that of the child … if she cannot do this, omnipotence continues' (p.38). Hence, the maturity of the mother is the basis of the future development of the child, but if the mother herself is unable to assert her own independence and recognise that of her baby, she will cause her children to remain in a state of symbiosis. Knox (2011) points out that if parents' development remains in the early stage and hence lacks the ability of mentalisation, they will treat their children as the absent internal parents and ask them to take care of their emotional needs. Under such circumstances, they cannot treat their children as independent beings and foster their individuation (pp.126–145). These arguments facilitate our understanding of how parents, as Giant Babies, are unable to foster their children's self-agency and sense of subjectivity and even become obstacles in their children's path of individuation. Alternatively, we could say that the parents are devoured by the omnipotent Great Mother, and hence, their mental age remains at an infantile level and they unconsciously engage their children in this symbiosis. Wu (2016) writes in detail that such symbiosis is the origin of collectivism which opposes individual will and a collectivistic group is the only residence for a Giant Baby (p.90). In China, a dominating mother figure is important for the unity of large families and the mother metaphor is used to represent the community and the state. Although such metaphors exist in other cultures, in China, devoting oneself to the extended family and the state and being filial to one's mother are the two basic ethical principles.

Hence, we can understand why Liniang's father was so stubborn in refusing his daughter's marriage. Idema (2005) suggested that this might be due to a form of 'Oedipal complex': the father has a secret, incestuous desire for his daughter (pp.309–312) and if this were a typical Western story, this might indeed be the case. However, in China, we can make another interpretation. Sexual encounter distinguishes mother-infant affection and intimate relationships between two adults (Colman, 1994, pp.511–512). As a man who shows no mature sexual desire and devotes himself to his work and his country, Liniang's father is still at the stage of being a mother's son and wants his daughter to remain innocent about sex and remain at the stage of a baby. However, he fails in this. Liniang has a strong determination to rid herself of the intergenerational symbiosis and to remain with the man who has initiated her sexual desires. This is the most extraordinary part of the story: although the parents are Giant Babies and try to keep their child in the same condition, the child has the opportunity to break free from this intergenerational curse and to enter the path of individuation. Ironically, Liniang's active pursuit of her sexual desire demonstrates her aggression and this aggression is the result of her identification with her father. Unfortunately, her father showed strong aggression but repressed his sexuality; hence, he did not have the same opportunity to break free as his daughter did.

Aggression: a two-edged sword

The split of sexuality and aggression among Chinese men

Samuels (2013) points out that the 'monolith of "men"' needs to be broken up: 'some are powerful …; others are manifestly powerless and oppressed' (p.121). Such a monolith has never existed in China, however. There is a long tradition of men being differentiated by their social class and career. Further, even in the elite class, the characteristics of different male images are quite divided; hence, power is not attributed evenly to all men.

In *The Peony Pavilion*, both Mengmei and Liniang's fathers belong to the elite class, but Liniang's father obviously has more power and demonstrates strong aggression while Mengmei is vulnerable and demonstrates little aggression. This is a typical split among the images of Chinese men in the extant literature. Usually, sexual desire and aggression are not carried simultaneously by a virtuous man. Hence, the hero of the romance story is Mengmei, the pretty and vulnerable boy who has been well educated. Liniang's father is a different figure. In the eyes of the Chinese mainstream, although he was against his daughter's marriage with Mengmei, he is not the villain of the story. On the contrary, he represents a good father and husband, a virtuous gentleman in the Confucian value system, who shows no interest in women and has great passion for the state.

As a director of the military, Liniang's father is quite similar to another typical male image, the warrior, who also shows no sexual desire, as mentioned in Chapter 2. There is a Chinese saying describing a common belief among warriors: 'You have to treat your brothers as hands and feet and your wife as a piece of clothing. Changing a piece of clothing is easy but replacing hands and feet is difficult'. This implies that a warrior's sexual desire for women is much less important than his sense of camaraderie bordering on brotherhood with other men. A prevalent and influential Chinese novel, *Water Margin*, which was also written in the Ming dynasty, tells the story of a group of warriors who have muscles and show strong aggression. They are very close to the image of Western masculinity, but most of these warriors show no interest in having sex with women. Some have experience of being cheated or betrayed by women for which reason they hate them, while others have lost their wives at the beginning of the story or their wives are unimportant or almost invisible in the stories. Hence, in this thick tome, it is difficult to find any romance and in the eyes of such heroes, a woman is either a slut who will bring damage to them or a shrew without sexual attraction. However, they admire their mothers and being filial to the mother is a notable virtue.

In contrast, a very important theme for Western heroes is to rid themselves of their mother complexes and to unite with the anima, the contrasexual image, depicted by the slaying of a dragon and rescuing a princess captured by the dragon. This is an important moment in which a hero can express his aggression directly and his aggression is in service of his sexual individuation. As mentioned above, the typical image of the Chinese mother is always positive; hence, this theme is lacking in Chinese culture. There are stories of Chinese warriors fighting against monsters or evil spirits and while such monsters and spirits sometimes represent the evil power of women, such power has nothing to do with motherhood. After annihilating this evil force, if the warrior has the opportunity to marry a girl in gratitude for his service, a man of honour should reject such a marriage to demonstrate his selflessness. Hence, in Chinese romance, there is no image akin to Sir Lancelot, the typical knight of Western literature, an attractive hero who is simultaneously equipped with both aggression and sexuality. In China, an aggressive man with sexual desires has always been a lecher, the villain of the piece who indulges in sex, the trafficking and raping of women, bullying and hurting their fathers and husbands and is thus exterminated by a warrior by the end of the story. Such figures represent another image of the omnipotent Giant Baby. None of the male figures in China mentioned above has a sense of separation from the mother. A decent man, whose first identity is as the son of his mother, may choose between either sexuality or aggression. However, without sexuality, a man cannot be mature, while without aggression, there is no opportunity for him to overcome the mother complex and hence of fostering a mature sexuality. Under these circumstances, a man remains faithful to his mother and as a mother's baby who is possessed by his mother complex. Hence, we may observe that, in *The Peony Pavilion*, Mengmei is Liniang's contrasexual image, but without any aggression, he is no equal to the Animus of Jung's idea, who denotes separation and independence. More precisely, he initiates Liniang's own will to separate from her natal family and become independent, while motivating her aggression and action. He represents the potential for a future from the other sex. While Chinese people create a split between masculine sexuality and aggression, their traditional attitude towards women's aggression has its own characteristics.

Women's aggression and the damage caused by their sexuality

As Austin noted, 'femaleness has been taken to be synonymous with non-aggression' (2005, p.25). However, women's active role in pursuing the fulfilment of their desires for love and sexuality has been a very common theme in Chinese stories, while the aggression that lies beneath the activeness and damage caused by their sexual power has also been emphasised. Therefore, while it is recognised that a woman can be the subject of desire, her sexuality should be oppressed lest her active sexual desire, her sexual attractiveness and her automatic aggression cause damage.

A typical pattern of Chinese romance stories is that a beautiful woman causes a disaster and she mostly does so actively and with a certain level of awareness. In *The Peony Pavilion*, to rescue Liniang, Mengmei opens her tomb. As an intellectual, this was disgraceful and criminal behaviour. Liniang insisted that Mengmei must meet her father, a government officer, and although it was not her intention to bring trouble to Mengmei, he was jailed for this action. To a certain degree, the relationship with Liniang does bring him disaster, although he eventually overcomes it. Nevertheless, this could serve as a lesson.

In other stories, women with active sexuality bring destructive results to a man or even to a whole dynasty. Chinese scholars (Boyang, 2010; Luxun,

1918; Yi, 1998b, pp.25–27) have concluded that this pattern shows Chinese men to be irresponsible and always blame women, a typically patriarchal attitude. From a different perspective, however, Chinese people tend to emphasise the primacy and power of female sexuality and aggression, a recognition that is not obvious in Western literature.

Boyang (2010) compared the story of Helen in *The Iliad* with the story of Daji in *Fengshen Yanyi*. There are certain similarities between the two stories: both occurred in the twelfth century and both heroines were beautiful women who caused a great war, which their current husbands lost. Boyang noted that the difference between them was that the Trojan warriors appreciated Helen's beauty and she returned to the arms of her ex-husband, who had won the war, while Daji was accused of being a fox fairy who had enchanted her husband, causing his demise, and was thus beheaded by the victor. Boyang claimed that the varying attitudes as shown in these disparate ends reflect the differences in attitude towards women between the West and China, i.e. the Western attitude is more merciful (pp.44–46). With further examination, another conclusion can be made, however: in *The Iliad*, the woman, Helen, is the passive victim of a man's desire. She never intended to cause the war; she was the one who was seduced and should thus be forgiven. The appreciation of her beauty proves that she is a trophy of war. However, in *Fengshen Yanyi*, Daji was sent by a goddess to seduce the emperor as a punishment; thus, in the beginning, as a representative of feminine power, she played an active role in her relationship to the man. She then pushed her husband into war and even fought in the war herself in an attempt to prolong her reign as queen. She is evil but strong, presenting her negative, destructive feminine power to challenge the patriarchal order.

On the surface, a more similar Western counterpart of Daji is Lady Macbeth, an evil woman in Shakespeare's play who manipulated her husband into killing the king and stealing the crown. However, she did not have her own name or identity and her ambition served her husband; thus, her desire for power was intertwined with his. She is dependent on her husband and is the victim of patriarchy. However, Daji's ambition and desire served herself. Further, Daji seemed quite similar to the male image of the lecher mentioned above, who carries both sexuality and aggression, but a typical lecher is still a mother's boy, who looks forward to being taken care of by women, while Daji is tougher and more independent. As an evil woman who should be defeated, her failure is inevitable, but her story shows the fear surrounding women's initiative and automaticity, which imply an awareness of those attributes in the first place. Hence, we can understand another function of the deep chamber and foot binding – to confine women's movement and limit the damage that may be caused by their sexuality and aggression.

Aggression turned against the self

Another cost of recognising the feminine power of sexuality and aggression is the high rate of female suicide in China. Suicide is an exemplary aggression which turns against the self. After studying the phenomenon of the 'faithful maiden' in China, Mann (2011) came to the conclusion that, for many, the decision to commit suicide was made to avoid moral reprehension and an unbearable lifetime of celibacy. She also said that '[h]igh rates of female suicide remain characteristic of Chinese culture' (pp.122–124) and in this she is correct. China might be among the few countries where the rate of female suicide is higher than that of male suicide (Cui, 2009; Phillips, Li & Zhang, 2002). Moreover, China has always had the highest rate of female suicide (Lee & Keinman, 2003, p.292; Wolf, 1975), which is quite unusual. Jung discussed why men have a higher tendency than women to commit suicide in the West, saying, 'in the soul … it is the man who feels, and the woman who reflects. Hence a man's greater liability to total despair, and a woman can always find comfort and hope; accordingly, a man is more likely to put an end to himself than a woman' (CW6, para. 805). In China, however, the situation is totally reversed. The reason for suicide amongst Chinese women might not be due to their inner feeling function, but rather due to the dynamics between them and the external world.

There have been two typical types of suicide amongst Chinese women. The first was common in the late Ming and Qing dynasties and complied with the requirements of the government and the voices of mainstream society – to be the 'faithful maiden' for her fidelity and purity. These women died for 'Jie' and 'Lie' to be the moral model to protect the patriarchal order, allowing their aggression to be used instrumentally by the patriarchal system. This type of suicide has not been heard of since 1949. However, there is another kind of suicide among Chinese women – 'a deliberate display of protest' (Mann, 2011, p.123). In *The Peony Pavilion*, Liniang also actively died in the middle of the story although there is no obvious suicide attempt, and after the story was published, she had female followers. Usually, such a protest is conducted for the sake of autonomy in marriage, which might have been the most available mode of protest for women in Chinese society for many years.

After her dream in the garden, Liniang could not accept an arranged marriage from her parents which seemed to be the only way for a lady to marry at that time, and the only way to escape her parents' arrangement was to die. Mann also points out that after the New Culture Movement, 'young girls would kill themselves to resist arranged marriages' (ibid.). In recent studies of rural female suicide in China, it has been shown that most such suicides comprise impulsive acts due to the conflicts within the women's marital families. Because of China's urbanisation, more and more rural women are now migrating and dwell in cities; thus, they have more choice over their own marriages and are less dependent on their husband's families. As a result, the suicide rate in China has decreased dramatically (Jin, Wu & Zhang, 2010; The Economist, 2014). For many Chinese women, death has for many years been the only way to attain freedom from liability to their families and marriages. Hence, if they find another way to escape from such liability, such as migrating to big cities, death becomes unnecessary.

Therefore, the recognition of women as the subject of desire and as having automatic aggression has not, in reality, brought more liberation or freedom to Chinese women; on the contrary, they must face severe oppression for many years due to the fear of and defence against feminine power, which shapes the persona of well-known Chinese women – a passive and obedient female image with no evident aggression – and as a consequence, brings their passive aggression and inhibited sexuality into their marital relationships.

Aggression in the context of individuation

The negative aspects of aggression have always been emphasised in both China and the West. However, more recent studies show that aggression can be a two edged-sword, bringing both creative and destructive results. Samuels (2001) argues that aggression 'is part of life and it is not all bad … Aggression is part of communication' (p.133). It is clear that aggression cannot be avoided in daily life and in relations with others and can be ambivalent. Austin elaborates the two sides of aggression and says there is a 'creative possibility and push towards embodied agency which dwells within aggression, alongside its destructive and annihilatory potentials' (2005, p.10). Such possibility and agency were clearly revealed by Liniang's story and prompt her to move forward, entering the path of individuation, while the image of Daji demonstrates how aggression can bring damage to others and to herself.

Here, the key questions are how to facilitate benevolent aggression, allowing creation and agency to merge in the service of individuation and to prevent the pure destructiveness of aggression. Let us compare the three different images of women: the Lady of Shallot, Daji and Liniang. The Lady of Shallot had some degree of activeness and little aggression. However, she was attracted by Sir Lancelot, a knight, and projected her aggression onto the other sex, her animus. She lived in a tower on an isle, like a deep chamber, which could be seen as a symbol of the mother's womb. She is a daughter of the Great Mother. Despite having some feminine awareness, she identified with the passive aspects of the Mother and was unable to assert her own aggression. Her only hope is to have a man in her fantasy to whom she can delegate her aggression. By denying her aggression, she loses her aliveness and is unable to become a complete individual. As a consequence, she loses her opportunity to connect with a real man.

Daji is sent by an angry goddess. She is also the daughter of a Great Mother. From the outset, she represents aggression and punishment from the mother's anger. (We must observe that in *Fengshen Yanyi*, although Daji is an evil woman, the goddess who sent her is an image of a good creating and rescuing mother. By the end of the story, she abandons Daji because she only sent her to punish the emperor who humiliated her and cannot accept Daji hurting others.) Daji's aggression is utilised to predominate over others and to enslave them for her own benefit. Her husband, the emperor, was used by her instrumentally and, like the Lady of Shallot, she had no opportunity to have a real, intimate connection with a man.

Of all three stories, only Liniang enters a process of sexual individuation. Her aggression serves her in a benevolent and creative way. As Austin describes,

> [A] capacity to hold and direct aggressive energy for the good of relationship is a significant human achievement, and ... an increasing capacity to do so correlates with an increasing capacity to build and sustain lively relationships without compromising oneself or one's values.
>
> (2005, p.1)

Liniang keeps her agency and establishes a solid relationship with Mengmei, showing her loyalty to him despite the pressure she is under from her father at the end. What makes Liniang different from the other two women is that she is not only her mother's daughter but also her father's daughter. Her father cares for her very much. As Samuels (2001) points out, 'fatherly warmth leads to a recognition of daughters as people in their own right ... Fatherly recognition of the daughter as other than a mother can enable women to break out of the cycle of the reproduction of motherhood' and lead them to other pathways, such as, 'the spiritual path, the work path, the path that integrates her assertive side, the path of sexual expression ... maybe the path of celibacy' (p.109). Hence, being recognised by the father and receiving affection from him open various opportunities for the free choice of the daughter and allow her to dare to be herself and to rid her of the solely culturally assigned role of a woman.

Further, as a daughter of a military director, Liniang's aggression is more likely to stem from her identification with her father. Benjamin applies Anna Freud's case to illustrate a daughter's wish to be her father's son and points out that such an identificatory bond can be healthy, having nothing to do with Oedipal compulsion and can foster the daughter's self-assertion and her 'sense of being the subject of the desire' (1995, pp.130–135). Hence, we can understand why Liniang is able to face her sexual desire directly and pursue her love actively. In a certain way, as the only child, she was cherished by her parents as a son and could become the successor to her father. Because of the son-preference in China, there is a tendency to treat the only daughter as the son of her family and the only successor to her father, particularly in modern only-child families. Only-daughters have more interaction with their fathers than daughters from non-only child families. These only daughters and their fathers have more opportunity to mutually recognise that the daughter could be the father's son.

Moreover, Samuels (2001) highlights that the daughter's aggression from her identification with her father serves 'to validate and reinforce their capacity to challenge and fight with men' and extends her 'capacity to confront the patriarchy stem' (p.114). This is exactly what Liniang did. Samuels also proposes 'the possibility of an element in fathering that can help to transform antisocial, sadistic, unrelated aggression into socially committed, self-assertive, related aggression' (ibid., p.113). This is the key difference between Liniang's aggression and Daji's. Daji's aggression comes from the Great Mother, which is the unconscious realm and thus, once unleashed, it is very difficult to control the damage caused by her. However, Liniang's aggression is identified with her real father. It is used more consciously and instrumentally to serve a clear purpose, which is to have a marriage based on free choice with a man she loves, and thus serves a mature sexuality and fosters her sexual individuation.

Conclusion

China is a country where the patriarchal system has dominated the collective consciousness, while the power of the Great Mother has occupied the unconscious realm and deeply affected the ethical awareness of Chinese people for many years. To be the mother's child is preferred in China. Chinese men are encouraged to split aggression and sexuality lest they rid themselves of their mother complex. Both women's sexual desire and aggression have been recognised but the dangers of such power have also been overemphasised. Hence, Chinese women have been oppressed for many years. *The Peony Pavilion* delivers an ambivalent attitude towards women in Chinese culture: on the one hand, women's innocence and obedience have been encouraged in daily life, while on the other, in literature, a girl who has awareness and is rebellious is the idealised female image. This might reflect Chinese people's secret eagerness to individuate.

From a psychological perspective, only mature and independent parents can foster their children's development and make their children independent. Immature and dependent parents harm their children's capacity to gain a sense of agency, cut off their opportunities for separation and place obstacles in their path to individuation. However, Liniang's story tells us that with enough love, even if it is from immature parents, the child dares to separate from her natal family and to be herself. In the process of separation and individuation, the affection from the father and identifying with his aggression are the two facilitating elements in an environment that overemphasises the importance of the nurturing mother. Although Liniang is an image of a Chinese woman, her experience could be borrowed by others, particularly by Chinese men.

Notes

1 A woman with modern consciousness of self means that she has feminine awareness in a modern way. Thus, she can recognise herself as a woman with autonomy, a sense of agency and desire, and these are not thought to be necessarily masculine characteristics.
2 A uroboros is a heavenly serpent eating its own tail. It is a mythical creation in ancient Egypt that was later applied to Western alchemy. Neumann applied this image to depict the undifferentiated state of early development of the psyche (Neumann, 1954, pp.5–38).
3 www.youtube.com/watch?v=A08oYsDKAzI&t=6s
4 It was believed that under certain guidance by a senior Taoist, the man could gain benefits for his health and longevity by keeping his sperm in his body and sucking the essence released from women during orgasm. This is a Taoist sexual practice, but was opposed by Confucianists and not approved by the mainstream of China.

Chapter 7

Unresolved Oedipal conflicts and narcissism-typical difficulties for marriage and individuation for young Chinese today

Two clinical case studies

In this chapter, I discuss two clinical cases to elaborate on the types of couple issues that prevail in contemporary China. Both are finished cases in which the patients came to me due to their relationship issues. I saw the female patient, Ting, for 4.5 years, 164 sessions in total, and the male patient, Peng, for 11 months, 37 sessions in total. I worked with them in my role as a therapist in the clinical department of a hospital that mainly focuses on psychotherapy. Following each session, I took clinical notes and discussed them weekly with my supervisor in the hospital, together with other cases. My theoretical orientation at that time was dynamic psychology, which means that I applied analytical psychology together with the theories and ideas of psychoanalysis to understand my patients. This combination is not new and can be seen in the work of other Jungians (Colman, 1996; Fordham, 1998; Frey-Rohn, 1974; Perry, 1970).

In both cases, I, the therapist, terminated the treatment and neither case can be deemed successful. I have selected these two cases because the problems they encountered in their relationships were quite typical. The female patient was from a one-child family and the effects of her natal and marital families on her are common among one-child families with an only daughter based on my observation. The male patient came to me because of his love affair, which is one of the principal reasons for failed marriages in China today. I discuss these two cases mainly to demonstrate the problems and difficulties in contemporary Chinese families rather than to present clinical solutions.

Case one: Ting

When I met her for the first time, Ting was 30 years old. A close friend of hers was a therapist in another hospital whom I had met at a conference and who then recommended me to Ting. A year before our work began, she and her husband had gone once to another hospital for couple therapy, but her husband had refused to do it again. Her chief complaint in our first session was that she and her husband had almost no sexual life. They had a two-year-old son and since his birth, she and her husband had only engaged in sexual activity two to three times per year. Her husband was quite aloof and showed no interest in sexual interaction with her. They went to couple therapy for this issue. She now felt quite desperate and had no clue how to deal with her marriage.

Ting's mother knew about the sexual issue between the young couple and felt sad about it but she did not think Ting should file for divorce, because it seemed that this was the only problem they had. She had said to Ting: 'After all, he doesn't beat you or have any affairs'. Furthermore, when Ting had tried to discuss her marriage issue with close friends, they had all persuaded her to simply improve her attitude towards her husband and suggested that this would be the best way to fix their relationship. Because of these opinions, in our first months of therapy, she kept telling me how she had tried to communicate with her husband to discuss what was wrong in their marriage, but without any apparent possible solutions. At first, her husband had resisted discussing the problem and had said that she valued her sexuality too much, which made Ting feel humiliated. Later, he accused her of being the cause of their sexual difficulties and said that his refusal of her body was due to her critical attitude. This claim made her fall into painful self-blame and helplessness. Usually, such conversations ended with her in tears and him snoring. Sometimes, the feelings of self-blame and desperation were so strong that she slapped herself after their fights.

The awakening of sexual desire and the absence of self-agency

In Ting's story, I saw echoes of a trapped Du Liniang in a contemporary young woman. Although the external, physical chamber has long disappeared from Chinese life, the internal, invisible chambers remain. For Ting, her desire to break out of the chamber and find the path to self-realisation caused her inner conflict and motivated her to attend psychotherapy.

Like Liniang, Ting was the only child in her family. Her family was richer than her husband's family for which reason Ting's parents had mainly paid for their apartment and car. After the birth of their son, her parents lived with the young couple to help take care of the little boy, which is quite a common scenario for young couples from one-child families. However, Ting felt quite ashamed of her dependence on her parents. Her mother was a very assertive and demanding woman, while her father was weak and withdrawn. He was distant to both the mother and daughter. Nevertheless, if there were any conflicts between the mother and daughter, he would ask Ting to obey her mother and to mind her mother's feelings. Her parents had both lost their jobs due to the transformation of the Chinese economy; later, when she was quite little, they had started their own business, running a small photo studio.

They worked very hard and had no patience with their daughter due to their exhaustion. Therefore, as a small child, Ting had been very obedient and had tried hard to avoid causing trouble and to fulfil her parents' expectations; nevertheless, she often bore the brunt of her parents' blame and she had finally realised, in desperation, that they would never be satisfied with her.

Ting's adolescence had been an extremely painful time for her. In high school, she had struggled with her academic studies and due to her academic failure, her parents had sent her to study drawing to ensure she could enter college. However, she had no aptitude for drawing and attending the drawing lectures had been torturous. In her final year of high school, she had spent most of her day sleeping, to the extent that her classmates had dubbed her 'sleeping god'. Ting's difficulties during puberty are not rare in China in the last 30 years. Schools do not encourage individual interests and young people are forbidden to date. Academic achievement is seen as the only valid goal for Chinese adolescents. At that time, Ting was quite sensitive but self-oppressed. The massive amount of time she spent sleeping was, in retrospect and from a psychological perspective, very meaningful.

In *The Peony Pavilion*, when Liniang realises her sexual desires, she falls asleep and finds fulfilment of her sexuality for the first time in a dream. However, Ting did not report any dreams from that period, and while Liniang's sleep was temporary, Ting's sleep was excessive and resembled more Liniang's death after waking from her dream. Idema (2005) drew parallels between Liniang's death and Sleeping Beauty's long sleep and suggested that both resulted from the first touch of sexuality for young maids (p.293). This analysis could also apply to Ting's situation. Her sleep comprised a defence against her desire because, as was the case for Liniang and Sleeping Beauty, the external world did not allow her to express her desire openly. Ting's academic failure and massive amount of sleep in high school could also be seen as symptoms of depression, but also a repetition of a more archetypal nature. The condition of falling into depression is quite similar to falling into the realm of death, or the underworld, with its darkness, lack of energy and lifelessness that inhibit the aroused sexual desires of puberty. This could be seen as a symbol comprised partly of passive obedience to the requirement to be inactive in sexual activities and partly a resistance to the pressure of academic achievement from the surrounding environment. As discussed in the previous chapter, Liniang's death could be seen as a gesture of protest. In ancient China, death was a common way for women to fight and show their determination to rid themselves of their dependence and to freely choose their own paths. Furthermore, in Jung's theory, death and rebirth are necessary for individuation.

Unfortunately, unlike Liniang, Ting remained lifeless and did not get the opportunity for rebirth, trapped as she was by her dependency on her parents. She was accepted into a college far from her hometown and studied interior design based on the drawing classes she had hated. After her graduation, she tried to move to Shanghai and find a job there with her boyfriend at the time. However, her parents ordered her to return to her hometown and found her a position as a college teacher there. They claimed that all these arrangements were for her own good, because a stable and secure job and a peaceful life in a small city were more suitable for a girl like her. She accepted the job offer, broke up with her boyfriend and returned to her hometown. She then found another boyfriend who lived in a big city near her hometown, 20 minutes away by high-speed train. However, they eventually broke up and she married her husband after they had dated for a year. Her husband, who lived in the same city as her, had lost his sexual interest in her in the latter half of their year of dating.

Here, for a young Chinese girl, the invisible chamber appears once more, in the name of stability and security. Her parents had asked her to return 'for your own good', a very typical phrase used by such parents. Ting felt quite pained and was unable to establish her self-agency. As Knox (2011) defines it, self-agency is 'the experience that we can influence our physical and relational environment, that our own actions and intentions have an effect on and produce a response from those around us' and she emphasised that the key element in this is 'intentional, action-based and related to the consequences of one's actions' (p.34). Therefore, self-agency is an individual's ability to make their own choices, take action towards those choices and accept the consequences. In Ting's case, this was lacking.

Knox pointed out that young children are afraid to assert their own agency in case their autonomy and independence cause them to lose their parents' love and evokes retaliation from them. The struggle between the call for agency and the worries and fears surrounding the parents' response will continue if the parents do not 'develop a secure sense of agency' and 'depend on ... their own child, to maintain a sense of their own identity' (ibid., pp.296–297). It was clear that Ting's parents feared her autonomy and undermined her attempts to take independent actions, asking her instead to be in tune with their own expectations of her. As Knox described it, this comprises 'a masochistic sacrifice of self to protect the caregiver, whose needs are felt to be paramount' (ibid., pp.299–300). Under such circumstances, as the only child, Ting carried the full weight of her parents' projections and had no one with whom to share her burden. Hence, she found it difficult to acquire her own sense of agency and establish her own identity.

On the one hand, as was the case for Liniang, since adolescence Ting had felt a strong temptation to be herself. She had realised what she did not want to do and what she was not suited to, such as her academic studies, the drawing courses and the teaching position. However, the fear and guilt she harboured towards her independent parents prevented her from finding her own path. Unlike Liniang, before coming to me, she had not found her own dream – her aspiration and internal life. Liniang's period of death lasted three years, but Ting's death-like depression and lack of vitality had lasted from her adolescence into her 30s. The failure of her marriage could be seen as a product of her inner death. Liniang found the man in her dream who fulfilled her sexual desires and brought her back to life but Ting had rejected men who had tried to be more intimate with her and made her leave her natal family and had instead married a man who strangled her lust for life and oppressed her sexual desires, as her parents secretly wished.

The temptation to be herself and the eagerness to come alive caused her continuous pain and prompted her to seek psychotherapeutic help. For generations in China, sexuality beyond the aim of reproduction has not been deemed necessary or important for maintaining a marriage; this explains why Ting was hard-pressed to find support from her family or peers and to take the issues seriously. Most of the advice she received in relation to her difficulty was that she should simply tolerate and adapt to it. However, she refused to do as she was told and resisted ceding her sexual desires. In this respect, she was quite similar to Liniang. When trapped in the chamber and not allowed to visit the garden, Liniang tried to cast off the role of an obedient lady, faced the pain of struggle and found a path to salvation. Ting now also decided to face her awakening sexual desires and to stop oppressing her inner conflict. By coming to my office, she was demonstrating a certain attempt to find salvation.

Transference and aggression

Ting lived in a small city in another province and travelled for an hour on the high-speed train between the two cities to attend therapy. Thus, her commute to the sessions took at least four hours. At first, she was strongly motivated to solve her problems. After the first 10 sessions, she asked to see me twice a week and suggested that we meet face-to-face in one session and by skype for the other. She said she was in a hurry to fix her marriage difficulties and furthermore, that more frequent meetings would bring the two of us closer. She said that between sessions, she was always eager to meet me and tell me what thoughts had emerged, in particular positive feelings such as attending a training program of interior design in Beijing and realising her feminine charms.

Through discussion with my supervisor, my understanding of this request was that she was treating me like a mother on whom she wanted to depend and whom she was trying to please like she did her own mother. She idealised me as an omnipotent mother and her fantasy was that the more she saw me, the more she could get from me and that, ultimately, she could use some of the magic power I gave her to diminish all her negative feelings and fix all her problems. Further, she demonstrated her intention to get close to me and emphasised the progress she was making in our sessions to please me; in this way, she saw me as she saw her real mother who pushed her to achieve in academic and drawing courses and who she also wanted to please. Therefore, she had to try her best to satisfy me, by seeing me more, paying me more and giving me confirmation regarding what I had done for her. I interpreted this understanding to her and told her it was unnecessary for us to meet twice a week.

While she accepted my interpretation, she felt abandoned by me and ashamed. Gradually, she came to speak less about her husband and more about her inner feelings, such as her shame and guilt, her eagerness to be independent and her worries that she would fail in every aspect of her life. In particular, she doubted her ability to be a good mother. It seemed that, all of a sudden, her relationship with her husband had stopped troubling her and the mother issue had become the core problem. This made me wonder if she was blaming me for not being a good mother and taking care of her.

Increasingly, Ting complained about my holiday leave. Every holiday break made her feel that she had been abandoned by me once more. She also complained that I maintained a distance from her and that she knew nothing about my personal life. She worried that I was good to her just because it was my job to do so. She had the same feeling towards her father who, in her description, was distant, aloof and isolated. She placed me in an ambivalent position as both the demanding mother and distant father and she felt simultaneously controlled and rejected by me. She then apparently entered an aggressive phase and later, she began to attack me. She said she disliked me and that I was just like her own mother, precisely because both of us were difficult to please. In the following months, she forgot her appointments with me for several months and postponed paying me.

This was Ting's first time expressing her aggression to someone so openly and directly. Previously, she had always turned her aggression against herself. As described by Austin, it is very common for women to express their aggression by attacking themselves: '[A]n inner critic or self-hater repeatedly tells a woman that she is useless, ugly, stupid, hopeless and ... fat' (2005, p.30). This was exactly the case for Ting. Now, however, she began to attack me, her therapist. As Austin noted, '[A]ggression might provide a link to the sense of aliveness and capacity for greater intimacy with other' (2005, p.3). For Ting, this external aggression brought something to her. She took some action in her life, asking for a long leave from the college at which she worked and found a job as an interior designer in a big city near her hometown. During this period, our relationship appeared closer and more real and she appeared to me to be more vivid.

However, the following six months in the big city were a disaster and our sessions were full of tension. She felt guilty toward her son and her parents, because she had to leave her son to be taken care of by her parents. All of a sudden, she was both a bad daughter and a bad mother. Obviously, I should take full responsibility for this disaster because I should have helped her to become strong and to acquire the ability to fix all of these problems as soon as possible, but I could not. Furthermore, I was unable to give her unconditional support. She gave up the job and returned to her hometown in frustration and shame. It was her way of telling me that I, as therapist, was a failure. She tried but had to go back to the demands placed on her by others. She then continued to forget her therapy once or twice every month. She accepted all the interpretations I gave to her and sometimes even made interpretations by herself, but her anger remained strong. Her anger at me was quite strong and irrational; she acted more like an angry baby who is frustrated by the realisation that neither it nor its mother is omnipotent. I realised that her many years of suppressing her aggression had caused it to swell and once this aggression lashed out, she did not know how to handle it appropriately. Meanwhile, I could not help her to use her aggression 'instrumentally' to get what she wanted and gradually her aggression lost its' potential.

In the third year of our therapy, her aggression expanded to everything around her. Her work in the college was disgusting, her son was annoying, her husband still had no emotional response to her and her parents were the reason for her terrible life because she had sacrificed her own life by not becoming independent and leaving them. In particular, however, I was the object of her anger. On several occasions, she was late to our sessions and twice, did not show up at all. She said she had done this on purpose, because she was trying to fight against me. She also aimed her aggression against herself. She had her freckles lasered off between our sessions and for several sessions wore a mask to see me. She told me the choice to undertake the operation was a self-attack. It reminded me that at the beginning of our sessions, when she had failed to communicate with her husband, she had slapped herself. When she tried to attack others, her guilt and self-reproach increased and she then attacked herself. She reported a dream in which she killed everyone in the dream including me and herself. Meanwhile, she had sex with her husband twice, both times initiated by her, and after they had finished, they had severe arguments. This time, she irritated her husband successfully and they almost had a physical fight.

As Samuels (1989) says, 'Aggressive fantasy can bring into play that interpersonal separation, without which the word "relationship" would have no meaning ... aggressive fantasy may want to make contact, get in touch, relate' (pp.208–209). Therefore, aggression is important both for separation and relationship. In this phase of our therapy, Ting expressed her aggression rather than oppressing it and used it to relate with others in her life. While she made some effort to be more active and to control her life, her way of expressing her anger was quite childlike. Her long-lived depression had mixed up both 'aggressive fantasy and destructive fantasy' as well as 'fantasy and action'. As Samuels warns, this is 'a distorted application of' aggression (ibid., p.210). Hence, her anger did not bring any distinction or separation. She relied quite heavily on others and kept asking others to be responsible for her. As her therapist, I was the one she blamed most often, but at the same time she had a strong desire to be close to me. She mentioned several times that she wanted me to hug her. Her aggression was quite ambivalent: the intention of attack and the longing for intimacy always coexisted.

The Oedipal dilemma: a trapped animus and oppressed femininity

The ambivalence of Ting's aggression could be related to her Oedipal conflict. As mentioned above, her father was aloof and his attitude to his wife and daughter was similar to the attitude of Ting's husband to her. However, Ting felt pity for both her husband and her father, because both had lost their mothers at a young age. She said her main reason for marrying this man was because if she had rejected him, no one would have wanted him because of his family circumstances. Her husband was also an only child whose mother had died of cancer of the uterus three years before they met, and whose father had thyroid cancer. The relationship between the father and son was distant. Ting's parental grandmother had died when Ting's father was little, her parental grandfather was an alcoholic and her father had previously been a tuberculosis patient. In a certain way, she had chosen her husband because he had many similarities with her father and she had tried to take care of him just as she had tried with her father. Her husband was also a doctor. Marrying him seems to have been an attempt to work through her Oedipal frustration and having a doctor husband could be seen to symbolise the potential to heal the traumatic past in both families.

However, her husband brought her even more frustration and traumatic experiences as he was too like her father. For a woman, the contrasexual archetype, or animus, must be distinct from her father, even if it is first embodied by him. This is an essential component for individuation (Colman, 1996, p.40) and means that the man upon whom the contrasexual images are projected must have similarities to the father but also have sufficient differences from him. Thus, the lover image must be detached from the father image. In Ting's case, the two images of her husband and father were merged; thus, she was unable to work through her Oedipal conflicts through her marriage. She was also unable to acquire her individual sense of self through being united with a proper man. Her libido remained fixed on her own father.

Ting reported a dream in which she had sex with her husband, but when she turned up her head, she realised that the man was her father. This dream recurred several times in the first year of our therapy. Her secret desires for her father emerged and she felt quite ashamed, scared and terrified. She also mentioned having a sexual fantasy about her director at work who was much older than her and with whom she did not get along well. Later, in her work in the big city, she had a crush on her boss who was an old married man. Both were replacements for her father. As Colman emphasised,

> [i]f anima and animus can be detached from the parental imagos, this fascinating archetypal power is exactly the element that will later fuel the longing for sexual union, a longing that pulls the child out of the charmed circle of the parents towards adult relationships.
>
> (ibid.)

Ting's situation was just the opposite; she was continually attracted by men just like her father, which means that her animus was trapped by her Oedipal compulsion, and the sexual union with another man was difficult to achieve due to her fear of incest. As a consequence, it was not possible for her to establish an adult relationship. As a young woman, her Oedipal compulsion and frustration had coexisted for a long time and there was no solution to her Oedipal conflict. This tension continued to traumatise her.

Idema (2005) says that in *The Peony Pavilion*, the theme of the Freudian family complex also pertains. Liniang's father's secret desire for his daughter leads him to insist that his daughter knows nothing about sex, to deny his daughter's marriage and to attempt to keep his daughter within the natal family (pp.309–311). Ting faced the same situation. Despite her continuous complaints about her father's aloofness and distance, she admitted that, like her mother, her father had insisted that she should remain in their hometown and had rejected all of her plans to become independent. However, Liniang's father is quite active and aggressive and his affection for his daughter made it easier for her to identify with him and his aggression. This ultimately led her to pursue her desire and autonomy. As Benjamin describes it, 'the more confirmation and the less humiliation a girl meets when she tries to fulfil the wish for identificatory love [with her father], the more the wish emerges free of self-abnegating or masochistic elements' (1995, p.134). For Ting, her situation was the opposite because her father gave her little confirmation and humiliated her. Little wonder then that she was trapped by her self-abnegation and masochistic relationships with him and other men. Nor did her relationship with her mother improve the situation. Her guilt towards her mother was also obvious. She said she felt sorry for her mother because she was also unhappy due to her aloof and distant husband. Ting had a dream that she was making out with her husband, but an older female cousin came into their bedroom two or three times and interrupted them until they finally gave up. She said the cousin could be her mother. She admitted that because of her mother's unhappiness, she did not dare to live a happy life herself. This was a typical compensation based on the guilt of the daughter in trying to replace the mother and possess the father.

On the other hand, she unconsciously identified with her mother – an austere woman who ignored her appearance and devoted all her time to hard work and taking care of others. Ting did not appreciate her lifestyle and got plastic surgery twice during her college years. Later, however, she felt quite ashamed about this and criticised herself for being vain, shallow and inauthentic. The surgeries were on her eyelids and nose to make her face clearer and sharper. However, after she married, she gained 10 pounds and said that 'the effect of the surgeries was neutralised by that'. Marcus (2004) proposes that 'the mother's capacity both to convey her own pride and pleasure in her female body, its sexual and procreative capacities, and to confer the privilege of passion on her daughter is requisite for a girl's full, pleasurable possession of her body and sexuality' (p.680). Ting's mother lacked this capacity and her feminine part was very oppressive. This caused a severe self-reproach and self-loathing in Ting. She rejected her own body and continuously attacked it, which in turn contributed to her issues surrounding her sexuality.

Marcus also argues that for a girl, her attachment and struggles for separation from her mother go beyond the preoedipal period. In the Oedipal phase, she will treat her mother ambivalently as a love object to attach to and as a rival with whom she competes for her father's love. For a mother, her function is not only 'to thwart [the daughter's] sexual desires for father', but also to pass 'the sexual baton to the daughter' and receive 'her libidinal desires toward the mother' (ibid., pp.704–705). Besides lacking passion in herself, Ting's mother also showed little affection for and a great deal of possession of her daughter. Ting's sexuality and libido had been stuck for a long time, while her attachment and separation from her mother had become distorted and twisted together. While on the one hand, she did not like her mother, on the other, she totally identified with her values and her destiny and had been bound to her both physically and emotionally for a long time.

Countertransference and the termination of our therapy

At the beginning, I felt quite sympathetic towards Ting and noticed my anger towards her husband and parents. I felt I could understand her dilemma as the only child in her family and as a young Chinese woman. When her anger towards me first emerged and she attacked me in our session, I was even glad for her because I thought she would now be able to face her real feelings and rid herself of her self-oppression. I thought this could be an opportunity for her to find her own voice through her courage to express her negative feelings. Although she missed our sessions and did not pay her bills on time, this did not trouble me because I knew that she would show up the next time and pay the bill eventually. Gradually, however, I also felt trapped and powerless in our sessions. In particular, in the third year of our work together, I realised that all her complaints and aggressive behaviour had not brought any real development in her life. She had twice attempted to leave her hometown and had moved out from her parents several times, but all these attempts had failed and she had always found reasons to return to her parents. The material convenience and childcare that her parents offered made it easy for her to give up making an effort. Without her parents' assistance, life was too difficult for her to handle.

Therefore, although she seemed to accept all the interpretations I made and expressed herself more openly, there was no real progress due to her lack of action. I felt quite frustrated and lost my patience with her. She noticed this and emphasised that all she needed from me was to believe in and support her unconditionally. She felt disappointed with me because I could not offer this to her. Gradually, I realised that our relationship had simply fallen into the same pattern as her relationships with her husband and parents. We were not satisfied with each other, but we both thought our relationship was important. So we were both equally culpable in maintaining it, with its regular complaints, displays of aggression and struggles.

In the middle of the fourth year of our work, she suddenly told me that she had submitted a resignation letter to her director in the college and that this time she had made up her mind to quit the job and find another in the big city. The following week, however, she told me that her parents had forced her to withdraw the letter and she had done as she was told. Her director had also persuaded her to ask for another period of sick leave rather than resigning. It would have been a pity to give up such stable and beneficial work no matter how much she hated being a teacher. She felt shame, frustration and self-hatred. Although I felt quite upset, I tried to avoid being another demanding mother, pushing her to accomplish something, despite my frustration at her inconsistency and withdrawal. By the end, her determination had disappeared once more and she lamented what she could not get. At the end of the fourth year, she told me she wanted to stop her therapy because she had never made any decision to end a relationship by herself and she needed to feel she could actively control something. After several months of discussion, I agreed that we could stop seeing each other for a while and see what happened. After saying yes to her, I felt quite relieved, although I believed she would return some day. I was even glad for her, because I thought she had found the courage to actively finish something that was making her uncomfortable and that this could be a new start.

However, she returned to me three months later and said she was not ready to terminate our work and wanted to continue her therapy. In the following months, she kept missing therapy sessions, sometimes because she had overslept or was too tired to make the journey, or because she had got stuck someplace and did not want to make the effort to come. Her passive aggression was very obvious in our relationship. I had to face the fact that she was not ready to continue our work and that she had lost her passion and energy to maintain our relationship. I was just like her husband, her parents and even her job, all of which she was dependent on passively and were difficult to get rid of, but towards which she lacked a deep connection and authentic interaction. My interpretation could not help her, nor were her payments for those sessions she did not attend helpful. I could foresee that in the following years, she would come back and forth to the relationship because she did not dare to lose anything. I thus became part of the stillness and death in her life, which my integrity could not tolerate.

After a painful rumination, when she did not show up for her sessions twice in a row, the next time I saw her, I proposed terminating our therapy and referred her to another therapist. It was not common for me, as a therapist, to decide to terminate long-term therapy by myself. I may have been wrong, but at that moment, I thought I had to do so. She felt shock and sadness and she said she felt abandoned. I told her she could treat it as abandonment if she wished, but for me, I would treat it as a lesson of separation. At a certain level, Ting's difficulties are common for girls from one-child families, who have close bonds with their parents and rely on them both materially and emotionally. Like Ting, however, they might not receive enough affection from their parents, while at the same time being spoiled by them. For such girls, being abandoned is not the core of their issue; the main challenge remains how to separate from an important object and to then rely on their own actions. Furthermore, I know how difficult it is, traditionally, for Chinese women to say no in a relationship and really mean it, even if they feel terrible about what has happened in that relationship. For Ting, her parents asked her to stay with them, her husband refused to file for divorce and even her director was reluctant to accept her resignation. In the eyes of some, femininity means being related and Chinese culture values such relation. However, I tried to show her a different model. As a Chinese woman, I valued our relationship, but once I found it could not bring life but was stuck in a deadlock and that the will to end it seemed more authentic than maintaining it, I decided to say no to her and terminate our relationship.

Again, I am not certain that I did the right thing for her. It might simply have been my acting out. Nevertheless, I still think that for Ting, a woman whose struggle lies in establishing her agency, action was more helpful than non-action.

Case two: Peng

Peng was in his late thirties when he came to see me. He had previously seen another female therapist for 40 sessions. However, gradually, they were unable to find a regular time to meet and he was unable to accept that the therapist had increased the fee for his therapy; hence, they both agreed to terminate the therapy. He then booked a session with me through the hospital.

Peng worked as a civil servant in the Department of Public Health in a small city, but he planned to become a psychotherapist in the future and had attended a psychotherapy training course, because he considered his own work to be boring and he was unable to attain any sense of achievement from it. His chief complaint in the first session concerned sexual issues he was having with his lover. By that time, they had been dating for nearly six months, during which time they had broken up once. They were now having difficulties in their sexual life; he was unable to satisfy her and had gradually developed erectile difficulties.

Peng's marriage was complicated. He had married his wife 14 years previously. At first, he had thought their marriage was happy and satisfying, but three years later, they had fought severely when he had had his first love affair with a female high school classmate. This fight lasted for three years, by the end of which time they had filed for divorce; however, they had continued to live together with their son who had been born after one year of their marriage.

Three months before coming to me, persuaded by a male friend of his, Peng and his wife remarried. At the same time, he kept up his relationship with his lover. He told me that he loved his lover and could not give up the relationship with her because he felt his relationship with women could be repaired through this relationship. Furthermore, his wife had placed many restrictions on their sexual activities and this frustrated him. However, he did not want to give up his marriage either and he planned to fix his own problems by re-establishing his relationship with his wife.

Chaotic relationships with women and the lack of mutual recognition

From what Peng told me in our first session, I came to the conclusion that his relationships with both his wife and his lover had been chaotic and that he was unable to recognise the 'intersubjectivity' in his relationships. Intersubjectivity, as defined by Benjamin (1995), 'refers to that zone of experience or theory in which the other is not merely the object of the ego's need/drive or cognition/perception but has a separated and equivalent center of self' (p.30). Peng was unsure what he could do for both women; he had objectivised them and seemed to have entirely ignored their subjectivity. He continually emphasised how they could facilitate his development and in what way they could fulfil his desires, in particular his sexual desires, but he was unable to imagine that these two women had their own feelings and desires. Despite professing to 'love' his lover, this had no impact on his behaviour toward her. As Benjamin notes,

> [I]n loving the other as an ideal 'love object' the self may take a position quite inimical to intersubjective recognition. To attribute difference to the other as sexual object, even to adore or idealize the difference, is not the same as to respect the other subject as equal.
>
> (ibid., p.8)

Hence, since he did not treat the two women as individuals with their own thoughts and needs, Peng had been unable to imagine the results of maintaining both relationships simultaneously. In other words, he was so focused on himself that the possible responses of the women to his unfaithful behaviour were beyond his imagining.

In our third session, Peng informed me that his wife had discovered his affair and had fought with him again. This time, she had been furious and had threatened to kill him with a knife. He was scared and blamed her for not accepting him unconditionally and for setting so many limits on their sexual life. Later, while the couple had been discussing divorce, his wife's whole family had come in and beaten him. Finally, the conflict had been settled by the police. Peng was furious and frustrated and complained to me that his wife had not spent any money on their family, while he had been the one to take full responsibility for supporting the family. He said that he had tried his best to fix the problems in his marriage and its failure was not all his fault. In our ninth session, he told me that he had completed the process of filing for divorce. However, two months later, he discovered that his now ex-wife had slept with the friend who had persuaded them to remarry. This secret relationship had already lasted for four years. Peng felt cheated, shocked and humiliated and he called his wife and arranged a meeting to confront her. After they met, they had sex again and this time his wife agreed to have anal sex with him.

Meanwhile, he continued to date his lover. She was now his formal girlfriend, but they had severe arguments because she refused to perform oral sex on him. He was angry and complained that she had done so previously for other men. At this moment, the roles of his lover and ex-wife seemed to be reversed. She was the one setting limits on him and being cheated by him. He also confessed to me that he was ashamed of the way they had begun their relationship. He had met her in a training program for psychotherapists and they had joined a group therapy together. They had slept together after one session of the group therapy because he had been drunk. Finally, the group had to be dismantled because their relationship had sabotaged the setting of the group therapy and he felt guilty about that. At that moment, he seemed to blame his lover for making him a bad person. At that time, he met the woman with whom he had had his first affair, asked her to have sex with him and was rejected. Further, he kept complaining that his lover was ugly, particularly in photographs. He also doubted her loyalty to him. She had previously been married and had had physical relationships with several men; during their last break, she had dated someone else. On the other hand, he told me that he planned to marry her in the future even though he worried that he would not be able to satisfy her financially, which had been the reason for her first divorce. His attitude towards his lover was full of paradoxes and oscillations. Again, he demonstrated a tendency to destroy a potentially stable relationship and put her in the position of blame for the possible failure of the relationship.

In Peng's narratives, he and everybody around him had been psychologically interconnected and connected in a physical way by sexuality and aggression. He had difficulties having really intimate relationships with women. His stories about women were replete with cheating, betrayal and revenge, with all the actors engaging in several physical relationships simultaneously. It was difficult for him to stop acting out and to let go because he lacked the ability to experience and facilitate mutual recognition. As mentioned, Peng did not recognise the intersubjectivity in any of the relationships he mentioned to me, which is a basic element in mutual recognition. Mutual recognition is a psychoanalytic notion, referring to the essential ability to develop one's faculties and 'to live in some degree free of domination and nonviolently'. It means preserving and transforming autonomy 'as a pole of the necessary tension of independence/dependence of subjects, of differentiation'. Moreover, mutual recognition requires 'acceptance of the other's independence and unknowability' (ibid., pp.21–22). Hence, it is important for one's sense of agency to find one's position in self-other relationships and to distinguish reality from fantasy in relationships with others. All of Peng's self-other relationships had been replete with domination and violence and they had harmed his sense of self-agency; hence, he was unable to take responsibility and kept placing himself in the position of victim. He was unable to treat others as real people and imagine the results of his behaviour, which led others to take unexpected revenge, or for him to be possessed by paranoid, destructive thoughts about others.

Further, mutual recognition 'includes the notion of break down, of failure to sustain that tension, as well as account for the possibility of repair after failure' (ibid.). Although Peng emphasised that he planned to repair his relationships with women, it was beyond his current ability to do so. Without mutual recognition, he was unable to really give up any relationship and accept his failure to connect with these women; instead, he became possessed by the tension of sexuality, violence and domination. When he continued to live with his ex-wife, while going back and forth to different women, he was not seeking real repair but was instead engaged in a compulsive repetition, haunted by his fantasy. This pattern could be traced back to his early development and his relationships with his parents.

Developmental history and identifying with both victim and persecutor

Peng described himself as a castrated man. He was the only son in his family and had a sister who was four years older. He had been born in northern China, where sons were highly valued (although the preference for sons has prevailed throughout China for many years, Peng's hometown is a region in which the value of sons is even more emphasised than else-where). He admitted that, from birth, he had been spoiled by his family. His mother and aunt had cared for him very well but had constantly babied him. He complained that, in daily life, he had been taken care of too well and had led a very comfortable life beyond what he deserved because of these two women. (In China, as discussed in chapter 2, the only son has been very precious for the mother, particularly when she lives in a traditional and conservative region. Her reputation in the neighbour-hood, her position within her marital family and her well-being in her older years are totally reliant on the son she has raised. Hence, taking care of the son as a baby and ensuring that he is absolutely safe and comfort-able are the main tasks and only life-time aim for the mother.)

On the other hand, his relationship with his father had been fraught and his parents' marriage had been terrible. In their relationship, his mother had done all the housework, while his father had done none of it, yet had constantly criticised his wife's work. In the family, the father was the blam-ing one while the mother was the grudging one. (This type of family dynamic is typical of the Northern region of China, where Peng's home-town is, which obviously holds traditional views that men are superior to women. As the housekeeper, the mother should take full responsibility for family affairs, take care of everyone in the family and take the blame for any dissatisfaction. Meanwhile, as the boss of the family, the father could do nothing within the family, yet have the right to judge his wife's work.) His father also criticised him constantly and as a result he took the side of his mother. However, he thought his mother had used him as a weapon against his father and complained that she had made him break up with his first girlfriend – a typical son-mother-'daughter-in-law' triangle in China as discussed in Chapter 2. As usual, due to the mother's interven-tion, the potential 'daughter-in-law' failed in the competition for the son and left his life. Based on what he had learned from his psychotherapeutic training course, he considered himself to be the victim of his parents' bad marriage and that all of his problems stemmed from his deep involvement in their relationship, with his father castrating him to demonstrate his own masculinity. When he said this, he seemed to be outraged, but also helpless.

Peng also had a terrible relationship with other men. From a very young age, he had been bullied by other boys. Later, although he had had some close male friends in college, his friendship with them all had ended by a severe conflict in which they had tackled him down and beaten him. This had been a huge humiliation to him. Recently, he had discovered that his close friend had cheated him and slept with his ex-wife. Another important man he mentioned was a lecturer in his training course. He had envied this teacher and felt small in front of him because this teacher was successful in the therapeutic realm, while he himself had not begun to earn money as a therapist despite having already spent a great deal of money on his training. Further, he suspected that his lover had a crush on the teacher and would choose the teacher over him if given the opportunity. In sum, the men in his life played the role of either hurting him, or in his fantasy, were going to hurt him eventually. The only man he admired was his grandfather, who had led a 'legendary' life – marrying several times, knowing how to practice Kongfu and wandering around China. However, his grandfather had contributed little to raising his own children (Peng's father had been raised by the grandmother alone and both he and his mother had been bullied by others in the village where they had lived because there was no male adult in the family). For Peng, this remote grandfather had been his male model.

To a certain degree, Peng resembles Mengmei in *The Peony Pavilion*, or a typical young male image in Chinese romance stories. In such stories, young males rarely show their aggression in society or in the broader world beyond their intimate relationships. They are weak and fragile, the very antithesis of the knight/warrior image that is typical of the masculine in Western countries. Mengmei types are bullied by others, in particular by father figures while they are taken care of by women, and mother figures in particular. Because of their close bond with the mother, while being distant from and terrified by the father, traditional Chinese boys are often dependent and helpless (Dien, 1992, pp.110–123). However, Mengmei had been raised by a loyal male servant and was rescued by another father figure (Liniang's tutor) when he was ill; therefore, he had both positive and negative father figures in his life. Thus, his experience of the masculine was integrated, which led him to show courage in taking responsibility and fighting the authoritative father figure with his wife. For Peng, nearly all the men around him, his father in particular, had demonstrated negative aggression towards him. He had had nearly no positive experience of a father in his life and, based on his narratives, even the ideal grandfather seemed to have been a bad father.

Klein (1945) says, 'For only if the boy has a strong enough belief in the "goodness" of the male genital – his father's as well as his own – can he allow himself to experience his genital desires towards his mother. When his fear of the castrating father is mitigated by trust in the good father, he can face his Oedipus hatred and rivalry' (pp.69–70). This is the reason that Peng considered himself to be a castrated man. He had lacked any experience of his father's goodness, while gaining the full experience of his badness; hence, he was unable to work through his 'Oedipal hatred and rivalry' and had expanded his experience of being the victim of the masculine to his relationships with other men.

This father-son pattern in Peng's family was intergenerational. Peng blamed his family for the fact that his father was a weak and castrated man; however, the ideal, legendary grandfather had treated Peng's father and grandmother in a similar way to how Peng's father had treated him and his mother. His was a typical Chinese patriarchal family and fathers in such families are tyrannical. As suggested by Colman (2000), in such families the father is the dominant partner, the master who devours, while the mother is merely a part of the dominant father, the salve and the devoured. Under these circumstances, the son was unable to obtain maternal assistance to defeat the terrible father and was thus devoured by him. He became intimidated and was ruled by guilt and fear (pp.522–523). In the father-son relationship, Peng identified himself as the victim, just as his father had identified himself in his own father-son relationship with Peng's grandfather.

As Colman proposed, 'the devouring father represents, at one level, being consumed by hatred and destructiveness and, at another, the son's wish to live in projective identification with a father who is more powerful than himself' (ibid., p.535). Hence, both Peng and his father identified their fathers as the persecutor. As a consequence of identifying with the negative aspects of the father, 'the boy's belief in the productive and reparative quality of his genital is diminished; he feels that his own aggressive impulses are reinforced and that the sexual intercourse with his mother would be cruel and destructive' (Klein, 1945, p.71). Peng's attitude towards the women who were close to him is evidence of this. He was intrusive and demanding in his sex life and wanted these women to treat him like a mother would, mainly, someone who would never say 'No'. However, when these women did take care of him as he wished, he either had erotic issues or immediately diverted his interest to another woman; this could be seen as both acting out sadistically and inhibition by incestuous anxiety.

On the one hand, like Ting, Peng invested his libido in the parent of the opposite sex and was unable to distinguish the contrasexual archetype – the anima – from his own mother. On the other hand, he was possessed by his father's anima, which Beebe (1985) referred to as 'the father's working sense of his life, the emotional attitude that the father takes towards his son' (p.100). Therefore, he treated the women close to him, including his mother, in the same way as his father had treated him and his mother – taking advantage of them without gratitude and attempting to enslave them. This demonstrated the fantasy of the 'tyrannical omnipotence' of 'the archetypal father', the cost of which is to eclipse and exclude 'the role of [the] maternal feminine' (Colman, 2000, p.521). Just like his father and grandfather before him, Peng was unable to recognise women as independent individuals and also drew revenge from them in the form of resentment, violence and betrayal. Further, as Henderson (1976) has pointed out, the basis of a mature relationship is that a man not only asks the mother to love him, but also has the ability to love the mother back (p.187). Peng had no such awareness in any of his relationships with women. As both the victim of tyrannical masculinity and the persecutor of femininity, he was unable to establish mutual recognition and develop a deep affection for others. This pattern also appeared in his relationship with me.

Transference and countertransference

From the outset, Peng seemed quite open in our sessions. He spoke to me directly about his unfaithful relationships and related the details of his sexual activity, which made me feel quite uncomfortable. Although other male patients discussed their sex life with me, he was the only one who was so straightforward and provided too many details in the first session. Thus, from the outset, I found it difficult to like him and my dislike increased in subsequent sessions. At first, I was astonished by the way he told his stories to me. He kept saying that he wanted to know himself more and be a better, more mature person, but he rarely demonstrated any real self-reflection. Instead, he placed himself in the position of a victim, spoke of his anger and frustration and blamed everyone around him. I felt I was working with a giant baby, who was obsessive in his omnipotent fantasy, and I began to suspect his real motivation for seeking therapeutic help.

Later, after he had finalised his divorce, he became very critical towards me. He said that I treated him in a perfunctory manner, that the effect of our work had been far below his expectations and that the sound insulation in my office was terrible. In a word, what I had done for him was disappointing. At this moment, I was just like his wife or his lover, or his mother, a woman who was difficult to please and could not satisfy him. Later, he made more and more comments about me, most of which focused on my appearance. In one session, he said, 'You look tired, you have dark circles under your eyes. I doubt that you can work for me under such circumstances'. In the next session, he said, 'Oh, you look prettier today. I feel less dissatisfied with you because you value my opinion and pay attention to yourself in order to work for me effectively'. He continuously commented on my clothing and make-up in a very disturbing and annoying way. He confessed that, 'I asked you to be my therapist because I want to have an attractive female therapist to learn how to be in love with a woman'. He said he wanted to call me 'darling' and kept telling me how much he missed me but he thought I was out of his league and he was unable to have any secrets from me which made him feel debased and helpless.

On the surface, the so-called 'erotic transference' was obvious, but in a very shallow and repulsive way; at times, I even felt it was harassment towards me. At this moment, he was possessed by intense feelings towards me and was unable to listen to any interpretation. After discussing it with my supervisor, I realised that this 'erotic transference' was a resistance that was sabotaging our therapeutic relationship as he was preventing me from working with him as a therapist. Although it is called 'erotic transference', it was not a real function of Eros but rather a misuse of Eros. It sabotaged his ability for relatedness and rendered him unable to connect with me in a genuine way.

Hence, I discussed with my supervisor how to terminate our relationship and transfer him to someone else. Before I spoke to him officially, two other events informed my decision. First, he brought his lover to one of my seminars in the hospital without informing me in advance. In our session after the seminar, he told me what had happened. I interpreted to him that he had attempted to situate me in his love triangle and to witness two women competing for him. This was a familiar pattern that he always created, such as with his mother and his aunt, his ex-wife and his lover. I told him that such behaviour had been invading our settings and he seemed to accept this. Nevertheless, I must confess that I was irritated by his arrogance; he always tried to put himself and others in a dramatic scenario and to centre himself in all of his relationships. Second, I had raised my fee slightly due to the policy of the hospital. I informed him that the charge would increase in three months, but he refused to accept this and insisted that he would pay me by the new standard in six months. This was not about money, it was about power; he tried to challenge the settings and to be the one who was in charge in our relationship. This sadistic and persecuting pattern appeared repeatedly in our relationship.

When I told him that I would not be able to work with him, he was surprised and rejected my decision. It took three months, 10 sessions in total, to terminate our therapy. During these sessions, I learned that his former therapeutic relationship with another female therapist had terminated in almost the same way. At first, he and the therapist had struggled for a time slot that suited both of them. Later, the therapist had increased the therapeutic fee and he had refused to accept this. By the end, the therapist had decided not to see him anymore. However, he then applied for an on-line administrative position in the company run by the female therapist, which he succeeded in procuring. In a certain way, I can understand his former therapist. In the transference and countertransference, the biological sex of both therapist and patient affects the therapeutic relationship. However, effective therapeutic work is based on more than biological sex and the integrating potential of the feminine and masculine. For Peng, his transference was concretely fixed on the biological sex of his female therapists, whom he treated like the real women in his daily life. Consequently, this aroused in both his female therapists an antipathy to such a negative masculine pattern and made us feel repulsed by him as a specific man. This, in turn, restricted the potential of the therapeutic work. By the end, his therapists had abandoned him, just as the other women had sought revenge on him. Further, as I mentioned above, due to his lack of mutual recognition, he was unable to accept the failure of his relationships with women and treated their 'no' as a serious refusal; instead, he kept reconnecting with them.

In our final 10 sessions, he attempted to change my mind. He said that he was regretful and sad and that he would try his best to obey the rules and pay me by the new standard. I told him genuinely that I was unable to work with him in a neutral and objective way based on what had occurred between us. Moreover, due to his old patterns of relating with women, which were extremely difficult to break, I highly recommended that he worked with a male colleague of mine. He spoke less about men in his life than women, but based on my understanding, I felt that a stable and caring father figure would open up a new possibility for him to amend his tyrannically-dominated masculine self. He finally accepted my advice and began to work with the male colleague that I had recommended to him. (Since then, he has kept working with my male colleague over the last five years and their work continues at the time of writing this book. This is the first time he has stayed in a stable relationship with a therapist.) After some time, his lover contacted me and asked to join my seminar. I said no, because I thought this might have been a ruse by Peng to connect with me in a different way. Setting clear boundaries and making him realise that when a woman says no she really means it are an important part of the work for him. Having open and honest dialogues with him that he should learn to stop acting out and to accept loss might give him the idea to establish a sense of intersubjectivity.

Discussion

Peng's story and his pattern seem to be totally opposite to Ting's. The two cases, in my opinion, mirror each other and are complementary. Everyone in Ting's narratives – herself, her husband, her parents and even her friends – lacked sexual energy, while the characters in Peng's narratives were full of sexual energy. As a woman, Ting was passive in accepting the role of victim to her father and husband, while as a man, Peng was identified with the role of victim of the patriarchal hierarchy and actively became a persecutor to the women around him. As discussed in Chapter 6, in China, male aggression has not been regarded as a valued masculine characteristic as it has in Western culture. In the two cases discussed, Ting's aggression was aimed more towards herself while Peng's aggression was aimed at the women around him. These resemble the patterns of aggressive expression described by Austin (2005, pp.4–5). Ting's main issue was that she was unable to take any action in her life or during her time in therapy, while Peng's issue was that he was acting out too much. On the surface, their stories demonstrate the typical differences between feminine and masculine narratives in China. However, under further examination, beneath these two extreme cases, the basic issues are the same.

Unresolved Oedipal conflicts

As some post-Jungians note, archetypes are intrapsychic structures and include behavioural and relational patterns revised by culture and environment (Colman, 2016, pp.49–51; Saayman, Faber & Saayman, 1988, pp.258–259). In Ting's and Peng's clinical narratives, the archetypal dynamic of the Chinese family constellation is demonstrated. Within this constellation, parents are not regarded as the most intimate couple; rather it is the mother and child who comprise the closest couple. In other words, the mother-child relationship becomes the most prominent in the family.

The premise of resolving Oedipal conflicts – giving up sexual desire towards the other sex parent – is that the child recognises the parents as a couple who have a sexual relationship (Britton, 1989, pp.84–85). In both Ting's and Peng's families, their parents had terrible relationships and did not act as a couple; hence, both of them fixed their sexual libido on the opposite sex parent. In Chapter 2, I mentioned that in China it was a common belief among older generations that marriages should serve the extended family and the state. The family was sometimes involved in political affairs or carried out political tasks; therefore, personal feelings had to be discarded and individual choice was impossible. From my interviews in Chapter 5, among the parents of these young interviewees, it was a common phenomenon that the relationships between husbands and wives were not intimate or it was difficult to say the relationships were good. Usually, they were full of unresolvable conflicts and tensions, making it difficult for their children to recognise them as a couple, not to mention imagining that they had a sexual connection. In the story of *The Peony Pavilion*, which was written 400 years ago, the atmosphere between the parent figures also lacks intimacy and sexual tension.

Therefore, under these circumstances, as Colman (1996) comments,

> [T]hose who carry the contrasexual archetype are equated with the parental object – a failure to distinguish between signifier and signified, carrier and what is carried ... sexual relationships are dogged by the threat that the love object will collapse into the original parental object, arousing the fear of incest.
>
> (pp.41–42)

Such confusion harms the sexual energy of children. Both Ting and Peng had sexual difficulties in their relationships, albeit in a different direction; this partly stemmed from their unresolved incest anxiety which caused them to avoid stable sexual relationships.

Further, the Oedipal drama must be ambivalent: both total gratification or total frustration of Oedipal desires are a disaster and close the ambivalent space. (ibid., p.50). For Ting, her father rejected intimacy with her and it was difficult for her to feel the bonds between her and her father. Peng, meanwhile, had an exclusive alliance with his mother and expelled his father from the mother-son space. Both Ting and Peng thus lost the possibility for ambivalence and were trapped by frustration, anxiety and guilt. Consequently, they were unable to relate with each respective parent or to relate to them as a couple; that is, to find a third position from which to observe the couple and to believe that all these relationships would not harm each other, as described by Britton (1989). Hence, they could not establish an internalised, creative image of intercourse; instead, the destructive intercourse in which they would either hurt or be hurt by one parent occupied their fantasies. They misused their sexual energy and it eventually withered.

The mother complex and the omnipotent fantasy

During my work with Ting and Peng, both emphasised their eagerness to be loved unconditionally. When they tried to develop a deeper connection with me, their therapist, they projected onto our relationship an omnipotent image of a relationship between a mother and her new-born baby and explicitly asked me to give them unconditional love. It was difficult for them to withdraw this projection solely through interpretation. Unconditional love is a popular term in psychotherapy training in China that is almost universally admired. However, to be loved unconditionally by the object suggests that the object must be submissive to the omnipotent power of the baby master and restrain its own will or needs. In other words, the object cannot be subjectivised and must be the carrier of a projection. While this fantasy is necessary for a new-born baby, it is harmful to an adult and prevents him/her from maturing. This is due to the mother complex, in which the person always puts him/herself in the position possessed by the longing for the mother, is trapped in 'a general fear of life' and then shrinks 'from adapting [him/herself] to reality'. Consequently, the fear increasingly besets his/her path at every point (Jung, CW5, para. 456). Both Ting and Peng, as middle-aged adults, were stuck in every aspect of their lives, because they both had difficulties separating from their own mothers and had been possessed by the mother complex. This is a particularly prominent problem in the context of China, mainly due to the strong bond with mother that is facilitated and, in many ways, admired.

As discussed in previous chapters, the inability to separate from the mother, psychologically or even physically, has been prevalent in Chinese families for many generations. On the other hand, both Ting's and Peng's mothers were typical Chinese mothers who were also secretly Giant Babies, as discussed in Chapter 6. They needed their children to identify, foster and nurture them. Both mothers and children were desperate for relationships and were unable to tolerate separation, perceiving a situation without relationship to be an unbearable one. This desperation was then transferred to the children's other intimate relationships. Hence, Ting was unable to file for divorce from her husband, regardless of how indifferently he treated her, while Peng was unable to tolerate any gap between the women with whom he was physically related, and his life was closely entangled with, and defined by, female relationships. However, all these relationships shared the same core – the unsacrificed, 'original "down state" of the psyche' and 'undifferentiated, unconscious state of primal being' – the image of a mother with her unborn child, as described by Jung, while their individual freedom was hampered by 'the unconscious endogamous relationship to the parents' on which their libido fixed (ibid., para.644–650). The fantasy of remaining in an omnipotent dyad – the mother and baby – made them fragile and brought trouble to their relationships as adults. Remaining in such a fantasy and denying the reality that others, even the mother, had their own subjectivity, could be recognised as a state of primary narcissism.

Narcissism

While Ting and Peng came to me individually, their respective situations were quite similar to the couple discussed by Colman (2014) in his case study of a couple in therapy. This couple, whom Colman named Bernard and Beatrice, came for therapy because they could no longer tolerate each other. The wife, Beatrice, had always tried to be good and took care of her husband but was ultimately disappointed by her husband's immaturity and irresponsibility. The husband, Bernard, had been obsessed by his own interest in becoming a rock musician and complained that his wife set limits on him and controlled him. In describing their relationship, Colman said that

> they each tried to negate the separate existence of the other in two ways – firstly by their own requirement that the other meet their needs in exactly the way that they required and secondly by projectively identifying the other with this demand and attacking them for it.
>
> (p.31)

This also occurred in Ting's and Peng's respective marriages. Every conversation that Ting initiated with her husband ended in his criticising her, while in all his relationships, Peng cheated or was cheated on. Both Ting and Peng made efforts to satisfy their spouses, but the spouses were not real, independent people in their eyes; moreover, they were unable to be satisfied themselves, as they held an image of the self which always demanded perfection and yet failed to obtain it.

Colman describes Bernard's case as one of 'extraverted narcissism' – 'the self is felt to be inside the object', while Beatrice's case was one of 'introverted narcissism'- 'the object is felt to reside within a private space inside the self' (ibid., 36). Peng's situation was similar to Bernard's: he had made an 'extraverted attempt to colonise his wife and force her to conform to his own image', in particular in their sexual relationship. In other words, he could not recognise women's subjectivity and treated them as 'his own masturbatory fantasies'. On the other hand, at first glance, Ting does not fit Beatrice's pattern – taking 'the introverted route of a retreat to a self-enclosed space where no other could intrude' (ibid.). Upon further examination, however, we find that Ting was unable to recognise her own subjectivity because she could not distinguish the object from herself. Like Beatrice, she always tried to be good – improving her appearance and her attitudes – and never gave up hope that if she became perfect, others, her husband in particular, would be satisfied with her and fit into her expectation of relationship. In other words, she imagined that in a relationship, she should take the main responsibility and that she could establish a perfect world by making herself perfect.

In such cases, extraverted narcissism is often typically masculine, owned by men, while introverted narcissism is usually observed in women, carrying feminine characteristics. The old Chinese saying 'male master outside, female master inside' reflects the longstanding belief that men should identify themselves through external achievement and through the reflection of others, while women should devote themselves to the marriage and family, making everyone around them fit within the cosy atmosphere they have created. In China in particular, women have been expected to initiate and maintain the relationship, as Liniang did in *The Peony Pavilion*. They should adopt the wills of their fathers, husbands, etc., as their own. However, without recognising their own subjectivity, it is not possible for them to understand others' subjectivity. As a result, the wills of others are merely their projection and they are unable to respect others as equally independent individuals. In both extraverted and introverted narcissism, 'the object is felt to be under the omnipotent control of the self' (ibid., p.36). Thus, both are obstacles to real connection.

In the arena of clinical work

Jung emphasised that the family constellation has a powerful influence (CW17, para. 474–475). Based on the development of his ideas on the archetype and the collective structures of the psyche in the Post-Jungian model of the intrapsychic system, individual minds and behaviours are affected by circumstance and environment. More precisely, they have been determined and modified by the net of archetypal images in the family, community and society. Further, exploration and discovery on developmental and relational models can reciprocally affect the archetypal constellation (Newton, 1975; Papadopoulos, 1989, 2011; Saayman, Faber & Saayman, 1988, pp.258–259; Knox, 2004). Hence, in clinical settings, to work with individual patients or couples, the collective, cultural and social context should not be ignored, while the knowledge gleaned from clinical work may facilitate our understanding of the psyche of the larger group in the current situation and inspire our future work.

As noted at the beginning of this chapter, the two cases here were not at all successful. The issues presented were not just personal issues but had been deep rooted in their families under certain cultural and social contexts. Papadopoulos (1989) noted that, according to Jung, within families, there are 'remarkable similarities between the patterns of responses among certain subgroupings' (p.96). In both Ting's and Peng's families, the children shared similar archetypal images of male and female as their parents and were related with the contrasexual other, just as their same sex parents were. Their respective marital difficulties were typical of young couples seeking therapy. In their families, from parents to children, recognising intersubjectivity and treating the spouse as an equal subject with their own agency have been lacking for generations.

However, we can tell the difference between the older generations and the younger ones. Both Ting and Peng realised that their patterns were problematic, that they should not take these issues for granted and that they could seek help and look for possible solutions. After we had finished our work, Ting found a local therapist to work with her, while Peng continues to work with my male colleague at the time of writing this book. Such self-awareness and effort are rarely observed among older generations.

On the other hand, as the only son in a two-child family, Peng's close bond with his mother is typical and prevalent of the relationship between mother and son in China for many years. However, the closeness and conflicts between a daughter and her parents, her mother in particular, as was the case with Ting, only began to be prevalent in recent years. This can be seen as the product of the one-child policy which has resulted in increasingly smaller family sizes. Dien (1992) says that in traditional Chinese families, the birth of a daughter has been more likely to be regarded as a disappointment to the mother because a daughter cannot improve the mother's status in her husband's family as a son can. However, due to their shared common destiny, Chinese daughters and mothers have been more likely to establish an alliance and have mutually supported each other. Therefore, the mother-daughter relationship in China is not as complex as in the West where such relationships can be quite stormy as the daughter strives to individuate (pp.114–116). It has not been shown that in such families, the mother and daughter have a better relationship; it is simply that mothers have valued their daughters less than their sons and their passion has been totally occupied by their sons. The diminished tension might, therefore, be due to less affection.

As an only child, Ting's relationship with her mother resembled that of a Western mother-daughter. In a certain way, I would say that this is progress. As a child raised among several children, Ting's mother never had the opportunity to seriously examine her pain and treated her lack of self-agency as normal. She told Ting, 'As women, we are born to suffer and should be blamed if we cannot maintain our family'. However, even if Ting identified greatly with her mother, as the only child she received the full attention and investment of her parents, Ting could feel the inner call to be herself and decided to struggle for her self-development. Despite sharing the same issues as her parents, it is possible for her to find a solution.

Hence, exploration of clinical solutions needs to start with an understanding of the cultural and social backgrounds of such patients and then to challenge the rigidity and stereotypes in the relatedness among generations. To help patients shed the role of Giant Babies who are dependent on both their literal and symbolic parents and to establish a sense of agency, psychotherapy's task in improving the ways in which individuals may relate to one another may be to foster intersubjectivity and mutual recognition. This is also the major theme of *The Peony Pavilion* – an opera demonstrating a possible way to establish and maintain an intimate relationship that includes self-realisation. The sense of agency, intersubjectivity and mutual recognition are all based on the differentiation between individuals. Marriages and families are both the stage and the fruit of individual psyches. How to become an individual, a human, more than a man or a woman in any relationship, is the major theme to grapple with in related difficulties.

Chapter 8

Some concluding reflections

Marriage as a psychological relationship in China

In 2016, the Chinese government replaced the one-child policy with a new two-children policy, and stated that in the near future, policies that set limits on reproduction would be abolished entirely. A year later, the Chinese government began to place an emphasis on mental health, abolished the old examination to become a psychotherapist, which was overseen by the Ministry of Labour and Social Security, and suspended the qualification programme for psychotherapists to await more professional regulation for such training. In terms of these two changes, the first has massive repercussions for society at large, giving young parents more choice in relation to their family planning, while the second indicates that, in the eyes of the Chinese government, psychotherapy is a profession rather than a specific technology, and they therefore prefer to offer more guarantees to people seeking psychotherapy due to the higher requirements of the training and qualification programme.

These two changes could be viewed as indicating progress in China. Nonetheless, the new policy has not been welcomed by young Chinese women as anticipated, and the birth ratio of girls and boys amongst second-born child is even more skewed in favour of males than amongst first-born children. According to the Sixth National Population Census of the People's Republic of China (2010) in Anhui province, among first-born children, the ratio of female to male babies is 100:108.78 in urban areas, while the same ratio among second-born children is 100:155.37 in urban areas, rising to 100:171.38 in rural areas. In 2016, the official website xinhua.net reported that since the implementation of the two-children policy, secret foetus gender testing has been prevalent, despite its illegality. Amongst ordinary Chinese families, the preferable family structure comprises one boy and one girl; however, the birth ratio demonstrates that, among second-born children, sex-selective abortion mainly targets girls. It is rare for male foetuses to be aborted based solely on gender. Hence, it may be imagined that in future generations, it will become even more difficult for men of marriageable age to find spouses, and marriage issues will increase as a result.

Regarding the new standard for training and qualification in psychotherapy, this has also been met with ambivalence. On the one hand, the increased government attention on this field means increased financial investment and more convenient procedures for handling relevant issues, which in turn brings more security to professionals. On the other hand, in the area of depth psychology, there is concern as to whether the typical terms and ideas, such as 'the unconscious', 'free association', 'individuation', etc., can fit within the remit of government ideology, not to mention the fact that healthy relationships, which are based on separation between children and parents, might challenge the traditional value of 'filial piety' which has once more been emphasised by the government. The question thus arises: under government supervision, will therapeutic methods oriented in depth psychology, which are rooted in Western culture, develop in accordance with their original pattern, or will government intervention force them to develop in a way that is more 'suitable'?

Currently in China, there is a fever of psychotherapy, and psychoanalysis in particular. In the coming years, will Freud's theory, like that of his Germany fellow Marx, be applied in a 'Chinese characteristic' way? And If this does occur, will such psychotherapy, which is either explicitly or implicitly interfered with by the government, really help those who seek it out as it does in the West and what results will accrue for clinical work in China? The answer remains, as yet, unclear.

The Chinese notion of 'integration'

As discussed in Chapter Two, China has been good at localising ideas from other cultures. In previous years, the concept of integration has been welcomed in the realm of psychotherapy. In 2017, I attended the fifth Chinese psychoanalytic congress in Wuhan, a city in the middle of China, for which more than 800 people were registered. The keynote speeches included studies from the Freudian, Kleinian, Jungian, Lacanian, and Winnicottian schools, amongst others. The techniques discussed at the congress covered infant observation, sandplay therapy, dream interpretation, family therapy and hypnosis; in short, almost every topic considered relevant to depth psychology. Most of the psychotherapists attending the congress followed a psychodynamic or psychoanalytic orientation, with most purporting to be integrated psychoanalytic therapists, which means that they learn and apply all techniques and theories known to them, regardless of the differences or even conflicts between them. In terms of 'integration', they might also profess to be interested in Buddhism, Taoism or Confucianism, while Chinese medicine was mentioned several times. The attendees were applying these relevant ideas to their psychoanalytic work. The most popular themes at the congress were how to understand these Western-rooted psychological ideas from a Chinese cultural perspective. The idea of 'localisation of psychotherapy' means that all ideas in Western psychotherapy have a counterpart in Chinese culture; therefore, the ideas and technologies of Chinese culture can be applied directly to clinical work without the need for adaptation. In discussing 'localisation' and integration, emphasis was placed on the similarities among different theories and how they can work together, while differences among them were ignored, conflicts denied, and disagreements set aside.

A similar attitude to 'integration' can be found throughout Chinese daily life, such as the government propaganda of 'establishing a harmonious society' and its suggested panacea for marital difficulties – adapting to and tolerating each other. Here, the definition of 'integration' is similar to that in the Longman Dictionary of Contemporary English:

1   the combining of two or more things so that they work together effectively.
2   when people become part of a group or society and are accepted by them.
3   the process of getting people of different races to live and work together instead of separately.

The key words in this definition are 'combination' and 'desegregation'. In China, this represents an inclusive attitude, with its underlying ideology of collectivism, which emphasises similarities, cooperation and the sameness within the group while ignoring individual differences and conflicts between individual members. People seek to have a common voice, and if new issues and conflicts emerge, they try their best to assimilate the new issues into the existing structure and to immediately annihilate potentially explicit conflicts.

To illustrate this further, let us examine the attitudes towards female images in China. When they are in high school, girls are required to wear school uniforms which are usually oversized to cover the shape of their young bodies. Schoolgirls generally have one of several basic haircuts, wear no makeup, and are asked to believe that a natural appearance is the ideal form of beauty. In September 2019, a video exploded on the internet, causing hot debate: it showed the principal of a high school in Guizhou province holding a piece of cloth and a bucket of water at the school gate, and washing the makeup off girls who were standing in a queue. By this extreme means, he sought to ensure that these young girls would obey the no makeup rule in the school.

Later, however, when they grow up, and in particular when they reach marriageable age, women are told that there is another standard of beauty, which is demonstrated in the pictures of Fan bing bing, a Chinese star: big eyes, wide eye-lids, small faces, a straight nose and pointed chin – these comprise the standard attributes deemed desirable for young women. (A Chinese star, Fan Bingbing, who is considered one of the most beautiful women in China, has been the model for plastic surgery among many

Chinese girls. My patient Ting also had two plastic surgeries in an attempt to resemble her. This has been the typical persona of Chinese women in recent years). However, these features are influenced by the Western aesthetic and are not natural for Chinese people, not to mention that they demonstrate the opposite standard to that promulgated at school. However, both standards of beauty express the same idea: there are certain ideal criteria that everybody should attempt to fit within.

More importantly, young people are expected to marry before age 30, but preferably before age 28 so that they can have a baby before 30; this is believed to be good for the baby. Once married, they should have a baby immediately and thereafter devote themselves to child rearing. If there is severe disagreement between the couple, they should remain together even if they do not talk for weeks on end. Filing for divorce is usually considered a bad choice, particularly for women. If a woman does divorce, she should find a new husband as soon as possible, although she is automatically devalued in the marriage market and therefore her new husband will often be a man who is 'below' her first husband. Beebe, an experienced analyst who has worked with many Chinese patients, told me of his shock when he realised the obsession with marriage among Chinese people and the cultural tendency to force young women into the mother role in a 'suitable' marriage (2017, personal communication). This could be called an archetypal expectation of Chinese marriage[1]– finding someone who is 'suitable' and with whom one remains together permanently and engages in the task of reproduction as soon as possible. This is not solely a woman's task, however; Chinese men are also expected to fit within a given pattern. Schoolboys wear the same over-sized school uniforms as their female counterparts. As they mature, they are expected to be 'Beckhams' (a reference to the English footballer and fashion icon, David Beckham) – tall, high earning, with a high social status, and preferably spending time with their wives and children. The female and male images have certainly been affected by Westernisation but marriage between Chinese women and men is nevertheless very traditional, with specific Chinese characteristics. In other words, as has occurred in the therapeutic world, in Chinese daily life, Westernisation might comprise a surface-level cosmetic persona. Chinese people adopt what they have learned from the West in a conscious and superficial way, but the deep-rooted Chinese cultural principles on ethical ideas and behavioural patterns have always dominated in our society, both consciously and unconsciously.

However, as times goes by, with more and deeper interaction with the rest of world, such cosmetic Westernisation has gradually changed. In recent years, the divorce rate has soared amongst the younger generations and an increasing number of young couples are seeking help from psychotherapy. This does not mean that young Chinese people have more marriage issues than their parents. It indicates, rather, that they realise that 'integration' will bring many painful and intolerable issues to their lives. This notion of 'integration' can be observed in the Chinese persona – 'a mask of the collective psyche, a mask that feigns individuality, making others and oneself believe that one is individual, whereas one is simply acting a role through which the collective psyche speaks' (Jung, CW7, para. 245). Individual will is sacrificed to the cultural expectation of marriage and how a marriage should work. The older generations cannot see any other option or way of being 'married', i.e. being independent yet still together, role reversals, etc. However, the younger generations do not want to yield to such sacrifice and attempt to find their individual positions within marriage and family. Here, the idea of 'integrity' has emerged in working with them.

The psychological notion of integrity

Integrity is an idea that is less common in China nowadays. From a philosophical perspective, Calhoune (2015) says that, as a personal virtue, integrity means, 'for the sake of my autonomy, my character, my agency that I stand by my best judgment'; acting with integrity is 'intimately tied to protecting the boundaries of the self', while 'loss of integrity signals loss of some important dimension of selfhood' (pp.145–146). As Colhoun describes, integrity focuses firstly on the self, stands for individual differences and one's best judgements, and values personal autonomy and boundaries. It is the basis of self-awareness, which allows a person to know who he/she is and what he/she wants to do and to be responsible for that, thus distinguishing self from others.

On the other hand, Calhoun continues, 'integrity is ... not just a matter of the individual's proper relation to herself but is a matter of her proper relation to common projects and to the fellows with whom she engages in those common projects' (ibid., pp.148–149). In terms of relationship, integrity emphasises the proper relationship to the self and to others and this is exactly what the two patients discussed in my case study lacked in their relationships. These cases are representative of the many young people who meet with relationship difficulties: without proper relationships to themselves or to their partners, they are full of disappointment with their spouses, complain about their lack of autonomy and free choice, and refuse to take responsibility and even blame their parents for their failure, which is sometimes, but not always, warranted.

Calhoun describes integrity as referring to a proper relation to the self and others from an ethical perspective. But what does 'a proper relation' mean? Regarding this question, the psychological notion of integrity can provide more detail. As Beebe (1992) notes, '[i]ntegrity involves our dealings with others, and ambition to win their respect is part of its archetypal constellation; integrity is a self-consistency that is effective interpersonally' (p.10). It demonstrates that there are two dimensions of relation in integrity: one is self-consistency, which is the elementary dimension; the other is having relations with others and earning their respect. Self-consistency is highly relevant to the ability to choose freely and take responsibility for that choice, not to be easily affected by others and not to be too flexible, always seeking to fit in within a group. In a word, being loyal to the self and protecting its boundaries are the basis of receiving respect from others. This does not mean, however, that integrity implies a self-defensive attitude towards others. In examining Jane Austen's definition of integrity from a feminine perspective, which suggested that integrity comprised 'amiability', 'constancy' and 'self-knowledge', Beebe concluded that 'integrity is part of the genuine interest in others ... and of continuity of identity' (ibid., p.70). Integrity implies the development of friendly and authentic relationships to others based on self-knowledge and self-consistency.

However, when we turn to the relationship between the individual and the group, integrity demonstrates a certain antagonism to collectivism. Even Calhoune (2015) highlights that integrity has social traits, but the community members to whom she refers comprise a group of 'deliberators who share the goal of determining what is worth doing' (p.151). Such a group is more likely to be selected by the individuals who join the group of their own free will and fit within its subjective criteria, rather than comprising a group determined by objective or external factors, such as blood, gender, geography, or social status. In a word, it is a group composed of independent individuals. Beebe (1992) expresses the clash between integrity and the collective in a more explicit way: 'we have to take the notion of integrity out of the realm of collective counsel, which supports a false self of superego expectation' (p.100). Hence, integrity should remain separate from collective influence; otherwise, individuals will be trapped in a rigid and inauthentic moral model and one's ability to face oneself honestly might be harmed by the wish to fulfil collective expectations.

How individual integrity can be eroded by collective power is revealed in Rangell's study of the Watergate scandal. Rangell (1980) thought that Nixon and his cabinet's attempt to lie to the public and cover up the truth of their decision-making demonstrated that the strength of the masses can force individuals to compromise their integrity. Such strength occurs not only in major events but also in daily life. Rangell suggested that it is essential for individuals to have the courage to maintain their integrity if they are to oppose collective pressure (pp.11–12). Here, the collective opposes integrity. The individual must make a great effort to maintain his/her integrity under collective pressure and this is no mean feat. Calhoune (2015) depicted in vivid detail how 'our own vulnerability to others' leads us to compromise our integrity and noted that 'people without integrity ... trade their own views too readily for the views of others who are more authoritative, more in step with public opinion, less demanding of themselves' (pp.142–144). Such scenarios are common in a society which always places the group above individuals, sometimes leading to disasters. In another article, Rangell noted that the consequence of compromising one's integrity is the 'forestages on the path to psychopathy or impulsive disorder' and may 'result in neuroses' (1974, p.7). Under such circumstances, an individual's judgement may be clouded by the decision of the group and his/her behaviour may become psychopathological in a bid to correspond with collective action. This is well illustrated in the insane pictures of mass violence against 'suspected reactionaries' during China's Cultural Revolution and of the huge number of coerced abortions under China's one-child policy. (Many non-fiction novels, such as *The Archives of the Red Guard*, by Wu Guo, *Ten Years of A Hundred People*, by Feng Jicai, etc., describe how people accused of being 'counter-revolutionaries' without sound evidence, were beaten, tortured and humiliated by those around them; in the Chinese countryside during the one-child policy, slogans could be seen expressing very similar threats, such as, 'if you choose not to abort an extra baby, we – the government – will destroy your house and take away your cattle'.) On the other hand, there are many stories of people with integrity who, in extreme circumstances, fought against the atrocity of the masses to tell the truth and protect victims.

In sum, integrity implies an exclusive attitude that stands for autonomy and separation, values consistency over flexibility, encourages people to deal honestly with difficulties, and places individual wills over collective requirements. Only when they have integrity can people be independent individuals, and only then can they establish decent relationships with other independent individuals.

Integrity in marriage

For many years, due to the typical Chinese marital expectation, integration – adjusting oneself to a long-term relationship which secures the happiness of the natal families – has been overemphasised, while integrity – being loyal to individual wills and choices – has been lacking. Hence, marriage lies beyond the unity between the two partners and carries with it many collective decisions of the two extended families and the burden of social expectations, including the following: people should marry at approximately the same age; reproduction and child-rearing are the main tasks of marriage; and the young couple's parents should be highly involved in both their daily affairs and major decisions, particularly for only children. There is a well-known joke that the wedding bed of a couple comprising two partners from one-child families must be large enough for six people. In my clinical work, on one occasion, an only-daughter came to me to seek help for her depression caused by her marriage. When she arrived, six other people squeezed into my office with her: her husband, her parents, her parents-in-law, and her one-year-old son who was held in her mother's arms. After speaking to her, I realised that her marriage difficulties were due very simply to the fact that there were too many people in her marriage, which should have been composed solely of herself and her husband.

Hence, how to relate with the other and other members in the extended family is essential for our clinical work on marriage issues. Regarding the different modes of relationship in marriage, Colman (2014) distinguishes between 'non-relating' and 'anti-relating'. The former refers to the need for 'space and solitude', which is 'an inherent – and essential – aspect of all relationships'; the latter comprises 'the intrusiveness of the other – when others intrude their difference and their own needs and demands into the private space of the self' (p.23). In a typical Chinese marriage and family, the unity and harmony of family members, which need to be demonstrated explicitly, are so important that private space and other possibilities of the relationships are excluded. Hence, the relatedness that occurs in a traditional Chinese family is, in fact, the anti-relating described by Colman, in which individual members are forced 'to be what is wanted to be under the control' of the collective will, while non-relating, or relating to others within certain limits, maintaining one's own autonomy and remaining beyond intrusion and invasion (ibid.), which is highly relevant to integral attitudes, is new to Chinese marriage.

In line with this development of a possible space of non-relating in marriage, two further archetypal patterns could prove useful complementary approaches. Schmidt (1980) suggested that the old parental model, which projects parental images onto the spouse as the basis of marriage, is not suitable on its own for modern relationships. A viable alternative could be the 'sister-brother' pattern in which the two spouses are equals. In this model, 'the brother and sister archetype would serve as a meeting place for the man and woman', covering 'fighting, testing, challenging and sexuality' between each other (p.18). In China, due to the one-child policy, many young people lack direct experience of having siblings, but they do have cousins, other children in the neighbourhood, and their peers at school, who have competed with them for appraisal from adults and their teachers' attention. Of course, the tension in such competition cannot compare with the tension in competition for parents' love, but it is nevertheless an opportunity for boys and girls to build relationships together and recognise each other as equal and real.

Another option in marriage relationships is to adopt the friendship pattern. As Johnson (1983) highlights, 'friendship ... within marriage, between husband and wife' which does not judge 'each other's difficult points and weaknesses and offers help, affirmation and support to each other, is necessary for human love and for a long-term relationship. The friendship pattern without romantic drama and intensity also takes away egocentric and unrealistic fantasy in marriage' (p.197). Friendship may be a more familiar experience for a child from a one-child family and could help couples to rid themselves of the ego-centred role cultivated by their parents. This would allow them to learn how to share, thus facilitating their ability to get along with their spouses.

Compared with the parental model, both the 'brother and sister pattern' and 'friendship pattern' are established through equal relationships between peers. One does not have to yield to the authority of the other, thus creating space between the two partners and excluding parents from the children's marriage. This has the potential to bring integrity into the marriage. However, each of these patterns has its own flaws, which is why I stated that while they may be useful as complementary approaches, they cannot serve for marriage alone. In the brother-sister pattern, as Schmidt conceded, the two spouses 'are permanently connected with each other; one does not divorce one's siblings' (1980, p.18). Such a pattern does not allow for the breaking up or failure of the marriage. In the friendship pattern, meanwhile, Johnson overemphasised the positive aspects of friendship, such as being nice to each other, acceptance of non-perfection, and offers of affirmation and support, while neglecting the necessary tension between couples and ignoring the difficult, negative aspects of marriage, such as disagreements, conflicts and fights.

However, in any real relationship, negative feelings are undeniable and failure is sometimes unavoidable. As Beebe (1992) says, 'failures in relationship also serve integrity ... Real work on integrity ... includes accepting the shadow and taking the impure parts of the collective human and animal character consciously into oneself ... [This] leads to a more conscious relationship to envy, shame, and anxiety' (p.124). In this view, none of the aspects of shadow in our inner world or our relationships with others are ignored or denied. Instead, they are seen and accepted and even failure in relationship is a viable option. This comprises a very authentic attitude that is open to disagreement. Getting married and remaining in a marriage are no longer of primary importance. Moreover, adapting to and tolerating grievances and complaints cannot fix marital problems and initiating communication without real dialogue cannot serve to connect husbands and wives. With such recognition, our clinical work on marriage would be helpful and practical for couples trapped in marital difficulties. Otherwise, a relationship without integrity can only be constructed on the false-selves of the two spouses and no real intimacy or security can develop between them. Therefore, for couples who meet difficulties in their relationships, a new approach would be to try to integrate their voices less, while demonstrating more integrity. This means, first, listening to one's inner voice, standing by one's best judgement, even if such judgement includes the possibility of breaking up, and taking responsibility for one's own choices. This is the basis for the further negotiation and cooperation which are necessary even in divorce cases.

Marriages as a relationship beyond gender difference

For negotiation and cooperation, recognising difference is the first step for any relationship. Saban (2016) compared Jungian psychology with psychoanalysis and noted, '[t]he single necessary condition for any healthy relationship is a clear awareness of the fundamental difference between the two partners; fusion, and especially unconscious fusion, is always an obstacle to relatedness' (p.345). Such a proposition can also be applied in marriage. The two partners in a marriage should realise and accept the differences between them. This is the basis of their recognition of the independence and subjectivity of each other and the establishment of their authentic relationship. However, the question arises: are such differences due to their biological body, or in other words, are they relevant to the differences between men and women? Further examination of this is required.

Williams (1989) noted that 'marriage itself is based on the archetypal theme of the union of complementary opposites' (p.257). Based on her understanding, the difference between the feminine and masculine – the opposites – and the complementary relationship between them are the two basic elements of marriage. Schmidt (1980) expressed a similar idea in a more explicit way, saying that 'marriage is the problem between a man and woman' and sets 'a stage where the problem between man and woman may be worked out' (p.17). However, while most marriages in the modern world are comprised of a man and a woman, as discussed in Chapter Two, a real man and real woman do not embody femininity and masculinity respectively, and the notions of masculine and feminine vary in different cultural/social settings. Thus, it is very difficult to define conclusively that the different identities of a man and woman, or the opposite stance of the feminine and masculine, are necessary for modern marriage.

It has been traditional to distinguish between the development of girls and boys in psychoanalysis and between the functions of the feminine and masculine. Benjamin (1995) noted that the binary gender oppositions 'play a major role in organizing our experience, that frame reveals many conflicts and provides a background for many other differences' (p.12). This is similar to the first levels of the feminine and masculine as discussed in Chapter Two, as two different elements form to help us understand the complexity of the world in a familiar and simplified way. The terms 'Yin' and 'Yang' also describe this role without the necessity of any gender implication. (In the system of 'Yin' and 'Yang', although 'Yin' is more often related with the feminine and 'Yang' with the masculine, both men and women have 'Yang' and 'Ying' sides within their biological bodies. Hence, these two terms are beyond opposite and binary gender certainty and difference). Benjamin considered that 'the terms of binary opposition men-women is likely to be as constricting as [it is] liberating' for women and suggested 'we may recognize that "Women" is not a unitary identity, and we may continually test the frame of gender' (ibid., p.11). I would add that such a constriction also applies to men and we can also not say that 'Men' is a unitary identity. The stereotype and certain category of the terms 'man' and 'woman' deprive all individuals of their potentials. Samuels asserts that 'gender certainty forms the oppressive heart of much neurosis' (1989, p.85). Based on past experience, it has brought to both men and women more constriction than liberation and made both sexes suffer from the narrow expectation of what a man or a woman should be like. Further, gender certainty can be viewed as a defence against gender confusion and the latter 'comes closer to capturing what contemporary people feel about their gender identity' (Samuels, 2001, p.41).

When we enter the realm of relationship, the tendency to distinguish gender roles within a marriage is prominent. Saayman, Faber and Saayman (1988) interviewed 62 parents, and described how marriage is 'ascribed to the intensely patriarchal orientation of Western Culture' (p.269). Thus, they concluded that the 'couple personified the clash between the impersonal feminine and masculine' and that in the failure of this marriage, the husband's 'instrumental and power aspects of Logos' constrained him from expressing any feminine affect to his wife and offspring, frustrated his wife and caused her to seek revenge by removing her affection from him and instead giving it to their child or another lover (ibid., pp.264–267). Based on these arguments, man and woman, husband and wife, feminine affect and masculine logos are in a split and opposite position, and the marital problem has always been due to the lack of the feminine principle – the principle of relatedness, which is quite essentialist.

However, as discussed in Chapter Six, in China, the principle of relatedness is essential in the Chinese family, while the Western feminine virtues of constancy, amiability, humility, etc., are as valuable for Chinese men as they are for Chinese women. In other words, such virtues do not have gender implications in Chinese culture. Further, as Dien says, 'Chinese society shares the same social structure of women mothering and men dominating in terms of social power', but 'Chinese women are psychologically more independent' than Chinese men (Dien, 1992, p.105). Sun, a historian who studied Chinese immigrants in the US, came to the same conclusion that Chinese women demonstrated more confidence and ego-strength in adapting to the new environment, while their husbands demonstrated a prevalent sense of disorientation and kept asking to return home (2004, pp.341–345). Such characteristics do not fit within the catalogues of the Western feminine, which refers to relatedness, or of the masculine, which refers to separation.

A common modern conflict found among young Chinese couples in my interviews and clinical work is that the husband asks his wife to relate more with his parents and to care for other members within the two extended families, while the wife wants to lead a life that is more separate from the parents and to maintain boundaries between their small nuclear family and the larger extended family. Hence, because the notions of feminine and masculine vary among cultures and societies, the Western 'feminine principle' based on the binary opposition of man and woman is not a universal solution for marital difficulties.

Moreover, even in the West, Samuels has challenged the overemphasis on the 'feminine principle', stating that, 'celebrating the feminine has raised it to the status of an ego-ideal, leading to a simple and pointless reversal of power positions' (1989, p.100). Hence, the emphasis on the difference between the feminine and masculine and the opposite positions of man and woman are based on the patriarchal ideology – situating man and woman in a rigid gender frame and asking them to behave according to certain patterns, thus devaluing behaviour that lies outside of such expectations.

Schmidt (1980) proposes that to apply 'quantitative differences (e.g. more or less "hard", more or less "soft")' to discuss the differences between feminine and masculine is more appropriate than applying 'contrast qualities (e.g. "hardness" for masculine v. "softness" for feminine)'. She also concedes that 'instinctive [sexual] differences have receded from today's young adult life' even though such differences can be observed in small children (pp.23–25). The differences between men and women have become increasingly vague today and, as noted by Samuels, have reached a position of 'fluidity or flexibility, or even androgyny' (2001, p.41). Hence, in modern times, it is difficult to state that modern marriage, as a relationship comprising two adults, demonstrates and resolves the conflicts between men and women. The difference between the two spouses in a marriage is not due to the difference between men and women as specific gender groups; rather, it is due to the differences between individuals. Moreover, the conflicts that occur between a couple are not due to the fact that one carries the feminine principle while the other carries the masculine; rather, they are due to the fact that each is a distinct and separate human being. Thus, it is natural for them to have conflicts and disagreements. In Chapter Seven, neither of the marital difficulties encountered by the two patients were really gender specific. The core of their issues was that they did not know how to be close to another individual while remaining independent individuals themselves. This is the core issue for contemporary Chinese marriage: to be a grown-up and find a balanced position between individual independence and interdependence with surrounding family members.

Further, as Guggenbuhl-Craig (1977) notes, '[m]arriage involves not only a man and a woman who happily love each other and raise offspring together, but rather two people who are trying to individuate, to find their "soul's salvation"' (p.124). This points to another direction: as a psychological relationship between two human beings, marriage not only requires individual independence and integrity but also serves and fosters individuation and integrity.

The way in which love and relationship can give people the courage and determination to fight against totalitarianism is not a new theme in literature or film. In George Orwell's *1984*, after the lead character, Winston, fell in love with Julia, he began to recall what had really occurred in the past, realised the manipulation of the Party and found his own recognition. In their love relationship, both were facilitated to have a sense of awareness, approached the truth and made attempts to fight against Big Brother. Their love stimulated their awakening integrity and fostered their attempts to become individuals – 'the real carrier of life' – and not 'infected by the leprosy of collective thinking and … an inmate of that insalubrious stud-farm called the totalitarian State' (Jung, CW 14, para.194). However, when their integrity was damaged by torture, their love disappeared, and they became totally subordinated to Big Brother and lost their sense of self.

The Chinese film, *Hibiscus Town*, which is based on historical reality, shares a similar theme but with a more positive ending. The two lead characters, Hu Yuyin and Qin Shutian, were unfairly accused of being counterrevolutionaries and enemies of the people during the Cultural Revolution. In a difficult and persecutory situation, moved by the kindness of Shutian, Yuyin fell in love with him and they made an attempt to get married despite the government's rejection of their marriage application. In this uncertain and difficult situation, they insisted on marrying by their own means and had a simple ceremony even though the people around them claimed that they did not deserve it. This determination to reveal their relationship rather than having a secret affair that would avoid trouble demonstrates their integrity, and also serves as a form of protest against the collective insanity. With such integrity and determination, both held onto hope and had the resilience to get through the most difficult period when they were forced to separate and were finally reunited.

1984 is a dystopian novel that portrays a pessimistic view of human nature, while *Hibiscus Town* attempts to reflect on and heal the psychological trauma of recent Chinese history. Both share the mutual influence of attempts at integrity and love relationships. Marriage, which should be the most officially recognised love relationship and, beyond that, a private matter, inevitably involves many complicated interactions between the two spouses, between the members of their natal families, between each spouse and his/her family-in-law, and even between the individual wills and collective expectations and requirements. Hence, marriage affords us the best opportunity for maturity but also has great potential to demonstrate the deficiencies and limitations of our characters. As Beebe (1999) notes, in analytical relationships, integrity embraces the limitations of the patient's character and contains its deficiencies 'in the midst of ambitions for [the patient's] psychological growth' (p.624). Marriage, as a psychological relationship, which also follows the model of 'container and the contained', albeit in a more flexible way (Jung, CW 17), could do the same.

A very Chinese dilemma?

In China, a very typical modern dilemma is how to achieve a balance between integration and integrity. Although the respective meanings of 'integration' and 'integrity' differ, and these differences lie beyond the scope of this book, their linguistic resources are similar and they share a common epistemological root. This commonality serves the discussion of the ethical notion of each to be provided in the following section.

As noted, there has been a long tradition of focusing on integration – the ideology of inclusive collectivism – and this has brought benefits to Chinese people. In the clinical world, therapists in contemporary China have many opportunities to learn techniques from different schools. Unlike their Western colleagues, few set limits on their study from the outset; new therapists find that they can learn techniques from different orientations at the same time, and even if they later identify themselves with one or more schools, they still have opportunities to dialogue with other schools and rarely develop hostile attitudes towards a certain school. These open attitudes by candidates during their training programmes bring a lively energy and the tendency to integrate every school fosters their curiosity. They may lack the spirit of criticism, but they also lack prejudice and bias, and do not reject from the outset the understanding or accepting of different perspectives within psychotherapy. This open attitude nurtures their future potential.

To return to the issue of marriage and family, it must also be noted that the close bonds within natal families are not unilaterally negative. The strong support that parents provide to young couples may constrain the internalised space within the family but gives young people more space in their lives outside of the family. In China, it is quite usual for parents to help the young couple with payments for their apartment and car, or at least to help them with the down payment. It is also the norm for parents to take care of grandchildren, particularly only children. With such support, young couples have less financial stress and less burden on rearing children, and this gives them more security as new parents. They also have more opportunities for career development, and more time for their social lives. Most young couples do not have to give up their careers because of the birth of a new baby; if they wish, they can rely on their parents to take care of the baby during the daytime, not to mention cooking, doing laundry, cleaning, tidying the apartment and other housework. Typical Chinese parents will do whatever they can to help their children and are not merely 'guests' in their children's homes. This brings particular benefits for their children, in making life physically easier for them. It was for this reason that Ting and Peng, despite complaining a great deal about their parents, found it difficult to separate from them. In China, a single woman is under a great deal of pressure, but a pregnant woman and the mother of a son will be carefully looked after and may accrue privilege in her husband's home where she can ask for whatever she wants. Chinese women are rarely moved to fight for their individual rights as women in the West do, perhaps due to the fact that when she gives birth to a son, a woman gets the opportunity to take charge of her husband's family, has a stable sense of security on the property and gains respect. Hence, in a certain way, integration brings security and means that the Chinese family constellation is organised in a mutually supportive pattern.

On the other hand, there is a danger of such integrity being misused. As Beebe warned, there is persona integrity – 'the mask for the ambitions to respectability which severs the status quo looks more attractive' and 'such integrity has grown rigid and inauthentic in the course of advancing psychological and moral development' (1992, pp.101–102). Here, integrity, and more precisely 'integrity in depth', does not comprise a rigid demand for morality, nor an adaptive attitude that serves for relationship. Both of these can be seen together in a collective persona of so-called 'integrity' that applies a single moral criterion to everyone and criticises those who are not adaptive to such a model. For example, while independence is essential for integrity, persona integrity overemphasises the financial independence and importance of careers for women, to the extent that women who prefer to be housewives or full-time mothers are looked down upon; or, the simple criterion that a man's mental health necessarily involves him maintaining a distance from his parents and that his affection for his mother renders him an abnormal 'mummy's boy'. Asking people to be independent from their families in this way comprises pseudo independence from a concrete small group, while remaining dependent on an abstract bigger group, or submitting to a consciously or unconsciously held collective belief. During the Cultural Revolution, the Red Guards jumped at the opportunity to challenge, or even beat up, authority figures, such as their parents, teachers, or even some government leaders; in so doing, however, they were being manipulated by higher authorities. These rebellious behaviours of adolescents may have allowed them to be seen within their gangs. Here, another dilemma arises: how can we know that for a woman the struggle to gain more financial independence in her marriage is her own choice rather than that she is forced to do so by the belief that 'all housewives are losers'? For a man, meanwhile, is his love for his mother and his attempts to take care of her an aspect of the goodness of his human nature or is he simply possessed by his mother complex, or is it a cultural obligation?

The concept of 'moral imagination' can help us to answer these questions. Moral imagination covers the attitudes of forgiveness without blame and embraces conflict and pluralism. It comprises a creative moral space, in which dialogues occur without the 'certainty [of] who speak[s] for what' (Samuels, 1989, pp.201–207). It also allows for illogical combination. As Samuels describes, 'What we admire and value in ourselves and others need not follow any logical format: warmth and openness together with careful attention to detail, driving ambition with pervasive self-doubt' (ibid., p.204). Simplification places both integration and integrity in a dangerous position, but with moral imagination, which places our moral choices in an imaginative space, an open and ambivalent space, dialogues between different voices are facilitated. In such spaces, integration does not simply combine everything and integrity is not a single criterion; hence, people can find their individual positions within a collective context. The following vivid picture of the ideal Chinese relationship between young couples and their parents illustrates this space: the best distance between the home of a young couple and the home of their parents is that if freshly boiled soup were delivered from one home to the other by walking, the soup would still be warm upon arrival: not too hot, not too cold, just warm. This beautiful metaphor demonstrates that warmth lies on a spectrum between hotness and coldness. It is a complex and ambivalent temperature that is difficult to define, in which tension, challenges, arguments, debates, conflicts and even clashes first occur to increase the heat and then gradually calm down so that dialogue can continue in a sustainable way.

Moral imagination has to and will be achieved gradually in China in the coming years. In previous years, the traditional belief in integration has been greatly challenged. As discussed in Chapter 2, the first generation of one-child families, as 'the first world youth in the third world' (Fong, 2004, p.154), demonstrate more obvious self-awareness than previous generations and subsequent generations have even more self-awareness because they live in better circumstances. With the development of the economy and the employment of the internet, information is delivered via various channels and people can see different aspects of the world and listen to a variety of voices. The younger generations have opportunities to communicate with people from other countries and regions around the world and have a broader vision with which to facilitate the creative space described above.

When my mother was young, she watched a film about twin sisters who lived separately in North Korea and South Korea. The sister in North Korea, as an ordinary person who was the owner of the state (referring to the communist idea), led a happy life; meanwhile, her sister in South Korea was a slave to the rich and lived a miserable life. Together with her peers, my mother totally believed this story because she had no other channels of information and had to believe everything she was told. Today, however, no young person would believe such a story and Seoul is one of the most popular cities for young Chinese people to go shopping. They have more direct experience of what is happening both inside and outside of China. Hence, the simple combination of exterminating disagreement, repressing conflicts and creating harmony on the surface is becoming increasingly difficult to sustain.

The same phenomenon is apparent in the clinical world. Most of the first generation of therapists completed their training in China. They learned from Western teachers who visited China and whose interests lay in China. By remaining in a Chinese setting and having lecturers whose passion was for Chinese culture, their unavoidable tendency was to focus on the similarities and to assimilate what they had learned with the world they saw around them. Although some trained in Western countries, upon returning they would practise in accordance with their preferences in an adaptive way, particularly if they received funding from the government. However, young therapists today have many more opportunities to study and train abroad with private funds and with local lecturers and trainers who may not have a particular passion for China. This increases their awareness around the differences between each school and rids them of the inclination toward 'localisation', because they are in a location outside of China, both physically and psychologically.

Under such circumstances, when young generations speak of 'integration', they have more potential to discover a pattern with which to integrate what they have learned with 'integrity', creating a space to balance separation and combination with an attitude of first admitting the difference. This will lead to the individuation process – 'open conflict and open collaboration at once' (Jung, CW9, para. 522–523).

The most popular history book in contemporary China, *Stories about the Ming Dynasty*, which was first published on the internet in 2006 and completed in 2009, was written by an author who was born in 1979. It has now sold more than five million copies and is the best-selling history book since Chinese open reform. As such, it has had a phenomenal influence on Chinese readers. Instead of relating the termination of the Ming Dynasty, the stories of the emperor and national heroes, the young author concludes the book with the story of a traveller, Xu Xiake. In this story, Xu does not consider it important to be filial to his parents, to get married, to have offspring, to be rich and famous, or to be recognised by the government – all of those things that are considered valuable in Chinese culture. Instead, Xu spends most of his time travelling around China taking notes because that is where his passion lies and thus he prefers to devote his life to this. This is his personal choice. The author says that after he had finished writing stories about major political events, about emperors, ministers and heroes, he finished his book by telling people: the most important thing for a human being is to spend your life in your favourite way. In Chinese culture, this is a rebellious statement and calls upon the young Chinese psyche. Individuation often entails a battle with one's culture. For young Chinese people who attempt to find their individual position within a context dominated for thousands of years by collectivism, and trapped by the dilemma between integration and integrity, balance is sometimes difficult to achieve. That being the case, choosing integrity over integration is another solution.

'[I]ndividuation (becoming who you authentically are) … is very different from mental health or social adaption and may, for some individuals, involve a non- or even anti-relational passage through life' (Samuels, 2017).

Is this only a Chinese dilemma?

While writing this book and researching the issue of coerced abortion among Chinese women, I noticed that women in other countries, such as the US, Ireland and Brazil, were also fighting for the right to abortion. Basic individual rights, even the right to own and take charge of one's own body, has not been fully achieved around the world. Collective forces are difficult to bend.

In the past years, the world outside of China has also undergone many changes: the Trump presidency, Brexit and the emergence of the new Tsar in Russia. Suddenly, nationalism seems to have become prevalent in every corner of the world. Upon studying the madness that has occurred throughout history, Zoja (2014) came to the following conclusion: '[T]he psychological space occupied by collective paranoia is the same one in which nationalism resides' (p.345). Nowadays, the fever pitch of nationalism has spread dramatically: the overemphasis on the term 'we' and the suspicion and hostility toward the 'not we' form the basis of a collective narcissism that threatens to poison individual independence and harm integrity. There is great danger that extreme forms of collectivism are being fostered – a totalitarianism in which there will be no space for integrity.

That being the case, a major challenge for China and for the whole world, in the coming years,

> will be that of maintaining, amid the indifference of the masses and anaesthesia of consumerism, a capacity for indignation. This should have two directions: an impulse towards rectifying wrongs committed by others, but at the same time shame for our own transgressions. Ultimately, the mobilization of credible moral feelings arises in the solitude of the individual conscience; and it mistrusts crusades aimed at the masses, propagated by media multipliers.
>
> (ibid., p.327)

Note

1 Here, I prefer to use the term 'archetypal expectation' rather than 'cultural practice'. As mentioned in Chapter 7, I adopt the post-Jungian notion of the 'archetype', in which archetypes comprise intrapsychic structures and behavioural and relational patterns modified by culture.

References

Akhtar, S. (1995). 'A third individuation: Immigration, identity, and the psychoanalytic process'. *Journal of the American Psychoanalytic Association*, 43: 1051–1084.

Amman, R. (2004). 'On resonance', in E. P. Zoja (ed.), *Sandplay Therapy: Treatment of Psychopathologies* (pp.245–267). Einsiedeln, Switzerland: Daimon Verlag.

Austin, S. (2005). *Women's Aggressive Fantasies: A Post Jungian Exploration of Self-Hatred, Love and Agency*. London and New York: Routledge.

Barrett, T. (2005). 'History', in D. S. Lopez Jr (ed.), *Critical Terms for the Study of Buddhism* (pp.139–157). Chicago, IL: The University of Chicago Press.

Beebe, J. (1985). 'The father's anima', in A. Samuels (ed.), *The Father: Contemporary Jungian Perspectives* (pp.95–111). London: Free Association Books.

―――――. (1989). 'Editor's introduction', in J. Beebe (ed.), *Carl Gustav Jung: Aspect of the Masculine*, trans., R. F. C. Hull (pp.viiii–xxii). London: Routledge.

―――――. (1992). *Integrity in Depth*. College Station: Texas A & M University Press.

―――――. (1999). 'Integrity in the analytic relationship'. *Psychoanalytical Review*, 86: 607–625.

―――――. (2008). 'Individuation in the light of Chinese philosophy'. *Psychological Perspectives*, 61: 70–86.

―――――. (2011). 'Archetypal aspects of masculine and adaption', in C. Blazina & D. S. Sher-Miller (eds.), *An International Psychology of Men: Theoretical Advances, Case Studies, and Clinical Innovations* (pp.289–314). London: Routledge.

―――――. (2015). 'Returning to China', in C. Crowther. & J. Wiener (eds.), *From Tradition to Innovation: Jungian Analyst in Different Cultural* Settings (pp.255–271). New Orleans, LA: Spring Journal Books.

Beijing News Weekly Review. (2015). 'The history of sex after 1949'. https://mp.weixin. qq.com/s?__biz=MjM5NTUxOTc4Mw==&mid=400467868&idx=1&sn=78c1 c780299e461251b00fe0a2fd4d55&scene=2&srcid=1110VbjUgm3RtPTlmlNhwSnk# wechat_redirect

Benjamin, J. (1995). *Like Subjects, Love Objects: Essays on Recognition and Sexual Difference*. New Haven, CT and London: Yale University Press.

Berger, J. (1972). *Ways of Seeing*. London: British Broadcasting Corporation and Penguin Books.

Bhugra, D., & Bhui, K. (2002). 'Is the Oedipal complex universal? Problems for sexual and relationships psychotherapy across cultures'. *Sexual and Relationship Therapy*, 17(1): 69–86.

Blowers, G. (1993). 'Freud's China connection'. *Journal of Multilingual and Multicultural Development*, 14(4): 263–273.

———. (2000). 'The prospect for a Jungian psychology in China'. *Journal of Analytical Psychology*, 45: 295–306.

———. (2015). 'Jung and Chinese culture', in M. E. Mattson (ed.), *Jung in the Academy and Beyond*. New Orleans, LA: Spring Journal, Inc.

Blowers, G., & Wang, X. (2014). 'Gone with the West wind: The emergency and disappearance of psychotherapeutic culture in China (1938–68)', in H. Chiang (ed.), *Psychiatry and Chinese History* (pp.143–160). London: Routledge.

Blue Book of Youth: The Development Report on Chinese Youth in the New Century (2012). China Youth Research Centre.

Bly, R. (1990/2001). *Iron John: A Book about Men*. Thompson, CT: Rider (2001).

Bowlby, J. (1973). *Attachment and Loss: Volume II: Separation, Anxiety and Anger*, The International Psycho-Analytical Library, 95: 1–429. London: The Hogarth Press and the Institute of Psychoanalysis.

Boyang. (2010). *The Death of Chinese Queens*. Beijing: People's Literature Publishing House.

Bradshaw, W. (1978). 'Training psychiatrists for working with blacks in basic residency programs'. *The American Journal of Psychiatry*, 135: 1520–1524.

Braun, V., & Clarke, V. (2006). 'Using thematic analysis in psychology'. *Qualitative Research in Psychology*, 3(2): 77–101. ISSN 1478-0887.

Britton, R. (1989). 'The missing link: Parental sexuality in the Oedipus complex', in R. Britton, M. Feldman, & E. O'Shaughnessy (eds.), *The Oedipus Complex Today: Clinical Implications* (pp.11–82). London: Karnac Books Ltd.

Brook, T. (1993). *Praying for Power: Buddhism and Formation of Gentry Society in Late-Ming China*. Cambriage, MA: Harvard University Asia Center.

Brownell, S., & Wasserstrom, J. N. (2002). 'Introduction: Theorizing femininities and masculinities', in S. Brownell, & J. N. Wasserstrom (eds.), *Chinese Femininities/ Chinese Masculinities: A Reader* (pp.1–42). Berkeley, LA and Oxford: University of California Press.

Buss, D. (2015). *Evolutionary Psychology: The New Science of the Mind*. London and New York: Routledge.

Cai, C., & Shen, H. (2010). '"Garden of the Heart-Soul" in the earthquake area of China'. *Jung Journal: Cultural and Psyche*, 4(2): 5–15.

Cai, J. (2009). 'The butterfly lovers: Psychodynamic reflections on the ancient Chinese love story "Liang-Zhu"', in S. Akhtar (ed.), *Freud and the Far East: Psychoanalytic Perspectives on the People and Culture of China, Japan, and Korea* (pp.105–114). Boulder, CO, New York, Toronto and Plymouth, UK: Jason Aronson.

Calhoune, C. (2015). *Moral Aims: Essays on the Importance of Getting It Right and Practicing Morality with Others*. New York: Oxford University Press.

Cambray, J. (2001). 'Enactments and amplification'. *Journal of Analytical Psychology*, 46(2): 275–303.

———. (2005). 'The place of the 17th century in Jung's encounter with China'. *Journal of Analytical Psychology*, 50: 195–207.

Chaffee, J. W. (1991). 'The marriage of sung imperial clanswomen', in R. S. Watson, & P. B. Ebrey (eds.), *Marriage and Inequality in Chinese Society* (pp.133–169). Berkeley, LA and Oxford: University of California Press.

Chen, F., & Li, T. (2007). 'Martial enqing: An examination of its relationship to spousal contributions, sacrifices, and family stress in Chinese marriages'. *Journal of Social Psychology*, 147: 393–412.

Chen, G. Y. (1936/1966). *History of Chinese Marriage*. Taibei, China: Taiwan Commercial Press. 1966.

Chen, J., Xie, Z., & Liu, H. (2007). 'Son preference, use of maternal health care, and infant mortality in rural China, 1989–2000'. *Population Studies*, 61(2) (July): 161–183.

Chen, Y. (2007). 'Parent-child relationships in single-child families in China'. *WCPRR*, 2(4) (Oct.): 123–127.

Chen, Y. X., & Ling, W. (2006). 'Parent-children relationships in one-child families'. *Shanghai Education Science*, 12: 57–58.

Clarke, J. (1994/2005). *Jung and Eastern Thought: A Dialogue with the Orient*. London: Routledge. 2005.

————. (1995). 'Introduction', in J. J. Clarke (ed.), *Jung on the East* (pp.1–32). London: Routledge.

Clarke, V., Braun, V., & Hayfield, N. (2015). 'Thematic analysis', in J. A. Smith (ed.), *Qualitative Psychology: A Practical Guide to Research Methods* (pp.222–248). Los Angles, LA, London, Washington, DC, New Delhi and Singapore: Sage.

Clulow, C. (1989). *Marriage Inside Out: Understanding Problems of Intimacy*. London: Pelican.

————. (2001). 'The sense of connection', in C. Clulow (ed.), *Adult Attachment and Couple Therapy: The 'Secure Base' in Practice and Research* (pp.276–284). Hove, UK: Brunner-Routledge.

Colman, W. (1994). 'Love, desire and infatuation'. *Journal of Analytical Psychology*, 39(4): 497–514.

————. (1996). 'Aspects of anima and animus in Oedipal development'. *Journal of Analytica Psychology*, 41(1): 37–57.

————. (2000). 'Tyrannical omnipotence in the archetypal father'. *Journal of Analytical Psychology*, 45(4): 521–539.

————. (2014). 'The intolerable other: The difficulty of becoming a couple'. *Couple and Family Psychoanalysis*, 4(1): 22–41.

————. (2016). *Act and Image: The Emergence of Symbolic Imagination*. New Orleans, LA: Spring Journal Books.

Coward, H. (1996). 'Taoism and Jung: Synchronicity and the self'. *Philosophy East and West*, 46(4) (Oct.): 477–495.

Croll, E. (1978). *Feminism and Socialism in China*. London: Routledge Kegan & Paul.

————. (1981/2010). *The Politics of Marriage in Contemporary China*. Cambridge: Cambridge University Press. 2010.

————. (1983). *Chinese Women since Mao*. London: Zed Books Ltd.

————. (1985). 'Introduction: Fertility norms and family size in China', in E. Croll, D. Davin, & P. Kane (eds.), *China's One-child Family Policy* (pp.1–36). Basingstoke and London: Macmillan.

Crowther, C., & Wiener, J. (2015). 'From tradition to innovation: What have we learned', in C. Crowther, & J. Wiener (eds.), *From Tradition to Innovation: Jungian Analyst in Different Cultural Settings* (pp.273–295). New Orleans, LA: Spring Journal Books.

Cui, W. (2009). 'Women and suicide in rural China'. *Bulletin of the World Health Organization*, 2009–2012.

Cushman, P. (1996). 'More surprises, less certainty: Commentary on Roland's paper'. *Psychoanalytic Dialogues*, 6: 477–488.

de Varela, Y. (2004). 'The splitting function of the dyad versus the containing function of the couple: A case of combined concurrent couple and individual therapy'. *International Journal of Applied Psychoanalytic Studies*, 1: 234–246.

Denis, D. R. (1983). *Love in the Western World*. Princeton, NJ: Princeton University Press.

Dien, D. (1992). 'Gender and individuation: China and the West'. *Psychoanalytic Review*, 79(1): 105–119.

Dixson, B., Dixson, A., Li, B., & Anderson, M. (2007). 'Studies of human physique and sexual attractiveness: Sexual preferences of men and women in China'. *American Journal of Human Biology*, 19(1) (Jan.–Feb.): 88–95.

Douglas, C. (1990). *The Women in the Mirror: Analytical Psychology and the Feminine*. Boston, MA: Sigo Press.

Ebenstein, A. (2008). 'The "missing girls" of China and the unintended consequences of the one child policy'. *The Journal of Human Resouces*, 45(1): 87–115.

Ebrey, P. B. (1991). 'Introduction: Marriage and inequality in Chinese society', in R. S. Watson, & P. B. Ebrey (eds.), *Marriage and Inequality in Chinese Society* (pp.1–24). Berkeley, LA and Oxford: University of California Press.

The Economist. (2014). 'Back from the edge: A dramatic decline in suicides'. pp.6–28.

———. (2015). 'Sex: Dream of the bed chamber'. pp.11–21.

Edlund, L., Li, H., Yi, J., & Zhang, J. (2007). 'Sex ratios and crime: Evidence from China's one-child policy'. *IZA Discussion Papers*, No. 3214.

Epstein, M. (1988). 'Attention in analysis'. *Psychoanalysis and Contemporary Thought*, 11: 171–189.

———. (1990). 'Beyond the oceanic feeling: Psychoanalytic study of Buddhist meditation'. *International Review of Psycho-Analysis*, 17: 159–165.

———. (1995). 'Thoughts without a thinker'. *Psychoanalytic Review*, 82: 391–406.

———. (2013). 'The devil we know'. *Psychoanalytic Perspectives*, 10(2): 285–290.

Estes, C. P. (1992/2008). *Women Who Run with the Wolves: Contacting the Power of the Wild Women*. London: Rider. (2008).

Evans, D. (1985). 'Psychotherapy and black patients: Problems of training, trainees, and trainers'. *Psychotherapy: Theory, Research and Practice*, 22: 457–460.

Evans, H. (2002). 'Past, perfect or imperfect: Changing images of the ideal wife', in S. Brownell, & J. N. Wasserstrom (eds.), *Chinese Femininities/Chinese Masculinities: A Reader* (pp.335–360). Berkeley, CA and Oxford: University of California Press.

Faludi, S. (1991/2006). *Backlash: The Undeclared War Against American Women*. New York: Three Rivers Press. 2006.

Farrer, J. (2014). 'Love, sex, and commitment: Delinking premarital intimacy from marriage in urban China', in D. S. Davis, & S. Friedman (eds.), *Wives, Husbands, and Lovers: Marriage and Sexuality in Hong Kong, Taiwan and Urban China* (pp.62–96). Palo Alto, CA: Stanford University Press.

Feeney, G., Wang, F., Zhou, M., & Xiao, B. (1989). 'Recent fertility dynamics in China: Results from the 1987 one percent population survey'. *Population and Development Review*, 15(2) (June): 297–322.

Feng, W., Cai, Y., & Gu, B. (2012). 'Population, policy, and politics: How will history judge China's one-child policy?'. *Population and Development Reviews*, 38(Supplement): 115–129.

Feng, Y. (1925/2009). *The Chinese Curses. The Frenzy of Psychoanalysis: Freud in China* (pp.115–117). C. Wu (ed.). Nanchang, China: Jiangxi University Press. 2009.

Fishkin, R. E., & Fishkin, L. P. (2014). 'Introducing psychoanalytic therapy into China: The CAPA experience', in D. E. Scharff, & S. Varvin (eds.), *Psychoanalysis in China* (pp.244–255). London: Karnac Books Ltd.

Fong, L. V. (2002). 'China's one-child policy and the empowerment of urban daughters'. *American Anthropologist*, 104(4) New Series (Dec.): 1098–1109.

————. (2004). *Only Hope: Coming of Age Under China's One-Child Policy*. Palo Alto, CA: Stanford University Press.

Fordham, M. (1998). *Freud, Jung and Klein – the Fenceless Field: Essays on Psychoanalysis and Analytical Psychology*. London and New York: Routledge.

Freud, S. (1924). 'The dissolution of the Oedipus complex', in *The Standard Edition of the Complete Psychological Works of Sigmund Freud, volume XIX (1923): The Ego and the Id and Other Works* (pp.171–180). London: Hogarth Press.

————. (1995). *New Introductory Lectures on Psychoanalysis (Complete Psychological Works of Sigmund Freud)* (Standard Edition). New York: W. W. Norton.

Frey-Rohn, L. (1974). *From Freud to Jung: A Comparative Study of the Psychology of the Unconscious (C.G. Foundation Books)*, trans., E. K. Engreen. Boston, MA and Shaftesbury, UK: Shambhala.

Fu, Y. (2016). 'General and gender relationships in the development of one-child generations'. http://mp.weixin.qq.com/s?__biz=MzA4MzA0MTYyMA==&mid=2651065742&idx=1&sn=655e6767e2f9fe18ddf652eb46f66782&scene=1&srcid=0611dX8Vl1E6TLQVc1o5T1g0#rd

Gates, H. (1993). 'Cultural support for birth limitation among urban capital-owning women', in D. Davis, & S. Harrell (eds.), *Chinese Families in the Post-Mao Era* (pp.251–276). Berkeley, LA and London: University of California Press.

Gerlach, A. (2014a). 'Collective castration anxieties: An ethnopsychoanalytic perspective on relations between the sexes in China', in D. E. Scharff, & S. Varvin (eds.), *Psychoanalysis in China* (pp.130–142). London: Karnac Books Ltd.

————. (2014b). 'German psychoanalysts in China and the start of group therapy work', in D. E. Scharff, & S. Varvin (eds.), *Psychoanalysis in China* (pp.256–265). London: Karnac Books Ltd.

Giegerich, W. (2008). *Soul-Violence*. New Orleans, LA: Spring Journal Books.

Gu, M. D. (2009). 'The filial piety complex: Variations on the Oedipus theme in Chinese literature and culture', in S. Akhtar (ed.), *Freud and the Far East: Psychoanalytic Perspectives on the People and Culture of China, Japan, and Korea* (pp.115–136). Boulder, CO, New York, Toronto and Plymouth, UK: Jason Aronson.

Guarton, G. B. (1996). 'Masculinity, femininity and change in psychoanalysis'. *Journal of American Academy of Psychoanalysis*, 24: 691–708.

Guggenbuhl-Craig, A. (1977/1981). *Marriage: Dead or Alive*. Thompson, CT and Dallas, TX: Spring Publications. 1981.

Guo, M. (1921/2009). 'Artistic critique on the story of the West wing and analysis of the author's character' in C. Wu (ed.), *The Frenzy of Psychoanalysis: Freud in China* (pp.115–117). Nanchang, China: Jiangxi University Press. 2009.

Haag, A. (2014). 'Psychoanalytically oriented psychotherapy and the Chinese self', in D. E. Scharff, & S. Varvin (eds.), *Psychoanalysis in China* (pp.44–56). London: Karnac Books Ltd.

Harding, M.E. (1955/1971). *Women Mysteries: The Inner Life of Women Revealed in Religious Myth and Ritual.* Thompson, CT: Rider. 1971.

Hannah, B. (2011). *The Animus: The Spirit of Inner Truth in Women*, Vol. I. Wilmette, IL: Chiron Publications.

Hansen, M. H., & Pang, C. (2014). 'Idealising individual choice: Work, love, and family in the eyes of young, rural Chinese', in D. E. Scharff, & S. Varvin (eds.), *Psychoanalysis in China* (pp.24–43). London: Karnac Books Ltd.

Harding, M. E. (1952). *The Anima And Animus: A Curtain Lecture* (pp.25–43). New Orleans, LA: Spring.

Henderson, J. (1976/2005). *Thresholds of Initiation.* Wilmette, IL: Chiron Publications. 2005.

Hesketh, T., Lu, L., & Zhu, W. X. (2005). 'The effect of China's one-child family policy after 25 years', *The New England Journal of Medicine*, September 15, 1171–1176.

Hillman, J. (1985). *Anima: An Anatomy of a Personified Notion.* Dallas, TX: Spring Publications.

———. (1989/1991). *A Blue Fire.* New York: Harper Perennial. 1991.

———. (1996/1997). *The Soul's Code: In Search of Character and Calling.* New York: Grant Center Publishing. 1997.

Holmes, D. E. (1992). 'Race and transference in psychoanalysis and psychotherapy'. *International Journal of Psycho-Analysis*, 73: 1–11.

Holmgren, J. (1991). 'Imperial marriage in the native Chinese and non-Han State, Han to Ming', in R. S. Watson, & P. B. Ebrey (eds.), *Marriage and Inequality in Chinese Society* (pp.58–96). Berkeley, CA and Oxford: University of California Press.

Hong, S. (1935/2009). 'Sadism and masochism in Chinese literature', in C. Wu (ed.), *The Frenzy of Psychoanalysis: Freud in China* (pp.201–209). Nanchang, China: Jiangxi University Press. 2009.

Honing, E. (2002). 'Maoist mapping of gender: Reassessing the red guards', in S. Brownell, & J. N. Wasserstrom (eds.), *Chinese Femininities/Chinese Masculinities: A Reader* (pp.255–268). Berkeley, CA and Oxford: University of California Press.

Hua, W. (1998). 'The discovery of the author of Caizi Mudan ting'. *China's Research and Development Journal*, 13 (Sept.): 1–36.

———. (2006). 'How dangerous can the Peony be? Textual space, Caizi Mudan ting, and naturalizing the erotic'. *The Journal of Asian Studies*, 65(4) (Nov.): 741–762.

———. (2015). *A Close Examination on Tang Xianzu.* Shanghai: Shanghai People's Publishing House.

Hubback, J. (1984). 'Amplification'. *Journal of Analytical Psychology*, 29(2): 135–138.

Hvistendahl, M. (2010). 'Has China outgrown the one-child policy?'. *Science*, 329 (17 Sept.): 1458–1461.

Idema, W. (2005). 'Suiqing Shui Jian: Du Liniang, Meigui Gongzhu Yu Ni'a Fuqin De Fannao', in W. Hua (ed.), *Tang Xianzu Yu Mudanting* (pp.289–321). Zhongguo

Wenzhe Zhuankan. Taibei, China: Zhongyang Yanjiu Yuan, Zhongguo Wenzhe Yanjiusuo.

Igra, L. (1992). 'The silent kill. Male and female destructiveness in psychoanalysis practice'. *International Forum of Psychoanalysis*, 1: 139–147.

Jeffreys, E., & Yu, H. (2015). *Sex in China* (China today). Cambridge: Polity Press.

Jia, X. (2016). 'Psychoanalytic training in China: Cultural colonialism or acculturation'. *Journal of Neuroscience and Mental Health*, 16(4): 377–382.

Jin, J., Wu, X., & Zhang, J. (2010). 'The migration of rural women and the decrease of suicide rate in China'. *The Journal of China Agricultural University (Social Sciences)*, 4: 20–31.

Johnson, K. (1993). 'Chinese orphanages: Saving China's abandoned girls'. *The Australian Journal of Chinese Affairs*, 30 (July): 61–87.

Johnson, K., Huang, B., & Wang, L. (1998). 'Infant abandonment and adoption in China'. *Population and Development Review*, 24(3) (Sept.): 469–510.

Johnson, R. (1983). *We: Understanding the Psychology of Romantic Love*. New York: HarperOne.

Jung, C. G. *Collected Works* (CW). H. Read, M. Fordham, G. Adler, & W. McGuire (eds.), trans. (in the main), R.F.C. Hull. London: Routledge & Kegan Paul; Princeton, NJ: Princeton University Press. (Except as below, references are to the Collected Works (CW) and by volume and paragraph number.)

————. (1931). *The Secret of the Golden Flower* (2nd Edition). New York: Harcourt Brace & Company, 1962.

————. (1932). *Visions: Notes of the Seminar Given in 1930–1934*, Vol. II. Princeton, NJ: Pinceton University Press.

————. (1934). *Nietzche's Zarathustra: Notes of the Seminar Given in 1934–1939*, Vol. I. Princeton, NJ: Pinceton University Press.

————. (1968/2014). *Analytical Psychology: Its Theory and Practice*. London and New York: Routledge. 2014.

————. (1985). 'The significance of the father in the destiny of the individual', in A. Samuels (ed.), *The Father: Contemporary Jungian Perspectives* (pp.229–248). London: Free Association Books.

————. (1995). *Memories, Dreams, Reflections* (MDR). London: Fontana Press.

————. (2008). *Children's Dream: Notes from the Seminar Given in 1936–1940*. L. Jung, & M. Meyer-Grass (eds.), trans., E. Falzeder. Princeton, NJ and Oxford: Princeton University Press.

Kam, L. Y. L. (2014). 'The demand for a 'normal' life: Marriage and its discontents in contemporary China', in M. McLelland, & V. Mackie (eds.), *Routledge Handbook of Sexuality Studies in East Asia* (pp.77–86). London: Routledge.

Kawai, H. (1982/2007). *The Japanese Psyche: Major Motif in the Fairy Tales of Japan* (Chinese Edition), trans., Z. Fan. Beijing: Sanlian Publishing House. 2007.

Kawai, T. (2006). 'Postmodern consciousness in psychotherapy'. *Journal of Analytical Psychology*, 51(3): 437–450.

Kirsch, T. (2000). *The Jungians: A Comparative and Historical Perspective*. London: Roultedge.

Kirsner, D., & Snyder, E. (2009). 'Psychoanalysis in China', in S. Akhtar (ed.), *Freud and the Far East: Psychoanalytic Perspectives on the People and Culture of China,*

Japan, and Korea (pp.43–60). Boulder, CO, New York, Toronto and Plymouth, UK: Jason Aronson.

Klein, M. (1945/1989). 'The Oedipus complex in the light of early anxieties', in R. Britton, M. Feldman, & E. O'Shaughnessy (eds.), *The Oedipus Complex Today: Clinical Implications* (pp.11–82). London: Karnac Books Ltd. 1989.

Knox, J. (2004). 'From archetypes to reflective function'. *Journal of Analytical Psychology*, 49(1): 1–19.

————. (2011). *Self-Agency in Psychotherapy: Attachment, Autonomy, and Intimacy.* New York and London: W. W. Norton.

Lavely, W. (1991). 'Marriage and mobility under rural collectivism', in R. S. Watson, & P. B. Ebrey (eds.), *Marriage and Inequality in Chinese Society* (pp.286–312). Berkeley, CA and Oxford: University of California Press.

Layton, L. (2006). 'Racial identities, racial enactments and normative unconscious process'. *The Psychoanalytic Quarterly*, 75: 237–269.

Lee, C., & Liang, Q. (2006). 'The managed fertility transition in rural China and implications for the future of China's population', in D. L. Poston, Jr, C. Lee, C. Chang, S. L. McKibben, & C. S. Walther (eds.), *Fertility, Family Planning, and Population Policy in China* (pp.159–171). London: Routledge.

Lee, S., & Keinman, A. (2003). 'Suicide as resistance in Chinese society', in E. Perry, & M. Selden (eds.), *Chinese Society: Change, Conflict, and Resistance* (2nd Edition, pp.289–311). London: Routledge Curzon.

Leichty, M. M. (1978). 'The effect of father absence during childhood upon the Oedipal situation as reflected in young adults', in S. Fisher, & R. P. Greenberg (eds.), *The scientific evaluation of Freud's theories and therapy* (pp.212–217). Hemel Hempstead, UK: Harvester Press.

Li, Q., Yin, F., & Shen, H. (2015). 'Death dreams from a manifest perspective: A cross cultural comparison between Tibetan and Han Chinese dreamers'. *Dreaming*, 25(1) (Mar.): 32–43.

Li, T. S., & Chen, F. M. (2002). 'Affection in marriage: A study of marital enqing and intimacy in Taiwan'. *Journal of Psychology in Chinese Societies*, 3: 37–59.

Li, X. (2007). 'The Peony Pavilion in the eyes of female readers in the Ming and Qing dynasties'. *Journal of Southeast University (Philosophy and Social Science)*, 9(5): 107–123.

Li, Y. (2014). "The encounter of psychoanalysis and Chinese cultural', in D. E. Scharff, & S. Varvin (eds.), *Psychoanalysis in China* (pp.266–272). London: Karnac Books Ltd.

Liang, Q., & Lee, C. (2006). 'Fertility and population policy: An overview', in D. L. Poston, Jr, C. Lee, C. Chang, S. L. McKibben, & C. S. Walther (eds.), *Fertility, Family Planning, and Population Policy in China* (pp.8–20). London: Routledge.

Liang, W. (2017a). 'A classic causing the suicide of female readers'. https://mp.weixin. qq.com/s?__biz=MzA3MDM3NjE5NQ==&mid=2650820234&idx=2&sn= c3e757d4388960f8527dd87e81908ce4&chksm=84c920e6b3bea9f092188 f9a79f24353113fcd9ab3f1da588e03cb0fd0b7f27efed1e9cbb47a&mpshare=1&sce ne=1&srcid=0901k7EzOCQnO74eb7GUZb3C#rd

————. (2017b). 'What a person could be if he or she has nothing except his/her dream?'. http://mp.weixin.qq.com/s?__biz=MzA3MDM3NjE5NQ==&mi

d=2650820291&idx=1&sn=2260b056ca82a691a7708f1422ae2577&chksm=84
c920afb3bea9b9dbe9dcf7d8486b1cc2fb12cbc586fe43bb4466a9cb0c81098c1a9a
d2a749&mpshare=1&scene=1&srcid=1021LE8CIebixrAcbil0ATvb#rd.

Lin, T. (2014). 'The encounter of psychoanalysis and Chinese culture', in D. E. Scharff, & S. Varvin (eds.), *Psychoanalysis in China* (pp.81–89). London: Karnac Books Ltd.

―――――. (2015). Interview with Huan Wang. March 13, 2015. London.

Liu, S., & Gao, H. (2015). 'Changes of the factors influencing the first marriage risk of the Chinese: A reseach based on CGSS2010'. *South China Population*, 30(1) 2005, General No. 127: 1–14.

Luxun. (1918/2001). 'My Opinion on Jie and Lie'. *The Tomb*. Guilin, China: Lijiang Publishing House. 2001.

Ma, J. (2012). *The Dark Road*. Taibei, China: Asian Culture Press.

Ma, S. (2010). *Footbinding: A Jungian Engagement with Chinese Culture and Psychology*. London: Routledge.

Mann, S. L. (1991). 'Grooming a daughter for marriage: Brides and wives in the mid-Ch'ing period', in R. S. Watson, & P. B. Ebrey (eds.), *Marriage and Inequality in Chinese Society* (pp.204–230). Berkeley, CA and Oxford: University of California Press.

―――――. (2002). 'Grooming a daughter for marriage: Brides and wives in the mid-Qing period', in S. Brownell, & J. N. Wasserstrom (eds.), *Chinese Femininities/Chinese Masculinities: A Reader* (pp.93–119). Berkeley, CA and Oxford: University of California Press.

―――――. (2011). *Gender and Sexuality in Modern Chinese History*. Cambridge: Cambridge University Press.

Marcus, B. F. (2004). 'Female passion and the matrix of mother, daughter, and body: Vicissitudes of the maternal transference in the working through of sexual inhibitions'. *Psychoanalytic Inquiry*, 24(5): 680–712.

Miles, R. (1988/2001). *Who Cooked the Last Supper? The Women's History of the World*. New York: Three Rivers Press. 2001.

Mitchell, J. (1971/2015). *Woman's Estate*. London and New York: Verso Books. 2015.

Mo, Y. (2012). *The Frog*. Shanghai: Shanghai Literature & Art Publishing House.

Monick, E. (1987). *Phallos: Scared Image of the Masculine*. Boulder, CO: Inner City Books.

Moore, R., & Gillette, D. (1992). *King, Warrior, Magician, Lover: Rediscovering the Archetypes of the Mature Masculine*. London: Bravo Ltd.

Naftali, O. (2016). *Children in China*. Cambridge: Polity Press.

Neumann, E. (1951/2017). *The Fear of the Feminine*, trans., Q. Hu. Beijing, Guangzhou, Shanghai and Xi'an, China: World Publishing Corporation. 2017.

―――――. (1954/1989). *The Origins and History of Consciousness*, trans., R. F. C. Hull. London: Maresfield Library. 1989.

―――――. (1956/1971). *Amor and Psyche: The Psychic Development of the Feminine*. Princeton, NJ: Princeton University Press. 1971.

Newton, K. (1975). 'Separation and pre-Oedipal guilt'. *Journal of Analytical Psychology*, 20: 183–193.

Ng, K. M., Peluso, P., & Smith, S. D. (2010). 'Marital satisfaction, intimacy enqing, and relationship stressor among Asians', in J. Carlson, & L. Sperry (eds.), *Recovering Intimacy in Love Relationships* (pp.331–352). New York and Hove, UK: Routledge.

Ng, M. L. (1985). 'Psychoanalysis for the Chinese – applicable or not applicable?'. *International Review of Psycho-Analysis*, 12: 449–460.

Ocko, J. K. (1991). 'Women, property, and law in the people's republic of China', in R. S. Watson, & P. B. Ebrey (eds.), *Marriage and Inequality in Chinese Society* (pp.313–346). Berkeley, CA and Oxford: University of California Press.

Osnos, E. (2011). 'Meet Dr. Freud: Does psychoanalysis have a future in an authoritarian state?'. *New Yorker*, January 10, 2011. www.newyorker.com/magazine/2011/01/10/meet-dr-freud

Ownby, D. (2002). 'Approximations of Chinese bandits: Perverse rebels, romantic heroes, or frustrated bachelors?', in S. Brownell, & J. N. Wasserstrom (eds.), *Chinese Femininities/Chinese Masculinities: A Reader* (pp.226–250). Berkeley, CA and Oxford: University of California Press.

Pan, G. (1924/2009). 'Study on the story of Feng Xiaoqing', in C. Wu (ed.), *The Frenzy of Psychoanalysis: Freud in China* (pp.142–150). Nanchang, China: Jiangxi University Press. 2009.

Pan, S. (1999). *Existence and Absurdity: Investment on Chinese Prostitution*. Beijing: Qun Yan Publishing House.

Papadopoulos, R. (1989). 'Archetypal family therapy: Developing a Jungian approach to family therapy'. *Journal for Jungian Studies*, 35(1989): 95–120.

———. (2006). 'Jung's Epistemology and Methodology', in R. K. Papadopoulos (ed.), *The Handbook of Jungian Psychology* (pp.54–73). London and New York: Routledge.

———. (2011). 'The umwelt and networks of archetypal images: A Jungian approach to therapeutic encounters in humanitarian contexts'. *Psychotherapy and Politics International*, 9(3): 212–231.

Parsons, A. (2010). 'Is the Oedipus complex universal?', in R. A. LeVine (ed.), *Psychological Anthropology: A Reader on Self in Culture* (pp.131–153). Chichester, UK: Wiley-Blackwell.

Pattis-Zoja, E. (2014). 'After mass violence and displacement: How a "safe place" emerges through symbolic play', Analysis and Activism: Social and Political Contributions of Jungian Psychology, London.

People's Daily, (July 2, 2011). *Boost of Divorce in China*. http://paper.people.com.cn/rmwz/html/2011-07/01/content_901668.htm?div=-1

People's Daily, (May 14, 2013). *Don't Be Getting Old When You are Still Young*. http://opinion.people.com.cn/n/ 192013/0514/c1003-21470995.html

Perry, J. W. (1970). 'Emotions and object relations'. *Journal of Analytical Psychology*, 15(1): 1–12.

Phillips, M., Li, X., & Zhang, Y. (2002). 'Suicide rates in China, 1995–99'. *The Lancet*, 359(9309) (March): 835–840.

Pimentel, E., & Liu, J. (2004). 'Exploring nonnormative coresidence in urban China: Living with wives' parents'. *Journal of Marriage and Family*, 66(3) (Aug.): 821–836.

Plankers, T. (2013). 'When Freud headed for the East: Aspects of a Chinese translation of his works'. *The International Journal of Psychoanalysis*, 94: 993–1017.

——————. (2014). 'China – a traumatised country? The aftermath of the Chinese Culture Revolution (1966–1976) for the individual and for society', in D. E. Scharff, & S. Varvin (eds.), *Psychoanalysis in China* (pp.57–70). London: Karnac Books Ltd.

Poston, Jr, D. L., & Glover, K. S. (2006). China's demographic destiny: marriage market implication for the twenty-first century, in D. L. Poston, Jr, C. Lee, C. Chang, S. L. McKibben & C. S. Walther (eds.), *Fertility, Family Planning, and Population Policy in China* (pp.1–7). London: Routledge.

Poston, Jr, D. L., & Walther, C. A. (2006). 'Prologue', in D. L. Poston, Jr, C. Lee, C. Chang, S. L. McKibben, & C. S. Walther (eds.), *Fertility, Family Planning, and Population Policy in China* (pp.1–7). London: Routledge.

Poulson, C. (1996). 'Death and the maiden: The Lady of Shalott and the Pre-Raphaelites', in E. Harding (ed.), *Reframing the Pre-Raphaelites* (pp.173–194). London: Scholar Press.

Rangell, L. (1974). 'A psychoanalytic perspective leading currently to the syndrome of the compromise of integrity'. *International Journal of Psychoanalysis*, 55: 3–12.

Rangell, L. (1980). *The Mind of Watergate: An Exploration of the Compromise of Integrity.* New York: W. W. Norton and Company, Inc.

Rawski, E. S. (1991). 'Ch'ing imperial marriage and problems of rulership', in R. S. Watson, & P. B. Ebrey (eds.), *Marriage and Inequality in Chinese Society* (pp.170–203). Berkeley, CA and Oxford: University of California Press.

Roesler, C. (2012). 'A revision of Jung's theory of archetypes in light of contemporary research: Neurosciences genetics and cultural theory – a reformulation', in P. Bennett (ed.), *Facing Multiplicity: Psyche, Nature, Culture: Proceedings of XVIIth Congress of the IAAP, Montreal 2010* (pp.71–91). Einsiedeln, Switzerland: Daimon Verlag.

Rofel, L. (2007). *Desiring China: Experiments in Neoliberalism, Sexuality, and Public Culture.* Durham, UK and London: Duke University Press.

Roland, A. (1996a). 'The influence of culture on the self and self-object relationships: An Asian-North American comparison'. *Psychoanalytic Dialogues*, 6: 461–475.

——————. (1996b). 'Culture, comparativity, and psychoanalysis: Reply to commentary'. *Psychoanalytic Dialogues*, 6: 489–495.

Roll, S., & Abel, T. (1988). 'Variations in secondary themes of the Oedipal legend'. *The Journal of the American Academy of Psychoanalysis and Dynamic Psychiatry*, 16: 537–547.

Rowan, J. (1989). *Subpesonalities: The People Inside Us.* London and New York: Routledge.

Rowland, S. (2002). *Jung: A Feminist Revision.* Cambridge: Polity Press.

Saayman, G. S., Faber, P. A., & Saayman, R. V. (1988). 'Archetypal factors'. *Journal of Analytical Psychology*, 33(3): 253–276.

Saban, M. (2011). 'Staging the self: Performance, individuation and embodiment', in R. A. Jones (ed.), *Body, Mind and Healing After Jung* (pp.110–126). London and New York: Routledge.

——————. (2016). 'Jung, Winnicott and the divided psyche'. *Journal of Analytical Psychology*, 61(3): 329–349.

Samuels, A. (1985a/2005). *Jung and the Post-Jungians.* New York: Routledge. 2005.

——————. (1985b). 'Introduction', in A. Samuels (ed.), *The Father: Contemporary Jungian Perspective* (pp.1–4). London: Free Association Books.

—————. (1986). *A Critical Dictionary of Jungian Analysis* (p.1986). London and New York: Routledge.

—————. (1989). *The Plural Psyche: Personality, Morality, and the Father*. London and New York: Routledge.

—————. (2001). *Politics on the Couch: Citizenship and the Internal Life*. London: Karnac Books Ltd.

—————. (2002). 'The hidden politics of healing: Foreign dimensions of domestic practice: America Imago'. *Studies in Psychoanalysis and Culture*, 59(4): 459–482.

—————. (2005). 'Amplification (Analytical Psychology)', in A. d. Mijolla (ed.), *International Dictionary of Psychoanalysis* (pp.67–68). Detroit, MI, New York, San Francisco, San Diego, CA, New Haven, CT, Waterville, ME, London and Munich: Thomson Gale.

—————. (2011). 'Introduction', in P. Young-Eisendrath (ed.), *The Cambridge Companion to Jung (Cambridge Companions)* (2nd Edition) (pp.1–18). Cambridge: Cambridge University Press.

—————. (2013/2015). *Passions, Persons, Psychotherapy, Politics: The Selected Works of Andrew Samuels*. London: Routledge. 2015.

—————. (2015). 'Global politics, American hegemony and vulnerability, and Jungian-psychosocial studies: Why there are no winners in the battle between Trickster Pedro Urdemales and the Gringos'. *International Journal of Jungian Studies*, 7(3): 1–15.

—————. (2017). 'The analyst is as much "in the analysis" as the patient (1929), Jung as a Pioneer of Relational Psychoanalysis', The International Association of Relational Psychoanalysis and Psychotherapy, San Francisco.

Sanford, J. A. (1980). *The Invisible Partners: How the Male and Female in Each of Us*. Nahwah, NJ: Paulist Press.

Saporta, J. (2011). 'Freud goes to China: Teaching psychoanalysis in a different culture – a dialogue'. *The Alonso Center for Psychodynamic Studies*, 9(1): 1–3.

—————. (2014). 'Psychoanalysis meets in China: Transformative dialogue or monologue of the western voice?', in D. E. Scharff, & S. Varvin (eds.), *Psychoanalysis in China* (pp.102–115). London: Karnac Books Ltd.

Scharff, D. E. (2014). 'Five things Western therapists need to know for working with Chinese therapists and patients', in D. E. Scharff, & S. Varvin (eds.), *Psychoanalysis in China* (pp.143–153). London: Karnac Books Ltd.

Scharff, J. S., & Scharff, D. E. (2014). 'The impact of Chinese cultures on a marital relationship', in D. E. Scharff, & S. Varvin (eds.), *Psychoanalysis in China* (pp.323–334). London: Karnac Books Ltd.

Schlosser, A.-M. (2009). 'Oedipus in China: Can we export psychoanalysis?'. *International Forum of Psychoanalysis*, 18(4) (Dec.): 219–224.

Schmidt, L. (1980). 'The brother-sister relationship in marriage'. *Journal of Analytical Psychology*, 25(1): 17–35.

Seidenberg, R. (1991a). 'Psychoanalysis and femininity, Part I'. *Psychoanalytic Psychology*, 8: 83–207.

—————. (1991b). 'Psychoanalysis and femininity, Part II'. *Psychoanalytic Psychology*, 8: 225–237.

—————. (1991c). 'Psychoanalysis and femininity, Part III'. *Psychoanalytic Psychology*, 8: 343–362.

Seligman, E. (1986). 'The half-alive ones', in A. Samuels (ed.), *The Father: Contemporary Jungian Perspectives* (pp.69–94). London: Free Association Books.

Settles, B. H., Sheng, X., Zang, Y., & Zhao, J. (2013). 'The one-child policy and its impact on Chinese families', in K. Chan (ed.), *International Handbook of Chinese Families* (pp.627–646). New York: Springer Science & Business Media.

Shang, W. (2005). 'The Tao between Yin and Yang: The subversive comments in Caizi Mudang Ting', in W. Hua (ed.), *Tang Xianzu Yu Mudanting* (pp.429–466). Zhongguo Wenzhe Zhuankan. Taibei, China: Zhongyang Yanjiu Yuan, Zhongguo Wenzhe Yanjiusuo.

Shen, H. (1996). 'Heart and psychology: The meaning of Chinese culture', Fulbright Scholar Presentation, University of Nebraska.

————. (2004). *Analytical Psychology: Understanding and Experiencing*. Beijing: SDX Joint Publishing Company.

————. (2007a). 'Analytical psychology and Chinese cultural', Academic Week on Analytical Psychology and Chinese Culture, Fudang University, China.

————. (2007b). *Psychology of Heart: The Happiness and the Cultural Psyche in China*. Eranos Round Table Session, Switzerland.

————. (2009). 'C.G. Jung and China: A Continued Dialogue'. *Jung Journal: Cultural & Psyche*, 3(2): 5–14.

————. (2011). *The Dreams of Xixin Island*. Guangzhou and China: Guangdong Technology Publishing House.

————. (2015a). 'Bao Chi'. *Analytical Psychology*, 1: 96–98.

————. (2015b). Interview with Huan Wang. April 9, 2015. South China Normal University, Guangzhou, China.

————. (2015c). 'Psychological implications of political policy: The impact on the soul and on relationships of China's one child policy'. Analysis and Activism: Social and Political Contributions of Jungian Psychology, second conference, Rome.

————. (2018a). *Jung and Chinese Culture*. Beijing: Capital Normal University Press.

————. (2018b). *The Psychology of the Heart*. Houston, TX: Fay Lecture.

Shen, H., Gao, L., & Cope, T. A. (2006). 'The *I Ching*'s psychology of heart and Jungian analysis'. *Psychological Perspectives: A Quarterly Journal of Jungian Thought*, 49(1): 61–78.

Shi, Q. (2014). 'The development of psychoanalysis in China', in D. E. Scharff, & S. Varvin (eds.), *Psychoanalysis in China* (pp.192–201). London: Karnac Books Ltd.

Shi, Q., & Scharff, D. E. (2014). 'Cultural factors and projective identification in understanding a Chinese couple', in D. E. Scharff, & S. Varvin (eds.), *Psychoanalysis in China* (pp.335–346). London: Karnac Books Ltd.

Shi, Q., & Scharff, J. S. (2008). 'Social change, intercultural conflict, and marital dynamics in a Chinese marriage in brief concurrent individual and couple therapy'. *International Journal of Applied Psychoanalytic Studies*, 5: 302–321.

Sies, C. (1992). 'Beyond pregenital determination of femininity and masculinity (discussion)'. *International Forum of Psychoanalysis*, 1: 148–150.

Silverman, M. A. (1986). 'Oedipus. A folklore casebook'. *The Psychoanalytic Quarterly*, 55: 313–318.

Simon, B. (1991). 'Is the Oedipus complex still the cornerstone of psychoanalysis? Three obstacles to answering the question'. *Journal of the American Psychoanalytic Association*, 39: 641–668.

Snyder, E. (2014). 'The shibboleth of cross-culture issues in psychoanalytic treatment', in D. E. Scharff, & S. Varvin (eds.), *Psychoanalysis in China* (pp.121–129). London: Karnac Books Ltd.

Sommer, M. H. (2002). 'Dangerous males, vulnerable males, and polluted males: The regulation of masculinity in Qing Dynasty law', in S. Brownell, & J. N. Wasserstrom (eds.), *Chinese Femininities/Chinese Masculinities: A Reader* (pp.67–88). Berkeley, CA and Oxford: University of California Press.

Stein, M. (1995). 'Report on IAAP visit to China'. *IAAP Newsletter*, p.15.

———. (2005). 'Some reflections on the influence of Chinese thought on Jung and his psychological theory'. *Journal of Analytical Psychology*, 50: 209–222.

———. (2006). *The Principle of Individuation: Toward the Development of Human Consciousness*. Wilmette, IL: Chiron Publications.

———. (2015). 'C. J. Jung, Richard Wilhelm, the *I Ching* – Following a process of transformation'. *Analytical Psychology*, 1: 17–27.

Steinfeld, J. (2015). *Little Emperors and Material Girls: Sex and Youth in Modern China*. London and New York: I. B. Tauris & Co. Ltd.

Stevens, A. (1994/2007). *Jung: A short Introduction*, trans., S. Yang. Beijing: Foreign Language Teaching and Research Press. 2007.

Su, Q. (1944/2009). *Marriage for Ten Years*. Beijing: International Cultural Publishing Company. 2009.

———. (1946/2009). *After Ten Years' Marriage*. Beijing: International Cultural Publishing Company. 2009.

Su, X. (1935/2009). 'Xiaoyan's poem of Partridge', in C. Wu (ed.), *The Frenzy of Psychoanalysis: Freud in China* (p.200). Nanchang, China: Jiangxi University Press. 2009.

Sudbeck, K. (2012). 'Effects of China's one-child policy: The significance for Chinese women', *Nebraska Anthropologist*. Paper 179, pp.43–60.

Sun, L. (1983/2011). *Deep Structure of Chinese Culture*. Guangzhou, China: Guangzhou Normal University Press. 2011.

———. (2004). *The Theodolite of a History*. Guilin, China: Guangxi Normal University Press.

———. (2006/2010). 'The gift from the devil', in B. Li (ed.), *Criticism on Chinese Food Culture* (pp.1–15). Beijing: Hualing Press. 2010.

———. (2010). *The Matricidal Culture of America: A History of the American Ethos in the 20th Century*. Nanchang, China: Phoenix Media Press & Jiangxi People's Publishing House.

Sun, Y. X. (1993). 'A campaign between Chinese and Japanese students in a summer camp'. *Reader* (Nov.).

Tang, X. (1598/2002). *The Peony Pavilion: Mudang Ting* (2nd Edition), trans., C. Birch. Bloomington, IN: Indiana University Press. 2002.

Teng, H. (2014). 'Conflict between extended families and couple identity in Taiwan – a psychoanalytic exploration', in D. E. Scharff, & S. Varvin (eds.), *Psychoanalysis in China* (pp.357–365). London: Karnac Books Ltd.

Tennyson, A. (1932). *The Lady of Shalott*. www.poetryfoundation.org/poems/45359/the-lady-of-shalott-1832

Thatcher, M. P. (1991). 'Marriage of the ruling elite in the spring and autumn period', in R. S. Watson, & P. B. Ebrey (eds.), *Marriage and Inequality in Chinese Society* (pp.25–57). Berkeley, CA and Oxford: University of California Press.

Theiss, J. M. (2002). 'Femininity in flux: Gender virtue and social conflict in the mid-Qing courtroom', in S. Brownell, & J. N. Wasserstrom (eds.), *Chinese Femininities/Chinese Masculinities: A Reader* (pp.47–66). Berkeley, CA and Oxford: University of California Press.

Tyson, P. (1997). 'Sexuality, femininity, and contemporary psychoanalysis'. *International Journal of Psychoanalysis*, 78: 385–389.

Varvin, S. (2014). 'Discussion on Chapter Seven', in D. E. Scharff, & S. Varvin (eds.), *Psychoanalysis in China* (pp.116–120). London: Karnac Books Ltd.

Varvin, S., & Rosenbaum, B. (2014). 'West-east differences in habits and ways of thinking: The influence on understanding and teaching psychoanalytic therapy', in D. E. Scharff, & S. Varvin (eds.), *Psychoanalysis in China* (pp.155–169). London: Karnac Books Ltd.

Veeck, A., Flurry, L., & Jiang, N. (2003). 'Equal dreams: The one child policy and the consumption of education in urban China'. *Consumption Markets & Culture*, 6(1): 81–94.

von Franz, M. L. (1970a/1992). *The Golden Ass of Apuleius*. Boston and London: Shambhala Publications, Inc. 1992.

————. (1970b/1996). *The Interpretation of Fairy Tales*. Boston and London: Shambhala Publications, Inc. 1996.

Waddell, T. (2006). *Mis/takes: Archetype, Myth and Identity in Screen Fiction*. London and New York: Routledge.

Wang, F., Zhou, M., & Xiao, B. (1989). 'Fertility dynamics in China: Results from the 1987 one percent population survey'. *Population and Development Review*, 15(2) (June): 297–322.

Wang, X. (2015). Interview with Huan Wang. 11/03/2015. London.

————. (2018). 'Shall we depend on the Western professionals to learn?', IPA Asia-Pacific Conference, Tokyo.

Wang, Z., & Zachrisson, A. (2014). 'Transference and countertransference in a Chinese setting: Reflections on a psychotherapeutic process', in D. E. Scharff, & S. Varvin (eds.), *Psychoanalysis in China* (pp.202–213). London: Karnac Books Ltd.

Wanlass, J. (2014). 'The intergenerational and cultural transmission of trauma in Chinese couples: Treatment considerations', in D. E. Scharff, & S. Varvin (eds.), *Psychoanalysis in China* (pp.347–356). London: Karnac Books Ltd.

Watson, R. S. (1991). 'Wives, concubines and maids: Servitude and kinship in the Hong Kong region, 1900–1940', in R. S. Watson, & P. B. Ebrey (eds.), *Marriage and Inequality in Chinese Society* (pp.231–255). Berkeley, CA and Oxford: University of California Press.

Wei, Y., Dong, J., & Jiang, Q. (2013). 'The transformation of China's first marriage pattern: Analysis on nuptiality table'. *Population & Economics*, 2(2): 21–28.

White, T. (2006). *China's Longest Campaign: Birth Planning in the People's Republic, 1949–2005*. Ithaca, NY: Cornell University Press.

————. (2010). 'Domination, resistance and accommodation in China's one-child campaign', in E. J. Perry, & M. Selden (eds.), *Chinese Society: Change, Conflict and Resistance* (pp.171–196). London and New York: Routledge.

Williams, M. (1989). 'The archetypes in marriage', in A. Samuels (ed.), *Psychopathology: Contemporary Jungian Perspectives* (pp.245–259). London: Karnac Books Ltd.

Winnicott, D. W. (1971). 'Creativity and its origins', in *Playing and Reality* (pp.65–85). London: Routledge.

Wolf, M. (1975). 'Woman and suicide in China', in M. Wolf, & R. Witke (eds.), *Women in Chinese Society* (pp.111–141). Palo Alto, CA: Stanford University Press.

Woo, M. Y. K. (2006). 'Contesting citizenship: Marriage and divorce in the people's republic of China', in E. Jeffreys (ed.), *Sex and Sexuality in China* (pp.62–81). London and New York: Routledge.

Wright, E. (1992). *Feminism and Psychoanalysis: A Critical Dictionary.* Chichester, UK: Wiley.

Wu, J., & Walther, C. S. (2006). 'Patterns of induced abortion', in D. L. Poston, Jr, C. Lee, C. Chang, S. L. McKibben, & C. S. Walther (eds.), *Fertility, Family Planning, and Population Policy in China* (pp.23–37). London: Routledge.

Wu, Z. H. (2016). *The Nation of Great Babies.* Hangzhou, China: Zhejiang People's Publishing House.

Wylie, M. (1962). *Children of China.* Decorah, IA: Dragonfly Books.

Xiao, H. (2015). 'Uterus never belongs to herself'. www.weibo.com/p/1001603904335888153528?pids=Pl_Official_CardMixFeedv6__4&feed_filter=1

Xie, Y. (2008). *The Peony Pavilion and Emotional Education among Women in the Ming and Qing Dynasties.* Beijing: Zhonghua Book Company.

Xin, F. (2012). *A Study on the Wives of Gay Men in China.* Chengdu, China: Chengdu Times Press.

xinhua.net. (2015). www.xinhuanet.com/politics/2015-11/08/c_128404355.htm

Xinran. (2003). *The Good Women of China: Hidden Voice.* London: Vintage Books.

————. (2011). *Messages from an Unknown Chinese Mother: Stories of Love and Loss.* London: Vintage Books.

————. (2016). *Buy Me the Sky.* London, Sydney, Auckland and Johannesburg: Rider.

Xu, F. (1987). *Further Examination on the Study of the Peony Pavilion.* Shanghai: Shanghai Classic Publishing House.

Xu, H. (2013). *The Seduction of the Body: The Politics of the Body in Chinese History.* Beijing: The Commercial Press.

Xu, J. (2007). *From Jin Ping Mei to Hong Lou Meng.* Nanning, China: Guangxi People's Publishing House.

Xu, J. (2012). *The Encounter of Freud and Buddha: A Dialogue between Psychotherapist and Buddhism.* Shanghai: Thread-Binding Books Publishing House.

Xu, Y., Qiu, J., Chen, J., & Xiao, Z. (2014). 'The development of psychoanalytic psychotherapy at Shanghai Mental Health Center', in D. E. Scharff, & S. Varvin (eds.), *Psychoanalysis in China* (pp.234–243). London: Karnac Books Ltd.

Yang, Y. (2014). 'The impact of psychic trauma on individuation and self-identity: How the psychic trauma of poverty affects individuation and self-identity in the context of the Chinese family', in D. E. Scharff, & S. Varvin (eds.), *Psychoanalysis in China* (pp.170–183). London: Karnac Books Ltd.

Ye, S. (1997). *The Goddess of Gao Tang and Venus.* Beijing: China Social Sciences Publishing House.

Yi, F. X. (2013). *The Big Country and The Empty Nest: Reflections on Chinese One-Child Policy.* Beijing: Chinese Developing Press.

Yi, K. Y. (1995). 'Psychoanalytic psychotherapy with Asian clients: Transference and therapeutic consideration'. *Psychotherapy*, 32: 308–316.

————. (1998a). 'Transference and race'. *Psychoanalytic Psychology*, 15: 245–261.

Yi, Z. (1998b). *Chinese Men and Women.* Beijing: China Federation of Literary & Art Circles Publishing Corp.

Yin, F., & Shen, H. (2015). 'Death dreams from an implicit perspective: A core cultural comparison between Tibetan and Han Chinese dreamers'. *Dreaming*, 25(2): 103–117 (June).

Yin, F., Shen, H., He, Y., Wei, Y., & Cao, W. (2013). 'Typical dreams of "being chased": A cross cultural comparison between Tibetan and Han Chinese dreamers'. *Dreaming*, 23(1) (March): 64–77.

Young-Eisendrath, P. (1984). *Hags and Heroes.* Toronto: University of Toronto Press Incorporated.

————. (1993). *You Are Not What I Expected.* New York: William Morrow & Co.

————. (1998). 'Contrasexuality and the dialectics of desire', in A. Casement (ed.), *Post-Jungian Today: Key Papers in Contemporary Analytical Psychology* (pp.199–213). London: Routledge.

Yu, W. (2015). 'Cheng Qiong's talents Peony Pavilion and its "eroticism"'. *Journal of Lanzhou University (Social Sciences)*, 43(1.): 26–34.

Yuan, L. (2014). 'There is no home for Nora'. www.21ccom.net/articles/lsjd/lsjj/article_2014011699031.html

Zabriskie, B. (2005). 'Synchronicity and the I Chin: Jung, Pauli, and the Chinese woman'. *Journal of Analytical Psychology*, 50: 223–235.

Zhai, F., & Gao, Q. (2010). 'Center-based care in the context of one-child policy in China: Do child gender and siblings matter?'. *Population Research and Policy Review*, 29(5) (Oct.): 745–774.

Zhang, J. (1992). *Psychoanalysis in China: Literary Transformations 1919–1949.* Cornell University East Asia Program.

Zhang, J. (2012). *Wild Swans: Three Daughters of China.* London: Harper Press.

Zhang, L., Feng, X., & Zhang, Q. (2006). 'Changing patterns of desired fertility', in D. L. Poston, Jr, C. Lee, C. Chang, S. L. McKibben, & C. S. Walther (eds.), *Fertility, Family Planning, and Population Policy in China* (pp.89–110). London: Routledge.

Zhang, S. (2005). 'Du Liniang in the garden', in W. Hua (ed.), *Tang Xianzu Yu Mudanting* (pp.267–268). Zhongguo Wenzhe Zhuankan. Taibei, China: Zhongyang Yanjiu Yuan, Zhongguo Wenzhe Yanjiusuo.

Zhang, W. (2006). 'Who adopts girls and why? Domestic adoption of female children in contemporary rural China'. *The China Journal*, 56: 63–82 (July).

Zhang, X. (2011). 'Masculinities in crisis? An emerging debate on men and boys in contemporary China', in E. Ruspini, J. Hearn, B. Pease, & K. Pringle (eds.), *Men and Masculinities around the world: Transforming Men's Practices* (pp.191–204). New York: Palgrave Macmillan.

Zhao, J. (1927/2009). 'Chinese new art and abnormal sexual desire', in C. Wu (ed.), *The Frenzy of Psychoanalysis: Freud in China* (pp.162–164). Nanchang, China: Jiangxi University Press. 2009.

Zhong, J. (2014). 'Working with Chinese patients: Are there conflicts between Chinese culture and psychoanalysis?', in D. E. Scharff, & S. Varvin (eds.), *Psychoanalysis in China* (pp.184–191). London: Karnac Books Ltd.

Zhou, Z. (1923/2009). 'Literature and morality', in C. Wu (ed.), *The Frenzy of Psychoanalysis: Freud in China* (pp.126–128). Nanchang, China: Jiangxi University Press. 2009.

Zhu, W., Lu, L., & Hesketh, T. (2009). 'China's excess males, sex selective abortion, and one China policy: Analysis of data from 2005 national intercensus survey'. *British Medical Journal*, 338(7700) (April): 920–923.

Zoja, L. (2014/2017). *Paranoia: The Madness that Makes History.* London and New York: Routledge. 2017.

Zweig, C., & Wolf, S. (1997). *Romancing the Shadow: A Guide to Soul Work for a Vital, Authentic Life.* New York: Ballantine Books.

Index

Abel, T. 68–69

abortion(s): coerced 35, 36, 165; right to 176; sex-selective 12, 35, 36, 159

absent fathers 9, 14, 70, 88, 98

abstinence (sexual) 28, 31, 32, 119

academic achievement 37, 40, 134

acceptance of femininity 20

access to information 55

active imagination 58n3, 66

active interaction: urban couple interviews 88, 92

activeness: against oppression of passion 113–114; as both feminine and masculine 102, 105; as individuation 101; of men in Western romance stories 111, 112; of women in romantic relationships 107, 109–113, 115, 116, 122, 126

adaptation 99, 102

adjustment 102

adoption 12, 36

advice on relationships 96–97, 98

aesthetic activities: fulfilment through 119

aesthetic tradition 110, 118

After Ten Years' Marriage 33

age: at marriage 41, 162; of divorcees 2

agency: aggression and 128; immature parents and harm to development of 130–131; *see also* self-agency

aggression: in the context of individuation 128–130; feminine 123, 125–126; non-welcomed in imperial China 31; split of sexuality and 123–125; transference and (case study) 136–139; turned against the self 127–128

aggressive fantasy 138, 139

aging population 34, 35

all-good father 9

American culture *see* Western culture

Americanisation *see* Westernisation

amplification 107

Analytical Psychology 52

analytical psychology: attention to second level of femininity and masculinity 26; Chinese culture as key to understanding 63; contributions of Chinese team 65–68; debates about femininity and masculinity 21–24; in different cultural settings 72; Eastern psyche in 3–4; individuation 55; journals on 51–52; Jung's four stages of 67; schools 65, 74, 75, 79n3; similarity and togetherness 87; three frames in 18n4

analytical psychology in China 49; after 2003 50–54; applicability 1–2, 58, 71, 72; before 2000 49–50; contribution to understanding dreams 75; development 56; increasing importance 4; interest in 49; localisation/modification 56, 63–65, 78; strong enthusiasm for 56; understanding of basic concepts 50

anatomy: -destiny 23; feminine/masculine distinction 19; as not destiny 28

Anding Hospital (Beijing) 47

androgyny 28, 170

anima 1, 4, 22; as belonging to nature 25; as carried by both men and women 5, 23; characteristics in common with animus 6; eros appointed to 23; of the father, and son's own anima development 10; four stages of 11; love and freedom from 14; and otherness 24; possessed by father's (case study) 149–150; romantic love 10; shaping of

perception of femininity 19; importance in process of individuation 114
body language 91
body politic 118
Bonaparte, M. 112
bonds: within natal families 172; *see also*
mother-daughter bond; mother-son
bond
boundaries: analyst/analysand 62;
between individuals 95; integrity and
163; *see also* self-boundaries
Boyang 126
boyfriends 99
boys: dependence and helplessness 148;
women's sexual preference for pretty
122; *see also* over-quota boys; schoolboys; sons
Britton, R. 154
brother *see* sister-brother relationship
brotherhood 32,
122, 124
Brutsche, P. 79
Buddhism: Chinese cultural assimilation
64; experts/speakers at IAAP conferences 52; integration in analytical
psychology 57, 76; integration in psychoanalysis 60, 61, 75
Buss, D. 92
butterflies: symbolism of 111
Buy Me the Sky 39

Cai, J. 69
Caizi Mudan ting 111
Calhoune, C. 163, 164
capacity for indignation 176
care giving: archetypal feminine as
province of 4
career(s): achievement/development 14,
38, 89–90, 93, 98, 99, 172; differentiation of men by 123
castrated man 148, 149
castration: fear of 69; of self (child's) 70;
symbolic 44
causal-reductive method 106
censorship 55
chambers 113, 118, 121, 126, 128,
133, 135
chaotic relationships (case study)
144–147
chastity 28, 29, 111, 118,
119, 120

chastity 'package' 29
Chen, J. 59
Chen Zuiliang 108
Cheng, Q. 111, 115
Chengdu 48
chi 66
children: attitudes to 93–94; overemphasis of mothers in emotional
development of 26–27; paradoxical
attitude to incest during Oedipal
phase 27; *see also* boys; girls
China: analytical psychology *see* analytical psychology in China; difficulties
of developing western depth psychologies in 54–56; divorce 2; as lesson for
demographic transitions 35; psychoanalysis *see* psychoanalysis in China;
study of national characteristics 1; *see
also* imperial China; modern China
China American Psychoanalytic Alliance
(CAPA) 47, 48, 59, 62
China Society of Analytical
Psychology 54
China Society of Sandplay Therapy 54
Chinese culture: anti-Oedipal complex
105–106; exaggeration of influence on
Jung 58; filial piety 9; first conference
on Jungian psychology and 49–50;
idealised father 9; identification with
the father as disrespectful 71; impact
on young urban couples 99–100;
incompleteness of terms borrowed
from 57; influence on relationships 3;
interpretation of Western ideas 76; as
key to understanding Jungian psychology 63; sexual symbolism in 111;
Shen's knowledge of 74; symbiosis
with the mother 120; triangular relationships 70; understanding through
a Jungian lens 50; women and men in
27–34; *see also* cultural assimilation;
cultural identity; cultural integration
Chinese Economic Reform 2, 46
Chinese families: couple relationships as
the basis of 2; mutually supportive
nature of 173; non-clarity of boundaries 95; perceived as basic unity of society 29; political effects on 2, 12–13;
similarity of responses among subgroupings 157; study of trauma in 48;
triangular relationship 69; women's

For Product Safety Concerns and Information please contact our EU
representative GPSR@taylorandfrancis.com
Taylor & Francis Verlag GmbH, Kaufingerstraße 24, 80331 München, Germany

www.ingramcontent.com/pod-product-compliance
Lightning Source LLC
Chambersburg PA
CBHW070412270326
41926CB00014B/2794